College Graduates and Jobs

ADJUSTING TO A NEW LABOR MARKET SITUATION

A Report and Recommendations by
The Carnegie Commission on Higher Education
APRIL 1973

MCGRAW–HILL BOOK COMPANY

New York   St. Louis   San Francisco   Düsseldorf

London   Sydney   Toronto   Mexico   Panama

Johannesburg   Kuala Lumpur   Montreal

New Delhi   Rio de Janeiro   Singapore

This report is issued by the Carnegie Commission
on Higher Education, with headquarters at
1947 Center Street, Berkeley, California 94704.
The views and conclusions expressed in this report
are solely those of the members of the Carnegie Commission
on Higher Education and do not necessarily reflect the
views or opinions of the Carnegie Corporation of New York,
the Carnegie Foundation for the Advancement of Teaching,
or their trustees, officers, directors, or employees.

Library of Congress Cataloging in Publication Data
Carnegie Commission on Higher Education.
College graduates and jobs.

Includes bibliographical references.
1.   College graduates—Employment—United States.
I.   Title.
HD6278.U5C36   331.1'26'0973   73-3288 4/17/73
ISBN 0-07-010061-6

Additional copies of this report may be ordered from
McGraw-Hill Book Company, Hightstown, New Jersey 08520.
The price is $4.50 a copy.

But whether there be prophesies, they shall fail . . .

Contents

Foreword

For over three centuries, college graduates in the United States have had a preferred place in the job market—more interesting and prestigious jobs, higher incomes, less unemployment than the general population. For the first time, this preferred place—or at least the degree of preferment—is perhaps now being threatened. This creates a potentiality of traumatic experiences for college students and for higher education.

How serious is the situation? What adjustments can be made to it? What consequences may it have for college graduates, for other persons in the labor force, for higher education, and for American society?

Higher education is oriented toward much more than the employment of its graduates. It is also concerned with the quality of the personal lives and of the citizenship of its graduates, with research and service, and with much else. But one major purpose of going to college for many students is to get a better job. This report is concerned with this one aspect of higher education, without in any way implying that it is the only aspect. There is a connection between higher education and employment, and it is important both to understand it and to handle it effectively.

In the preparation of this report the Commission has benefitted from several studies undertaken under its auspices, including:

- **Mark S. Blumberg:** *Trends and Projections of Physicians in the United States, 1967–2002,* Carnegie Commission on Higher Education, Berkeley, Calif., 1971.

- Carnegie Commission Survey of Students and Faculty, 1969, conducted under the direction of Martin Trow and Seymour M. Lipset.

- **Margaret S. Gordon (ed.):** *Higher Education and the Labor Market,* a volume of essays prepared in cooperation with the Institute of Industrial

Relations, University of California, Berkeley, McGraw-Hill Book Company, forthcoming.

- **Gus W. Haggstrom:** *The Growth of Higher Education in the United States; School and College Entrance and Graduation Rates, 1900–2000;* and *The Growth of Graduate Education in the Post-Sputnik Era,* unpublished papers, Carnegie Commission on Higher Education, 1972.

- **Everett C. Hughes, et al.:** *Education for the Professions of Medicine, Law, Theology, and Social Welfare,* McGraw-Hill Book Company, forthcoming.

- **Thomas Juster (ed.):** *Education, Income, and Human Behavior,* a volume of essays prepared for the Commission by the National Bureau of Economic Research, McGraw-Hill Book Company, forthcoming.

- **Herbert L. Packer and Thomas Ehrlich:** *New Directions in Legal Education,* McGraw-Hill Book Company, New York, 1972.

- **Richard E. Peterson:** *American College and University Enrollment Trends in 1971,* Carnegie Commission on Higher Education, Berkeley, Calif., 1972.

- **Edgar H. Schein:** *Professional Education: Some New Directions,* McGraw-Hill Book Company, New York, 1972.

- **Stephen B. Withey, et al.:** *A Degree and What Else? Correlates and Consequences of a College Education,* McGraw-Hill Book Company, New York, 1971.

A conference of the authors of papers included in the volume, *Higher Education and the Labor Market,* in October 1971, was also very helpful in connection with the preparation of this report.

The Commission also wishes to express its appreciation to numerous consultants who provided information on various aspects of this report, and especially to those who read and gave us helpful comments on sections relating to their professions, including Professor G. Leland Bach, Graduate School of Business, Stanford University; Dr. David W. Breneman, Staff Director, National Board on Graduate Education; Dean Thomas Ehrlich, School of Law, Stanford University; George J. Maslach, Provost, Professional Schools and Colleges, and former Dean, College of Engineering, University of California, Berkeley; and Professor Mary K. Mullane, College of Nursing, University of Illinois at the Medical Center, Chicago.

The Commission expresses appreciation to a number of its staff members who assisted in the preparation of this report, and especially to Dr. Margaret S. Gordon.

1. Major Themes

1 *A new period* Historically, the labor market has not been a continuing source of concern for higher education. Except in times of depression, it has absorbed all the college and university graduates. It has been taken for granted as a generally adequate outlet for talent highly trained academically. This has now changed, and has probably changed for the foreseeable future; the labor market is now a serious concern for higher education and will remain so.

This report seeks to set forth this new situation as realistically as possible. Its central themes are (1) the many adjustments that will and should be made to alleviate the negative consequences inherent in some of the broad statistical prophecies about the future and (2) the good as well as the bad consequences that may flow from the new situation in the market for college graduates.

The temporary job crisis for college graduates of the last several years (1968–1973) now seems to have passed. However, continuing problems are in store for the future. We consider these underlying problems as they may affect both college students and American society. Although the short-term crisis is phasing out, the long-run situation still deserves careful attention.

2 *Official predictions of major surpluses of college-educated persons*
Three predictions, in particular, as well as the recent experience of college graduates searching for jobs, have highlighted the contemporary concern about the labor market prospects for college-educated persons:

(1) A *United States Bureau of the Census* study states: "It is necessary to make some estimate of the educational levels required for the occupations of 1975; the first and easiest assumption is that the educational attainment distribution within each occupation will remain the same

as it was in 1960. If this assumption turns out to be correct, there will be more high school and college graduates available in 1975 than will be required. In fact, there will be about 3.1 million more high school graduates, 850,000 persons with some college education, and 3.3 million more college graduates than will be required to maintain the 1960 educational status quo within each occupation" (1, p. 174).

It is not suggested that persons with college training will go unemployed in large numbers, but, rather, that nearly a doubling of the rate of "educational upgrading of occupations" that occured from 1950–1960 will be needed between 1960 and 1975, if their absorption is to be adequate (ibid., p. 176). There will more likely be underemployment of talent than unemployment of the college-educated person.

(2) *The Manpower Report of the President, 1972* estimates that 9.8 million college-educated persons will enter the labor force during the 1970s and that 9.6 million of them will be absorbed as follows: 3.3 million by replacement needs for persons retiring or otherwise withdrawing from the labor force, 3.3 million by expansion of employment opportunities, and *2.6 million by educational upgrading of positions that have not normally utilized college-educated persons in the past* (2, p. 114; italics added).

(3) The *U.S. Bureau of Labor Statistics* has estimated that "a high school education will be sufficient for 8 out of every 10 jobs" during the 1970s (3, p. 3). Stated the other way around, only 20 percent of the jobs will require education beyond the high school. Yet today, more than one-third of the 18 to 21 age group is in college at any one moment of time, and one-half attend college at some point; our Commission also estimates that two-thirds of this age group will take postsecondary educational training of some sort in the foreseeable future. We estimate this proportion by looking at recent trends in the ratio of those in the age group who attend college, at recent patterns of attendance by young persons from higher-income families — patterns that are increasingly being followed by young persons from lower-income families — and by looking at the rate of high school graduation (90 percent in Minnesota) and of college attendance by high school graduates (75 percent in California) in the most advanced states and assume that the national average will rise to these levels. The discrepancy between the estimated 20 percent of jobs requiring more than a high school education and these attendance rates is shown in Chart 1. The current discrepancy is 30 percent, and the estimated potential discrepancy is nearly 50 percent.

It should be noted immediately that flows are different from stocks, and that Chart 1 is concerned with flows. The labor force turns over completely within a 50-year cycle. Thus it takes a half-century for a change in the com-

CHART 1 *Matching jobs and postsecondary educational attainment*

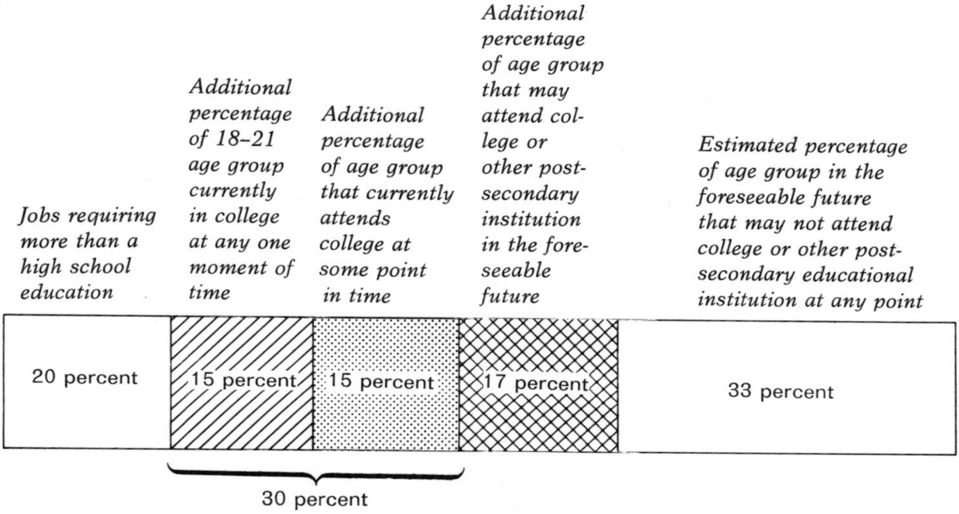

Jobs requiring more than a high school education	Additional percentage of 18–21 age group currently in college at any one moment of time	Additional percentage of age group that currently attends college at some point in time	Additional percentage of age group that may attend college or other postsecondary institution in the foreseeable future	Estimated percentage of age group in the foreseeable future that may not attend college or other postsecondary educational institution at any point
20 percent	15 percent	15 percent	17 percent	33 percent

30 percent

position of the flow to work out its complete impact on the stock. Changes in flow starting in 1960, for example, if continued will not have had their total impact on the labor force until about 2010.

Taken together, these three predictions indicate difficulties, even severe difficulties, particularly in the long run, *if* no adjustments are made.

3 *How serious is the situation?* Adjustments will be made; in fact, they are being made. Man is highly adaptable to changing circumstances.

The real problem for the current decade is the over 25 percent of the college graduates (and attenders) who will need to find jobs in "educationally upgraded" positions (2.6 million out of 9.6 million). The approximately 75 percent who will replace persons withdrawing from the labor market and who will take jobs in expanding occupations which are now normally filled by college-trained persons constitute no general labor market problem. But the 25 percent may be a problem.

Another way of looking at the problem is to refer, not to the occupations that will be "educationally upgraded," but to the persons who will be *occupationally downgraded* as compared with past experience. Some of these persons will go into jobs which have been genuinely upgraded, as into managerial levels formerly filled by noncollege graduates but where the assignments are of a truly higher order than in the past. Others will go into jobs which *could* be and may be redesigned. Some persons, however, will go into jobs that will not and perhaps cannot be raised to the level of their capacity. Some of this happens already. Nearly 30 percent of four-year male college graduates are now in blue-collar, sales, and clerical jobs, many of which do not make full use of their education.[1]

Thus, the realistic problem for the 1970s will be the necessity for the absorption of some college-educated persons into jobs which have not been traditionally filled by persons with a college education, but in a national context where such absorption has been occurring in the past and is less of a traumatic problem than in much of the rest of the world.

Some of the absorption of college graduates into the labor market will be relatively easy because the jobs will have been upgraded; but some will be frustrating for the persons involved because the jobs have not been or cannot be upgraded. Perhaps somewhere in the vicinity of 1 million to 1½ million college-educated persons, as a *very rough guess,* will face this frustrating experience. But the same number would probably have ended up in about the same types of jobs if they had not gone to college. They are no worse off occupationally—and often may be better off in other ways— for going to college than they otherwise would have been. The problem, then, may be concentrated on about one-half of the 25 percent of the college-educated persons who will enter "educationally upgraded" positions. The potential problem is thus one more nearly for 10 percent than it is for 100 percent of college-educated persons.

This is not to say that the resultant frustration will not be a negative experience for the persons involved—it will be. We only indicate the general proportions of the problem, and note that it is not a new problem.

Nor is this to say that the United States could never have a much more severe problem in the very long run. If inadequate adjustments are made, we could end up (1) with a situation in which additional expenditures on higher education for additional graduates would add nothing at all to the GNP—there would be no economic return at all on the expenditure—but only to the number of competitors for scarce jobs, or (2) with a political crisis because of the sub-

[1] See Appendix A, Table A-9.

stantial number of disenchanted and underemployed or even un-employed college graduates—as in Ceylon or in India or in Egypt, or (3) with both. Higher education will then have become counter-productive. The first possibility would mean a waste of resources; the second, greater political instability; the third, both. But, in the judgment of the Commission, we are far away from any of these possibilities. Higher education is still a good investment—with apparent monetary returns for the individual at the annual rate of about 10 percent or more of his investment and perhaps about the same for the economy as a whole. And the adaptability and realistic expectations of American students diminish the prospects of grave political repercussions as in Germany at the time of Hitler.

The United States is very fortunate in that there is no tradition of a one-to-one relationship between a college education and the jobs that are considered acceptable by the college-educated. In some countries, for example in Finland—where "white-cap" Finnish stu-dents expect "white-cap" jobs—or in India, the problem of ad-justment is far more serious because of the lack of the adapt-ability historically shown by American college graduates. The American tradition of the dignity of hard labor is a great national asset, as is the tradition of the worthiness of any useful position. We have a relatively "democratized" occupational structure, with-out clear class lines.

Two further factors ease the situation for the person just out of college. Many of the "best" of the new jobs opening up are taken by college graduates with their greater skills, rather than by per-sons already in the labor force. They have a differential advantage over older persons with lower educational attainments, whom they pass over. Also, new lifestyles make some otherwise less acceptable jobs not only acceptable but eagerly sought after. For example, postal positions, once filled by high school graduates, are now sought by some college graduates who find they fit into their chosen lifestyles and occupational interests. Some college graduates prefer the life of a craftsman, as another example.

We do have an enduring concern, and also some temporary and specific crises. But we do not face any general or even specific catastrophe at the moment, or the prospect of a major overall crisis—at least for a long time to come. We should not take any panicked actions. The budgets of higher education should not be cut because of the labor market situation. Student aid should not generally be reduced. We should not reverse the trend toward open-access admissions to the system of higher education—the 1 million or 1½ million college-educated persons of the 1970s who may take jobs well below their expectations and below their educational attainments still should have had the chance at the over 8 million educationally more appropriate jobs that will develop and at the higher-quality lives that more education can help make possible.

Adjustments, however, can and should be made. And the situation has some very positive aspects, as we shall set forth subsequently.

4 *Developments and prospects—1900-2000* The current period should be seen in the perspective of earlier periods and the prospects for later periods:

1900–1950 Demand for the college-educated person expanded generally along with the supply. Wage and salary differentials for the more highly educated declined steadily but moderately compared with those for the less highly educated.

1950–1968 Demand for the college-educated kept up with or ran somewhat ahead of the supply, which itself expanded greatly, and the long-run narrowing of wage and salary differentials ceased. Demand was buoyed up by these factors:

A rising GNP, more of which went into expenditures on services and the professions where college-educated persons are particularly employed.
An explosive increase of R&D funds and of aerospace employment that called, in particular, for more scientists and engineers.

An explosive increase in primary and then secondary and then tertiary school enrollments, requiring more teachers.

A greater increase in college graduates, as we moved into mass higher education, was met by an equally advancing market for their services—a most favorable period for the college graduate.

1968–1973 The favorable demand developments of the prior period stopped being so favorable, but the outflow of college graduates continued to increase:

A recession took place.

Research and development funds were cut back, and so were funds for the aerospace industry.

School enrollments and teaching positions began leveling off. Thus far the change has affected only the elementary level, but later there will be a decline at the secondary level and then at the tertiary level.

1973–1980? Predictions are dangerous in the labor market area, but we appear to be moving toward a more favorable employment situation economically; the recession is abating. We will spend increasingly more of our GNP on health services that require many college-trained persons. The output of college graduates will probably rise by 50 percent, not the 100 percent of the 1960s. The labor market situation for college graduates should improve somewhat—better than in 1968–1973; worse than in 1950–1968.

1980s? There will be *no* increase in the output of college graduates. Demand for college graduates, however, will presumably continue to expand on a long-term basis. The situation will be a generally favorable one, with at least one major exception—the need for college-level teachers. This one field will surely be in a crisis state. The market may also continue to be unfavorable for elementary and secondary school teachers, but we cannot be certain about that as yet.

1990 and beyond Long-term factors will be at work. The output of college graduates will expand more nearly with that of the total population. It has been expanding much faster than that as we have moved from 2 percent of the age group going to college in 1870 to 50 percent in 1970. But the rate of increase cannot go on forever—in fact we see it reaching a maximum likely rate in the near future of two out of three. This is a favorable factor for the market prospects of college graduates. The major unfavorable factor is that the stock of college graduates will have been fed for 30 years or more by the output of mass higher education. But many other things will happen before the year 2000; and many adjustments will have been made by then.

5 *Prospects by occupations* The outlook for individual occupations, as far as we can anticipate the 1970s, will vary considerably in some instances from the general picture:

- Some will go steadily up in their employment opportunities: computer operators, office machine operators, and recreation workers, among others.

- Some have dim employment prospects: primary and secondary school teachers, for example, and college faculty members.

- Some will have generally bright employment prospects: health care personnel and managers generally, for example. The case of managers is most interesting. More managers are now salaried and fewer are self-employed. The salaried manager increasingly tends to be a college graduate. The jobs are more complex but, also, the heavy rate of college attendance leaves less uneducated talent in the nonmanagerial ranks available for promotion into managerial positions—even into positions as foremen.

- Some will have their ups and downs: engineers, for example. Engineers have their own "corn-hog" cycle. Salaries go up. Students flood in. Students hit the market. Salaries go down. Students flood out. Several years later there is a scarcity of newly trained engineers. Salaries go up. And so on, seemingly ad infinitum. The length of the "production period" interferes with smooth adjustments. The current direction for engineers is up.

6 *Prospects by groups*   The prospects for women college graduates will be hurt by the teaching situation, but helped by the need for more health care personnel. The prospects for men are hurt by the employment trend for scientists, which is currently declining (but will turn up again), but helped by the strong demand for more salaried managers. Women and male members of minority groups will be helped in their employment prospects by national policies. College-educated black women appear to be in a particularly favorable position at the present time. A group especially to be hurt will be majority male Ph.D.'s—more in some fields than in others and possibly in some fields little or not at all. Their general prospects are dismal, particularly because of the high supply of and low demand for Ph.D.'s but also because of the current efforts at hiring women and minority males. They constitute a special potential crisis situation that will result in massive disappointments in the later years of the 1970s and the early 1980s. This is the most serious single problem area we see ahead.

7 *Adjustments—the role of public policy.*   Public policy has had and will have a major impact on the labor market situation for college graduates as it is influenced by:

- The degree of full employment and prosperity.
- The course of hours of work—usually led in modern times by federal policy. A reexamination of the standard 40-hour work week, which has prevailed for nearly 40 years now, may soon be in order. So might longer vacations, extension of sabbatical privileges to new groups of employees, and earlier retirement. Fewer hours of work per person, whether per week, or per year, or per lifetime, can create the possibility of more places to be filled by more persons.
- Expenditures on health care, including some form of national health insurance.
- Expenditures on teaching. The current period holds special opportunities, given the surplus of teachers, for moving generally available educational opportunities to the 4-year-old level, for massive extension of day-care

centers, for remedial work, for greater assistance to the handicapped, and for supplying needed teachers for vocational education programs.

- The flow of R&D funds, hopefully held at a steady rate and at a level appropriate for the long run.

- The flow of funds to support graduate-level education, also hopefully held at a steady rate and at a level appropriate for the long run—the spigot was turned on too hard in the 1960s and it should not be turned off too hard in the 1970s.

- The flow of funds for the creative and performing arts.

- The creation and improvement and support of other attractive channels into work and life than college attendance alone—such as a national service program.

- The extension of the doctrine of the Griggs case (Griggs et al. *v.* Duke Power Company, 1971). That case calls for "the elimination of artificial, arbitrary and unnecessary barriers to employment that . . . cannot be shown to be related to job performance" and of "devices and mechanisms . . . unless they are demonstrably a reasonable measure of job performance"; and that requires, instead, that "any tests used must measure the person for the job and not the person in the abstract." This doctrine, if extended into practice, will reduce the felt necessity of young persons to get a degree when a degree is an artificial requirement for the job in question; more jobs will be open without formal advance certification.

- The provision of data on occupational prospects for the guidance of students and counselors.

Constructive actions in each of these areas would add up to a policy of selective involvement, rather than total public responsibility and control.

8 *Adjustments—the role of private policy*
Young persons have the most at stake. When given the necessary information and reasonable options, at least those at the college level have shown themselves very adept at seeking out the better opportunities for themselves. They can assist effective adjustments by:

- Deciding carefully whether they really wish to go to college or not and by looking at other alternative channels as well as at college. Some young persons are reevaluating the necessity of going to college and, as a result, enrollments are now falling below recently projected levels.

- Seeking broad training in college rather than narrow specialization, unless they have a very carefully chosen goal in mind. Many graduates do not get jobs in the specific field of their undergraduate major.[2] Yet college can benefit them greatly by giving them skills and knowledge useful in many jobs, and by giving them training in how to benefit by training so that their subsequent on-the-job training will be more effective.[3] College helps both ways.

- Looking on college as much more than preparation for an occupation. It is also preparation for life. This means looking for opportunities to broaden interests that can enrich all of subsequent life. Higher education was once most helpful in entering a higher class status; subsequently, in entering into a better job; and increasingly now, in entering into a better life.

- Selecting occupational specializations carefully, including use of counseling services.

- Stopping-out after high school or while in college both to have an opportunity to try out occupational interests and to get experience that can help in getting a job; or by engaging in part-time work; or both.

- Developing realistic expectations about jobs. On the average, the jobs of college graduates do "pay off" at the rate of about 10 percent or more a year on the investment. They also tend to be more "satisfying," aside from income.[4] But many college graduates must be reconciled to not getting the job of their first choice.

By and large, students make career choices that are responsive to labor market changes. Their choices should be respected, in col-

---

[2] As Folger, Bayer, and Astin (4, pp. 232–235) have indicated, many college graduates are employed in occupations that "do not require degrees in the particular field in which they received their bachelor's or master's degree." Only 4 percent of the males with 1958 bachelor's degrees in the social sciences, for example, and only one-fourth of those with degrees in the natural sciences, were employed full-time in the same field five years after graduation. The proportions of graduates employed in their major fields of study were considerably higher for those with B.A.'s in engineering, education, and business administration.

[3] Among workers with three or more years of college, about one-fourth reported that they had learned their jobs through company training, and nearly two-thirds stated that they had learned substantially on the job. However, a substantial proportion indicated more than one way of learning (5, p. 20).

[4] A recent survey, for example, indicated that 89 percent of workers with a college degree responded that they found their work "enjoyable," as compared with 70 percent of workers with less than 12 years of schooling. In fact, the proportion finding their work enjoyable varied directly with educational attainment. College graduates were also considerably more likely to mention "meaningful, interesting activity" as a preferred job characteristic than were workers with less education, whereas those with less education were more likely to mention job "security" (6, pp. 67 and 68).

lege and by government, as they prepare themselves for occupations. We are totally opposed, with a few special exceptions, to a "manpower planning" approach to higher education; we believe that reliance on student choice is superior—it is a more flexible, a more constantly dynamic mechanism. Manpower planning leads toward rigidities and toward controls, and we find it, by and large, both an ineffective and a repugnant mechanism and probably also an unenforceable one as well. Student choice, in the long run and by and large, is superior to central planning of higher education to accord with centrally determined manning tables. The "free-choice principle" is generally superior to the "manpower principle" (7).

Parents can assist by not pressing their children to attend college against their will. We already have a situation in which 5 to 30 percent of our students are reluctant, to one degree or another, in their attendance (8): And the reluctant attenders are usually not very good students.

The campus can help adaptability to the new labor market situation by:

- Following, with a few exceptions, changing occupational interests of students. Students have already reduced their undergraduate enrollments in education and increased them in nursing, as an indication of quick and constructive responses. Such a policy will prove better, in the long run, than that of following guild like quotas developed by the faculty and administration. The exceptions to this rule, as we see them, are two:

   (1) When there are sudden shifts of student interests, as in the recent case of law, that cannot be sustained more than temporarily and where a full campus response to such a sudden demand would, in any event, be impossible in the short run

   (2) Where very great costs of a long-run nature are involved, as in the training of medical doctors and of Ph.D.'s

   In both types of cases, the college must exercise a restraining hand. In order to be guided by student interests, these exceptions aside, the campus must seek to avoid an excessively large proportion of tenured faculty and must retain flexibility in assignment of its budgetary resources.

- Not holding down places unduly for the sake of an external profession (as once for medicine) or building them up unduly for the sake of institutional prestige (as currently with the Ph.D.). The public was misled in the first case; Ph.D. candidates were misled in the second.

- Providing adequate counseling and placement services. A good placement service may also become a great competitive advantage, as it is for the Harvard and Stanford Schools of Business.

- Providing broad training opportunities for students.

- Providing "quality of life" courses, as in the creative arts. Each time there is a change in the focus of higher education (as from class status to job placement), there is a corresponding curricular change; so it will be again (job procurement to quality of life).

- Permitting, even encouraging, stop-outs.

- Providing a three-year degree option so that students may have more time to stop out to obtain work experience and so that time may be saved for subsequent adult training periods. (A three-year degree option will, of course, tend to put more persons in the labor market during the transitional period when colleges are shifting from a four-year bachelor's program.)

- Revising teacher education approaches to take advantage of the new opportunities for teaching noted earlier and to provide instruction in the use of the new technology.

- Curbing addition of new Ph.D. programs except under the most unusual circumstances.

- Adding D.A. programs, where appropriate, to provide teachers for the expanding community and comprehensive colleges.

Some types of colleges will be affected more favorably by current and prospective labor market developments and some less favorably. We expect that the occupationally oriented community colleges and comprehensive colleges will benefit most, as well as all colleges, including these, that emphasize adult education. We expect that the Ph.D.-oriented research university (excluding the health sciences center), the teachers college, and the liberal arts college heavily oriented toward teacher training will benefit least.

Professional associations can assist by (1) making careful labor market studies of their own as has been done in the case of physics and by (2) developing more effective career ladder opportunities such as are needed in the health service professions.

Coordinating councils and other agencies with statewide planning responsibilities can assist by:

- Being cautious about expectations for future enrollments until the impact of the new labor market situation and the prospect for the opening up of other cannels into work and life other than education become clearer

- Helping to consolidate teacher-training programs as enrollments contract

- Helping to expand training facilities for health care personnel and for managers, but being careful not to overexpand, as with Ph.D. training in the 1960s

- Halting further expansion of Ph.D. programs except under the most unusual circumstances

- Encouraging offering of the D.A. degree

- Expanding adult education and nontraditional training programs

- Collecting better labor market information

- Giving more attention to labor market prospects in planning and in approving new campuses and major new endeavors on existing campuses

Employers can assist by:

- Reviewing their hiring policies. Employers may genuinely need, and benefit from, the employment of college graduates. Graduates may have specific skills that the employer wants. They are likely to have the ability and experience to benefit from training on the job. Their talent has been sorted out. Their background tends to make them more flexible in their assignments. A pool of such people makes it easier to handle emergency situations (a "fail-safe" device), and it provides a competitive group from which promotions can be made. Also, the college graduate has demonstrated his willingness to accept functional authority, to postpone gratification, to work steadily. In addition, he tends to have accumulated more social skills and is more mature in age. Thus, even if no specific occupational skills are required, the college graduate may still be the preferable employee. We do not generally subscribe to the view of the "Great Training Robbery" (9). However, employers may misuse the college degree when hiring by making it an artificial screening device to reduce the number of applicants when the job does not require a degree either directly or indirectly; and their hiring officers may use the degree—or lack of it—as a substitute for their own judgment. For some jobs, of course, a degree is considered a disqualification.

- Looking at the implications of the Griggs case for them. Are they really measuring "the person against the job" and not against formal rules or informal prejudices? Employers should realize that we have entered a Populist period in our policy toward the labor market.

- Providing on-the-job training and opportunities for further education so that employees may prepare themselves to advance vertically or to move to other occupations.

- Engaging in job redesign to make jobs more interesting and less routine, to give them more responsibility and variety, to provide more promotional levels, and generally to enrich them. Employers also should provide job "options" as in hours of work, in alternative retirement plans, and in other ways. Some of this, of course, goes on almost unnoticed in day-to-day adjustments to actual situations. Historically, education has fitted itself to occupational requirements; increasingly, job situations may need to fit themselves to a more educated labor force.

- Providing short-term and part-time jobs for college students.

9 *Consequences* The new labor market situation for college graduates will have many repercussions, some of which can be only dimly seen. Certainly there will be some that cannot now be seen at all. Some likely consequences, as they now appear, are the following:

- Many adjustments, as noted above, will need to be made by many individuals and groups. Some will be both difficult and costly.

- Even after adjustments are made, some college graduates will be disappointed by jobs that fall below their expectations.

- Frustration may extend to other groups as well: to young persons without college experience who are pushed down by the pressure of college graduates in the labor market—even pushed into unemployment, and to older persons who are passed over by younger and more educated persons. These strains on society will be increased.

- Employers faced by many educated applicants may require more artificial certification rather than less.

- Labor force participation rates will rise, as they have in the past (10), as the labor force is more highly educated; geographic and occupational mobility will increase.

- The "brain drain" from abroad will be reduced; it may even be reversed, as has occurred already in the migration of some Ph.D.'s from the United States to Canadian universities.

- Equality of opportunity to secure the better jobs will be increased for the children of lower-income families, for women, and for members of minority groups. Higher education has been the first level of education in the United States to achieve largely effective integration of students, at least at the undergraduate level, and thus can serve as a model for the other levels. But there is still a need for greater progress toward integration in graduate and professional training, and on college faculties.

- With human capital now relatively more important in relation to physical capital, the distribution of opportunities to acquire it becomes more crucial. Policies for grants, for loans, and for access will all become more central within higher education and within society.

- The society will become more meritocratic. Land ownership once greatly influenced income and power; then capital ownership acquired such influence; now the possession of skill and ability are more influential. This skill and ability is not so easily passed on from one generation to the next: Thus, there will be greater competition within each generation. Children from families at the top will not be protected so much by property and status; children from families farther down the socioeconomic scale will have more of a chance to move up.

- Some young persons will slide backward in the competition to climb the meritocratic occupational pyramid, just as others will advance. Some will not make the attempt to climb at all. Participants in the counterculture may well grow in numbers. Society will increasingly face a major problem of how to handle the persons who are sliders and dropouts.

- There will be more "noneconomic personalities"—more persons not in the labor force at all, or more marginally attached to it and inclined to more turnover, more absenteeism, and less assumption of responsibility.

- In the face of the new labor market situation, society is less likely to favor heavy subsidies to higher education than it did when high-level manpower was scarce.

- To the extent that higher education is less job-oriented, both enrollments and curricula will be affected. If comparative wage and salary differentials for the college-educated are reduced, and if public subsidies are reduced, the benefit-cost ratio facing students will change considerably with additional potential impacts on enrollments. Education costs money and effort, but the comparative returns for both the money and the effort may go down, and the psychic costs of the effort—resulting from preferences for new lifestyles—may go up, and, as a consequence, new balances may be struck between attendance and nonattendance in college by many young persons.

- Jobs will be redesigned in the face of the pressures of the more highly educated labor force. They will improve in many respects. More job relationships will be of a collegial rather than hierarchical nature not only because of the increase in the number of persons in the professions but also because of the greater education of persons in nonprofessional occupations. "Job cultures" and "job styles" will change.

- Wage and salary differentials will gradually be more equalized, as they have been already in Israel and Sweden. This has also been the long-term tendency in the United States. The period from 1950 to 1970 has been an exception, as we have noted above. We do expect, however, that the long-term trend will be resumed. But there is the possibility that it may not be, or that it will be resumed but at a slower rate because of increasing rigidification of the wage and salary structure. It is possible that the job market will have no or little impact on the wage and salary structure, although we doubt it. Were this to be true, nevertheless, more college graduates would show up in longer "queues" for entrance to college-type jobs rather than as a factor reducing comparative wage and salary differentials for college-type jobs.[5] Under such conditions, college-type jobs could show a positive "rate of return" on the investment even though this was an artificial result of the wage structure and not the result of comparatively high productivity contributions as reflected in wages. Overinvestment in college education could then easily occur. However, we believe that the long-term trend toward more equality in the wage and salary structure will resume and, perhaps, even accelerate.

- We note the importance of flexibility in wage and salary differentials for the sake of absorption of college graduates. Some absorption takes place as a result of the long-run increase in demand — more employment at any given wage and salary level. But the behavior of demand for college-educated persons is such that some *comparative* reduction in wage and salary levels can also result in substantially increased employment.[6]

- This prospective renewed trend in equalization of wage and salary differentials will bring greater "social justice" within society, but at the cost of social tension as the differentials narrow, as Sweden has experienced. But, in the longer run, the inherent social tensions of a meritocratic society will be reduced as incomes are more equalized. Status and power may still vary greatly, but their variation will be easier to accept if access to material rewards is more equal. Democratization of income reduces both the need to democratize access (as in Sweden) and to democratize the status and power of jobs.

- In the process of the readjustment of wage and salary differentials, the rate of return on a college education will gradually go down — it is now 5 percent in Norway (12). The monetary incentives to go to college will be

[5] Lester Thurow has developed a "job competition" model of the labor market, which is based on the assumption that employers conceive of their job applicants as forming a labor queue in which the order of preference largely reflects identifiable background characteristics, among which education is important (11). In the Thurow model, an increase in the supply of college graduates relative to the availability of jobs for which college graduates have traditionally been hired would inevitably result in an extension of the types of jobs for which college graduates were either required or preferred. The incomes of college graduates would not necessarily decline in relation to those of workers with less education.

[6] In other words, in the terms of the economist, the demand schedule is elastic.

reduced, and this may come to discourage some college attendance, although there is no indication of this as yet in Norway. If college attendance is discouraged, the further narrowing of differentials from this cause will also be reduced.

- The quality of life of many individuals may well be increased as they have more education; their participation as citizens in both nonprofit and public endeavors may be enhanced; their tolerance for members of other religious, ethnic, and racial groups in our pluralistic society may be raised to higher levels (6, 13, and 14).

- More parents will be better qualified to teach their own children. And we have come to realize the great importance of the early home environment on the subsequent academic and career achievements of children.

- The quality of public and private bureaucracies will be improved with beneficial results in a society of large-scale organizations, although their greater quality may never show up in any measurement of the GNP.

- Higher education is ecologically sound—it uses few resources itself; it helps change tastes toward the literary and the artistic; it tends to reduce the birthrate.

- The opportunities to increase national welfare are substantial, given the larger and larger numbers of highly trained persons—to improve health, to improve the environment, to reduce poverty, to improve our system of justice, to aid the creative and performing arts, and in many other ways. This enlarged pool of talent, properly utilized, can be an enormous national asset—the greatest "wealth of a nation."[7]

- In the past, the educational system has always followed and adapted itself to the society of the time and place. Now for the first time in history, the educational system, in the several ways indicated above, may become a major force for changing society—may become a more dependent force in society. It may come to change society as much as it is changed by society.

The potential consequences are many—some are negative and some are positive. On the negative side we see particularly more social tension as some college-educated persons fail to find jobs for which they are academically qualified, as pressures accumulate for the redesign of jobs and work environments, and as wage and salary differentials are narrowed and otherwise readjusted. On the positive side we note the likelihood of greater social justice through more equal opportunity and through more equalized earned

[7] According to Adam Smith (15, p. lvii), "The annual labor of every nation is the fund which originally supplies it with all the necessaries and conveniences of life which it annually consumes. . . ."

incomes, of more tolerant attitudes among fellow citizens, and of greater human capacity to solve the many problems of postindustrial society. It is our belief that the positive potentialities outweigh the negative, provided the proper adjustments to the new situation are made. Instead of facing a catastrophe, we can secure an elevation of the quality of life for most of the people in the United States. Predictions of gloom and doom based on the new labor market situation for college-educated persons can be proved to be quite wrong.

2. The Issues to Which This Report Is Addressed

Throughout most of American history, the advantages of a college education, for those who have been fortunate enough to obtain one, have been largely taken for granted—by parents, by students, and by the general public. And foremost among these generally accepted advantages—though by no means the only attraction of a college education—has been access of the college graduate to a relatively remunerative and high-status job. Related to this faith in the economic advantages, as well as to other values of higher education, have been the extraordinary efforts that have been directed over nearly 350 years to the development of an exceptionally extensive and diverse array of colleges and universities that is without parallel in any other country in the world.

Particularly in the years since the Civil War, the development of the American economy and the expansion of higher education have proceeded hand in hand. In the era of the colleges before the Civil War, the student body consisted largely of "young men headed for the three learned professions"—law, medicine, and the ministry (16, p. 34). With the rapid industrialization that followed the Civil War, new demands were created for teachers, engineers, scientists, architects, and a host of other professionals. Thus it was scarcely an accident that the development of universities, which began in the latter part of the nineteenth century, accompanied, and to a degree was a response to, the emergence of increasingly complex manpower needs in an industrializing economy.

Since World War II, the link between the development of higher education and the rapid development of the American economy has been especially evident. Enrollments in colleges and universities increased at an unprecedented rate, but the demand for professionally trained workers was also rising in such a buoyant manner that, until the end of the 1960s, college graduates and holders of advanced degrees had little difficulty obtaining the types of jobs to which they aspired, except in recession years. This generalization applies more clearly to white males than to women or to members of disadvantaged minority groups. The relative position of black college graduates in the job market was clearly improving toward the end of the period, however, and there have been very recent indications that civil rights pressure and fair-employment legislation are beginning to have some effect in alleviating discrimination against college-educated women.

The economic recession that began at the end of 1969 had a distinctly adverse effect on job opportunities for college graduates, and there was evidence that the difficulties might not altogether disappear as the economy slowly recovered from the recession. In fact, most official and unofficial predictions suggested that the job market for college graduates in the 1970s would be somewhat less favorable than it had been in the preceding two decades. One of the purposes of this report is to attempt an assessment of those predictions.

However, preparation for the labor market is only one of the functions of higher education. Other functions of our colleges and universities are also extremely important. Some writers emphasize the distinction between the technical and critical components of higher education. In their view, the technical component is concerned primarily with preparing students to become economically productive citizens, while the critical component is concerned with stimulating students' "intellectual, moral, and emotional growth" (14, pp. 40–41). Other writers on the functions of higher education have emphasized its roles in (1) identifying and encouraging talent, (2) developing relatively informed citizens and potential leaders, (3) preserving our cultural and intellectual heritage, (4) contributing to the advancement of knowledge, and (5) extending to widely varied groups in the community the opportunity to enhance their understanding of social, economic, and technical problems through the public service activities of colleges and universities.

The Commission does not believe that colleges and universities should tighten their undergraduate entrance requirements because the job market for college graduates is likely to be less favorable in the future than it has been in the recent past. Nor should they restrict the flow of student aid for this reason. We have given high priority to the unfinished task of providing equality of opportunity to enroll in higher education to low-income and minority-group students, whose opportunities have been unequal in the past.[1]

In addition, as we shall point out in later sections, gloomy predictions about job prospects for college graduates toward the end of the present decade may not be fully warranted because of numerous possibilities of adjustments to changing trends on both the demand and supply sides of the labor market. And, looking forward to the 1980s, when enrollment in higher education is likely to be essentially stationary, we believe that the job market for college graduates will almost certainly improve as demand for educated manpower increases in the face of a relatively stable supply.

Recommendation 1: Institutions of higher education and governments at all levels should not restrict undergraduate opportunities to enroll in college or to receive student aid because of less favorable trends in the job market for college graduates than have prevailed in the recent past.

Nevertheless, shifts are clearly taking place in demand and supply relationships in many occupations in which college graduates are employed. Students are changing their career choices, and institutions of higher education are facing many adjustments as a result. In recent years, also, significant numbers of young people have been turning away from conventional career aspirations toward nontraditional careers or alternative lifestyles. And just in the last few years, new types of opportunities for participation in nontraditional patterns of higher education have begun to be provided. As a consequence, it is becoming increasingly difficult to predict the net effect of all these changes on higher education in the United States by, say, 1980 or 1985.

Recommendation 2: Individual institutions of higher education and state planning agencies should place high priority in the 1970s and 1980s on adjusting their programs to changing student choices of fields that will occur in response both to pronounced occupational shifts in the labor market and to changing student interests and concerns. High priority should also be placed on continued flexibility in the use of resources in order to facilitate such adjustments.

---

[1] See, especially, the Commission's report *A Chance to Learn* (1970).

The necessary adjustments will be difficult to achieve as the rate of growth of enrollments declines in the 1970s and as enrollments become essentially stationary in the 1980s. Adjustments can always be accomplished more easily in periods of rapid growth than in periods of declining rates of growth or of stationary enrollment.[2]

Thus the issues to which this report is addressed are complex. We are concerned with at least these major questions, as well as with related more minor questions:

(1) What is the long-term outlook in the job market for college graduates in general, looking in particular toward the late 1970s and early 1980s? How will this outlook be affected by prospective changes in demand and supply, and by possible adjustments on both the demand and supply sides of the market to a situation that may well be quite different from that which prevailed in the 1950s and 1960s?

(2) In which occupations can we anticipate surpluses? In which occupations shortages? In which occupations, a reasonable balance between demand and supply?

(3) What does available evidence suggest about the changing aspirations of young people and about the extent to which they have become disenchanted with traditional careers?

(4) What changes in the structures and policies of higher education seem indicated by the changing job market for college graduates?

(5) How should individual colleges and universities respond—in their admissions policies, in their curricula, in their counseling programs, in their relationships with prospective employers of college graduates, and in the extent to which they encourage college-age young people to seek combinations of work and educational experience?

(6) What is the outlook in the job market for Ph.D.'s? How should doctoral-granting institutions respond—in their policies for admission to graduate education, in their relative emphasis on Ph.D. and newly emerging D.A. programs, and in the restructuring of Ph.D. programs?

[2] The Commission has made a number of recommendations relating to this problem in its report *The More Effective Use of Resources* (1972). See Appendix B.

(7) How should state and federal governments respond in their policies relating to the support of graduate students and graduate education?

(8) How does the outlook for graduates of professional schools compare with the outlook for those receiving master's and doctor's degrees? Is there a danger that shifts away from master's and doctor's programs in liberal arts fields into professional schools will lead to oversupplies of lawyers, doctors, graduates of schools of business administration, and other professionally trained workers?

(9) More generally, to what extent and in what sectors of higher education should changing manpower requirements be a major criterion in determining public policy toward higher education? What alternative criteria should be given major emphasis? How can we adapt social policies so that they will be responsive to changing perceptions of national needs and at the same time create challenging jobs for young people, some of whom are unhappy with the kinds of jobs that have been traditionally available to college graduates?

3. Changes in the Job Market for College Graduates, 1900–1970

College graduates are employed primarily as professional and managerial workers, and the enormous increase in demand for the services of college-educated workers since the beginning of the present century has been closely associated with the rise in the relative importance of these two major occupation groups in the labor force (Chart 2). Among men, the share of these two groups in total employment rose from about 10 percent in 1900 to approximately 28 percent in 1970, while among women the share rose from about 10 to 19 percent during the same period.

The increase in the relative importance of the professional group among the major occupation groups in which men were employed proceeded much more rapidly between 1950 and 1970 than in earlier periods. For the male managerial group, the experience has been somewhat different. The data in Charts 2 and 3 suggest that the big jump occurred between 1940 and 1950, but this reflected in large part a heavy influx of men into small business following World War II, influenced by recovery of the economy from the Great Depression and from the restrictions of the war period, as well as a move on the part of veterans, aided by the G.I. Bill of Rights, into self-employment. In the late 1950s and in the 1960s, on the other hand, the number of self-employed managerial workers declined, among both men and women, whereas salaried managerial employment rose sharply (Charts 4 and 7).

The more moderate rise among women in the relative importance of the professional and managerial groups reflects a rather different historical experience. In 1900, the proportion of all female workers represented by the professional and technical group was 2.4 times as high as for men and by 1930 was 2.9 times as high as for men. In the following two decades, however, the percentage of female workers employed in this occupational group declined, and al-

CHART 2 *Professional and managerial workers as a percentage of all workers, by sex, United States, 1900–1970*

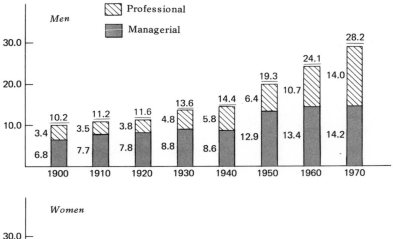

SOURCE: Appendix A, Table A-1.

though it rose again between 1950 and 1970, in the latter year it only slightly exceeded its 1930 level as a percentage of all female workers and also only slightly exceeded the percentage of male workers employed in the professional group.[1]

Employment opportunities for women in the managerial group have never been particularly favorable, as compared with those for men, and the decline in self-employment among women in the last two decades has been accompanied by a decline in the percentage of all female workers employed in the managerial group.

The reasons for these broad changes will be discussed more

---

[1] It is important to recognize here, however, that fine comparisons between data for the early part of the period represented in Chart 2 and the later part of the period are not justified, because of the shift from the "gainful worker" concept used in the early part of the period to the "employed worker" basis in the later part of the period (See Appendix A, Table A-1).

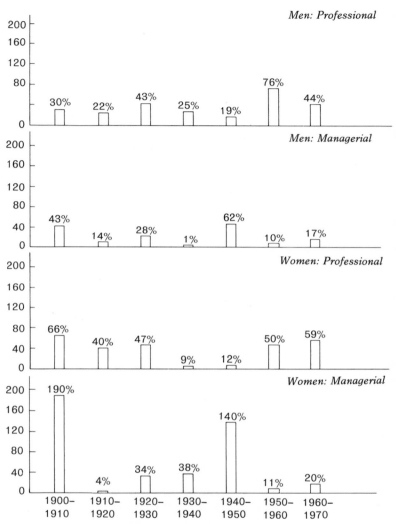

CHART 3 *Percentage changes in the number of professional and managerial workers from decade to decade, by sex, 1900–1970*

Men: Professional

Men: Managerial

Women: Professional

Women: Managerial

| | 1900–1910 | 1910–1920 | 1920–1930 | 1930–1940 | 1940–1950 | 1950–1960 | 1960–1970 |

SOURCE: See source references for Appendix A, Table A-1.

fully at a later stage. For the present, the important point is that, despite the enormous increase in enrollment in higher education and in the number of college graduates in the postwar period, the demand for college graduates was also rising rapidly. Degree-credit enrollment in higher education rose from about 1.5 million in 1940 to nearly 8 million in 1970, while the number of recipients of bachelor's and more advanced degrees increased from 217,000 in 1940 to slightly more than 1 million in 1969–70. Even so, not only did college graduates, for the most part, fare well in the job

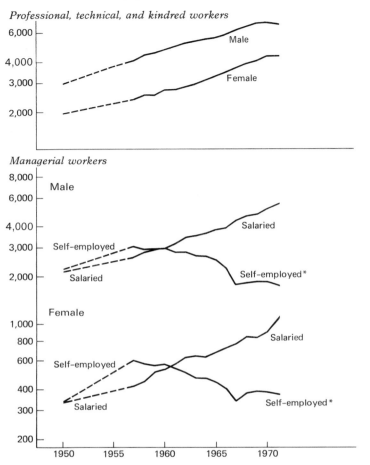

CHART 4 *Number of employed professional and managerial workers, by sex, 1950 and 1957 to 1971 (logarithmic scale, in thousands)*

Professional, technical, and kindred workers

Managerial workers

* A change in classification in 1967 shifted about 750,000 self-employed managerial workers to the salaried managerial category.

SOURCES: U.S. Bureau of the Census (17, Table 128); U.S. Department of Labor (2, p. 171); and U.S. Bureau of Labor Statistics (18).

market, but, especially in occupations such as engineering, demand was rising *more* rapidly than supply during certain short-run periods.

PATTERNS OF OCCUPA- TIONAL CHANGE The capacity of our economy to employ steadily increasing numbers of college graduates, especially in professional and managerial occupations, can be understood only by examining patterns of occupational change in some detail. Unfortunately, available statistics, especially for years before 1940, are far from ideal for this purpose.

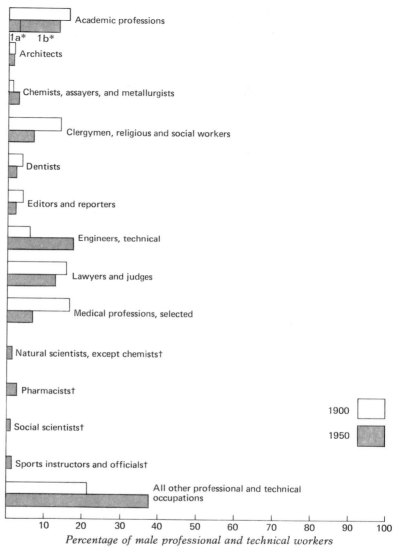

CHART 5 *Percentage of male professional and technical workers in selected occupations, 1900 and 1950*

Academic professions

1a* 1b*

Architects

Chemists, assayers, and metallurgists

Clergymen, religious and social workers

Dentists

Editors and reporters

Engineers, technical

Lawyers and judges

Medical professions, selected

Natural scientists, except chemists†

Pharmacists†

Social scientists†

Sports instructors and officials†

All other professional and technical occupations

1900

1950

10   20   30   40   50   60   70   80   90   100

Percentage of male professional and technical workers

* 1a. College presidents, professors, and instructors, not elsewhere classified.
1b. Teachers, except college.
† Data not available in 1900.

SOURCES: Edwards (19, pp. 120, 128, and 178); and U.S. Bureau of the Census (17, Table 3).

Changes in Occupational Trends: Men

If we consider first the professional occupations in which most workers tend to be college graduates, we find that, among men, the most significant development in the first half of the present century was a rise in the number of these college-graduate occupation groups that were significantly represented in the male professional group (Chart 5). Particularly striking was the increase in the relative importance of engineers. Natural scientists (other than chemists) and social scientists probably also gained relative ground, but we cannot be certain, because they were not classified separately until 1950. Some of them were probably included among college professors in earlier years.

Changes in the relative importance of professional fields over this period are also indicated by data on changes in the distribution of bachelor's and first-professional degrees awarded by field (Appendix A, Table A-5). In the early years of the century, nearly two-fifths of these degrees were awarded in three traditional professional fields—medicine, dentistry, and law. Humanities and arts accounted for about 28 percent and natural sciences for about 13 percent. By the late 1940s, degrees in social sciences, engineering, applied biology, and business and commerce accounted for more than two-fifths of all degrees awarded at these levels, while the share of natural sciences, humanities and arts, medicine, dentistry, and law had declined—in some cases dramatically. The rise in the relative importance of the field of education and the decline in humanities and arts may be regarded as to some extent complementary, because many of those majoring in humanities and arts in the early 1900s were probably preparing to be teachers.

Somewhat less dramatic changes occurred during the first half of the century in the distribution of doctor's degrees awarded (Appendix A, Table A-6). The natural sciences accounted for about 44 percent at the beginning of the period and for a somewhat smaller proportion in the late 1940s. Next in relative importance in the early years of the century were humanities and arts, but their share fell quite markedly over the years. The proportion of all doctorates awarded in the social sciences did not change greatly, while such fields as engineering, applied biology, and education gained substantially in relative importance.

Although both the 1950s and the 1960s were characterized by pronounced increases in demand for highly educated men, patterns of occupational changes differed somewhat between the two decades. Between 1950 and 1960, there were relatively high percentage increases in the employment of designers, draftsmen, engineers, personnel and labor relations workers, religious workers (other than clergymen), social scientists, elementary and secondary school teachers, technicians, and miscellaneous professional workers (Appendix A, Table A-2). These changes reflected two main sets of forces—(1) the sharp increase in the percentage of the gross

CHART 6 *Research and development expenditures as percentage of gross national product in current dollars, 1940–1971*

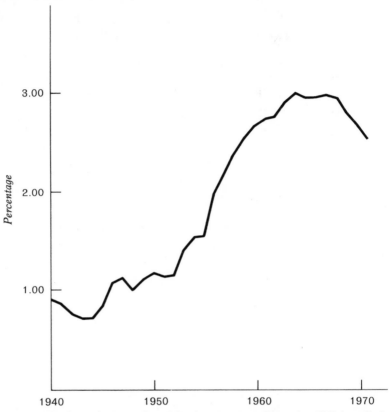

NOTE: The figure for research and development expenditures for 1970 is preliminary; for 1971 it is estimated.

SOURCES: Folk (20, pp. 33–34); National Science Foundation (21, p. 25); and *Economic Report of the President* (22, p. 195).

national product expended on research and development from 1952 on (Chart 6) along with the overlapping influence of expansion of the aerospace industries and (2) the pronounced increase in elementary and secondary school enrollment.

On the other hand, in the 1960s the percentage increase in employment of engineers was below the average for professional workers, reflecting the cutbacks in aerospace employment and in the proportion of GNP expended on research and development toward the end of the decade (Appendix A, Table A-4). But relatively pronounced rates of increase occurred in the employment of men as architects, librarians, biological scientists, computer specialists and operations and systems researchers and analysts,[2] personnel and labor relations workers, dietitians, therapists, social scientists, social workers, school and college teachers, airline pilots, and public relations workers. Major influences in inducing these increases were the generally rapid advance of the economy, technological change, a very pronounced rise in health expenditures during the decade, continued sharp increases in school enrollment, and a burgeoning of college enrollments, which created a brisk demand for faculty members.

Natural and social scientists employed in institutions of higher education are grouped with other college professors in Appendix A, Tables A-2 and A-4, i.e., only those in other types of employment are shown separately. In Chart 7, however, the data on natural and social scientists include those in all types of employment and thus overlap with the data on college professors. Actually, there were very pronounced increases in the employment of natural and social scientists both inside and outside of institutions of higher education in the 1960s, although the proportions employed in government and industry vis-à-vis education varied greatly by field, as we shall see in Section 7.

Both decades were characterized by quite pronounced increases in the number of men employed as salaried managers—the 1960s somewhat more than the 1950s—and by declines in the number of self-employed managers. The especially sharp increase in the employment of college graduates as salaried managers in the 1960s, to be noted subsequently, was important in stimulating increases in enrollment in schools of business administration, as we shall find in Section 7. But in this connection it must be recognized that there have also been very pronounced increases in a number of professional occupations for which training is provided primarily by schools of business administration, including personnel and labor relations workers. The market for accountants has also been very favorable in recent years, even though the percentage increase in men employed as accountants was below the average for all professional workers in the 1960s.

Also affecting enrollment in schools of business administration has been the development of two new professional occupations, which were not classified separately in the 1960 census—computer

[2] Precise percentage increases are not available for computer specialists and operations and systems researchers and analysts, but they are known to have been very large.

CHART 7 *Percentage changes in employment in selected professional and managerial occupations, actual, 1950 to 1960, 1960 to 1970, and projected, 1970 to 1980 ***

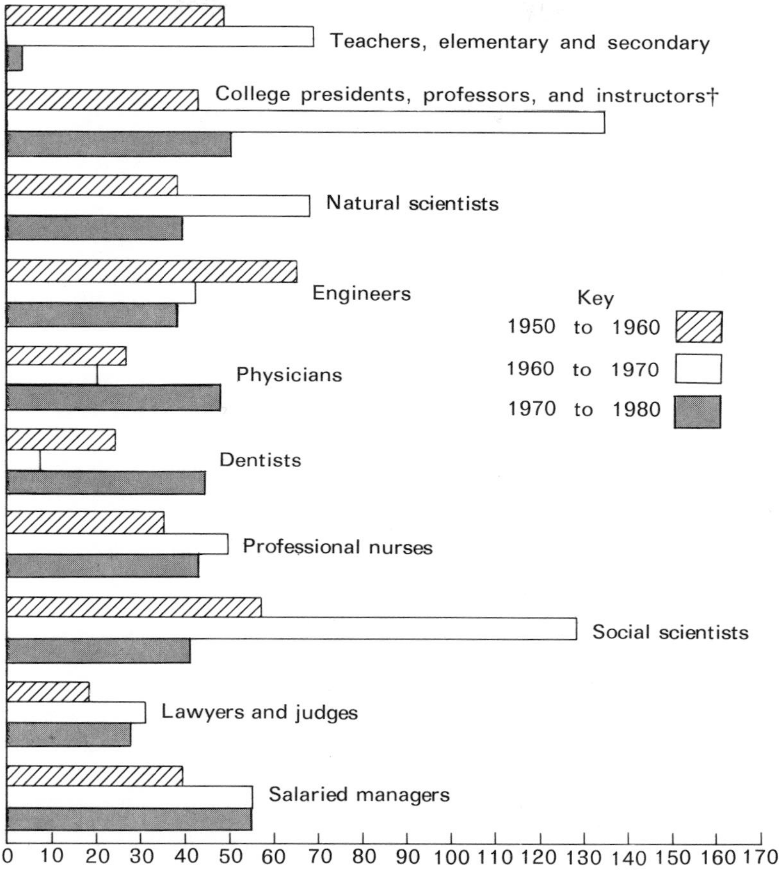

*The projections relate to manpower requirements.

† Projection includes full-time faculty only.

SOURCES: U.S. Department of Labor (2, pp. 107 and 112); U.S. Bureau of the Census (17, Table 3); U.S. Bureau of the Census (24, Table 3); U.S. Bureau of the Census (25, Table 8); U.S. Bureau of Labor Statistics (25, p. 1); and U.S. Bureau of Labor Statistics (26, p. 58). In some cases, estimates have been developed by the Carnegie Commission staff.

specialists and operations and systems researchers and analysts. Computer specialists are frequently trained in separate departments rather than in business schools, but operations and systems researchers and analysts tend to be trained in schools of business administration.

Turning specifically to the employment of college graduates, a highly significant aspect of the changes in their employment in the 1950s was the predominant role of the professional occupation group in accounting for the huge increase. More than three-fifths of the rise in the employment of men with four or more years of college was found in the professional and technical group, which appreciably increased its share of all college graduates employed:

Male college graduates in the experienced civilian labor force, by major occupation group, 1950 and 1960	*1950*	*1960*
All college graduates	100.0	100.0
Professional, technical, and kindred workers	54.6	57.0
Managers, officials, and proprietors, except farm	17.7	17.7
Salaried managerial workers	11.7	14.0
Self-employed managerial workers	6.0	3.7
Clerical and kindred workers	6.5	5.5
Sales workers	8.7	8.4
All other occupation groups	12.6	11.4

SOURCE: Appendix A, Table A-2.

However, the failure of the proportion of male college graduates employed as managerial workers to increase reflected the conflicting changes that we have noted for salaried and self-employed managerial workers.

The pattern of changes from 1959 to 1971 was significantly different (we have used data for 1959, 1968, and 1971, because comparable figures are available for those years, and because a slackening demand for scientists and engineers and for other professional workers began toward the end of the 1960s):

Employed male college graduates by major occupation group, 1959, 1968, and 1971	*1959*	*1968*	*1971*
All college graduates	100.0	100.0	100.0
Professional, technical, and kindred workers	59.8	60.4	57.6
Managers, officials, and proprietors, except farm	18.3	22.7	25.3
Salaried managerial workers	13.1	19.9	22.7
Self-employed managerial workers	5.2	2.8	2.6
Clerical and kindred workers	5.4	4.4	3.8
Sales workers	7.9	6.7	7.3
All other occupation groups	8.6	5.8	6.0

SOURCE: U.S. Bureau of Labor Statistics (18). The data are not precisely comparable with those in the preceding table because they relate to employed male workers rather than to the experienced civilian labor force.

Between 1959 and 1968, the proportion of college graduates employed as professional and technical workers increased only slightly, while between 1968 and 1971 it fell off quite sharply. Meanwhile, the proportion employed as managerial workers rose markedly, and, once again, this reflected a rise in the percentage of college graduates employed as salaried managerial workers, whereas the percentage employed as self-employed managerial workers fell. But the rise in the proportion of college graduates employed as salaried managerial workers was much more pronounced than in the 1950s. Between 1959 and 1968, the professional group accounted for slightly more than three-fifths of the increase in employment of college graduates, as it did between 1950 and 1960. But from 1968 to 1971, it accounted for only 36 percent of the gain, while the salaried managerial group accounted for 46 percent. The relatively pronounced increase in employment of salaried managerial workers in the 1960s was probably greatly influenced by the more rapid annual average rate of increase in the real gross national product (about 4 percent) in the 1960s than in the 1950s (about 3.2 percent). A close relationship between the rate of growth in real GNP and in the employment of salaried managers would be expected.

Additional light is shed on these changes by Chart 4, which shows that the employment of male professional workers rose relatively slowly from 1969 to 1970 and declined appreciably from 1970 to 1971, reflecting the impact of the recession on job opportunities in a number of fields. There was little change between 1959 and 1971 in the percentage of male professional workers with either four years of college or five or more years of college, but the percentage with one to three years of college crept up over the course of the period—from 15.7 percent in 1959 to 18.1 percent in 1971 (Chart 8).

In contrast with the relative stability in the educational composition of the professional group, there was a pronounced increase in the proportion of college-educated workers in the salaried managerial group. Those with four years of college constituted 14.5 percent of the group in 1959 and 19.7 percent in 1971, while the proportion of those with five or more years of college rose from 6.5 percent in 1959 to 10.5 percent in 1971. Only a slight increase occurred in the percentage of those with one to three years of college.

But, the most interesting feature of Chart 8 is the sharp rise in the percentage of salaried managerial workers with five or more

CHART 8 *Professional and salaried managerial workers, by years of college, and by sex, 1959 to 1971*

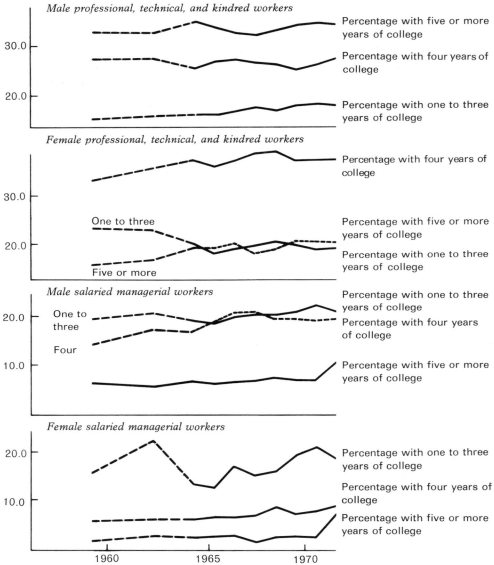

SOURCE: U.S. Bureau of Labor Statistics (18).

years of college between 1970 and 1971.[3] This suggests that employers took advantage of the relatively unfavorable job market to

[3] The data are subject to sampling variability, but the rise in this proportion, for both men and women, was large enough to indicate the general direction of change, even if the exact percentage increases may not be reliable.

upgrade the educational composition of their managerial personnel by hiring men with master's degrees in business administration or other appropriate advanced degrees. They were responding, in the manner suggested by the results of a number of postwar labor market studies, by increasing their selection standards in a relatively loose job market. But there are also longer-run factors that suggest that employers are likely increasingly to prefer applicants for managerial positions with specialized graduate training.

The increasing use of large-scale computers, not just for routine record keeping and payroll operations, but also for the analysis of complex managerial problems, is creating a situation in which training in such specialties as systems analysis and operations research is regarded as essential for many managerial openings. We shall return to a discussion of the implications of these developments for the 1970s in Section 7.

We shall consider future job prospects for college men after discussing past trends for women, but the data presented thus far suggest rather clearly that the increase in demand for male college graduates in the 1950s and 1960s was probably unusual in extent. The sharp increase in the percentage of GNP going into research and development expenditures between 1952 and 1964 — stimulating as it did the employment of scientists and engineers — is not likely to be repeated on anything like that scale. Another major impetus to increased employment of male college graduates was the rising demand for elementary and secondary school teachers. But here again the prospect for the future is quite different, given the decline in the number of children entering school, which we shall consider at a later point.

Patterns of Occupational Change, 1900 to 1970: Women

The overriding factor in the history of employment patterns of female college graduates has been the predominance of elementary and secondary school teaching among their career destinations. At the beginning of the century, when about three-fourths of the women classified as professional and technical workers were school teachers (Chart 9), completion of two-year normal school training, if that, was all that was required for teachers in most cases. But, over the decades, state public school systems gradually increased their requirements to call for a four-year college degree plus a teaching certificate; two-year normal schools became four-year teachers colleges, and later, in many cases, comprehensive state colleges. However, throughout the entire period from 1900 to 1970, the large proportion of women engaged in school teaching has been a major factor in explaining the relatively greater percentage of all women workers than of all men workers in the professional and technical group.

As the years went on, another professional occupation, nursing — not shown separately in Chart 9 because it does not consist predominantly of college graduates — came to play an important role within the female professional and technical group. Other occupations that gradually acquired an increasingly significant role in the female professional group *and* in the employment of female college graduates were librarians, social welfare workers, and miscellaneous health workers. All these occupations played a relatively more important role in the female than in the male labor force. But, as is well known, women have tended to be very poorly represented in the traditional professions of law, medicine, and the ministry. And, despite an increase in the relative representation of women on college faculties during the 1960s, by 1970 they represented only 28 percent of all faculty members (Appendix A, Table A-4), and all

CHART 9 *Percentage of female professional and technical workers in selected occupations, 1900 and 1950*

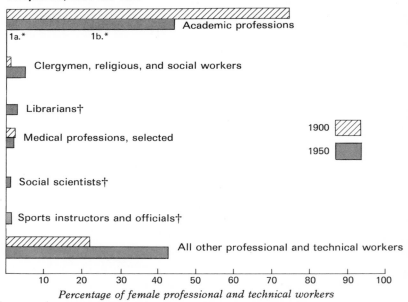

* 1a. College presidents, professors, and instructors, not elsewhere classified.
* 1b. Teachers, except college.
† Data not available in 1900.

SOURCES: Edwards (19, pp. 120, 128, and 178); and U.S. Bureau of the Census (17, Table 3).

the available data indicated that they tended to be concentrated in the lower faculty ranks.

Again, as in the case of men, patterns of occupational changes in the 1960s differed somewhat from those in the 1950s. In the former decade, particularly large percentage gains were experienced in the employment of female personnel and labor relations workers, recreation and group workers, sports instructors and officials, technicians, and therapists and healers, but the largest numerical gains were made among elementary and secondary school teachers and nurses (Appendix A, Table A-3). In the 1960s, the largest numerical increases once more occurred in the employment of school teachers and nurses, but pronounced, and in some cases very spectacular, percentage gains were made in many professions in which women had been either very poorly or rather slightly represented in earlier decades (Appendix A, Table A-4). These included accountants, architects, engineers, lawyers and judges, biological scientists, chemists, other life and physical scientists, personnel and labor relations workers, dentists, pharmacists, physicians, social scientists, college and university teachers, engineering and science technicians, airline pilots, radio operators, and public relations workers. In many of these occupations, the total number of women employed, as well as their relative representation, continued to be small, but the changes were so pronounced, especially in the latter part of the decade, that former patterns of sex differentiation in employment were clearly beginning to break down.

The percentage increase in the number of women employed as salaried managers was also relatively large in the 1960s, and, as Chart 4 indicates, the gain was particularly pronounced toward the late 1960s and early 1970s. Other indications that sexual patterns of employment were changing occurred among blue-collar workers, where the percentage increases in employment of women as skilled craftsmen and laborers—two groups in which they had been very much underrepresented in the past—were large.

However, there were also impressive percentage gains in professions in which women had previously been comparatively well represented, including therapists and health technologists and technicians—again reflecting the impact of the sharp increase in health expenditures in the 1960s.

From 1950 to 1960, even more than in the case of men, a very large proportion of the increase in employment of female college graduates (88 percent) was in the professional and technical group, which increased its share of all female college graduates employed.

**Female college
graduates in the
experienced
civilian labor
force, by major
occupation
group, 1950
and 1960**

	1950	1960
All college graduates	100.0	100.0
Professional, technical, and kindred workers	69.5	74.9
Managers, officials, and proprietors, except farm	4.0	3.5
Salaried managerial workers	2.6	2.6
Self-employed managerial workers	1.4	0.9
Clerical and kindred workers	16.9	12.3
Sales workers	2.7	2.0
All other workers	6.9	7.3

SOURCE: Appendix A, Table A-3.

Moreover, female college graduates were more heavily concentrated than male college graduates in the professional group in both years.

Again, as in the case of men, patterns of change were somewhat different from 1959 to 1971:

**Employed
female college
graduates
by major
occupation
group, 1959,
1968, and 1971**

	1959	1968	1971
All college graduates	100.0	100.0	100.0
Professional, technical and kindred workers	79.1	81.0	76.0
Managers, officials, and proprietors, except farm	4.1	4.1	5.3
Salaried managerial workers	2.6	3.4	4.6
Self-employed managerial workers	1.5	0.7	0.7
Clerical and kindred workers	11.8	10.4	10.8
Sales workers	2.3	1.2	2.7
All other workers	2.7	3.3	4.4

SOURCE: U.S. Bureau of Labor Statistics (18). The data are not precisely comparable with those in the preceding table because they relate to employed female workers rather than to the experienced civilian labor force.

Between 1959 and 1968, the percentage of all employed female college graduates in the professional and technical group continued to rise, but very slowly, and after 1968 it dropped quite sharply. Meanwhile, between 1968 and 1971 the percentages of female college graduates employed in other major occupation groups rose, especially in the sales and "all other" groups. The percentage of female college graduates employed as salaried managerial workers rose modestly throughout the 12-year period.

Interestingly, also, total employment of female professional and technical workers rose sharply between 1969 and 1970 and slightly between 1970 and 1971 (Chart 4), in contrast with the behavior of employment for the corresponding male group. Also, in contrast with the changes for males, the percentage of female professional workers with four years of college, and with five or more years of college, rose significantly over this period, while the percentage with one to three years of college declined (Chart 8).

The percentage increases in employment of teachers indicated by U.S. Bureau of Labor Statistics (BLS) data from 1969 to 1970 and from 1970 to 1971 (for men and women combined) were considerably larger than those shown by U.S. Office of Education (OE) data (27, p. 60). Significantly, also, the total number of teachers shown by the BLS data has been exceeding the number shown by OE data by a widening margin in recent years. We shall consider the reasons for these differences in Section 5.

As in the case of males, the number of women employed as salaried managerial workers increased in 1970 and 1971, and there was a similar sharp rise in the percentage of managers with five or more years of college between 1970 and 1971. Among other things, the data suggest that civil rights pressure on behalf of the employment of women in managerial positions is having some effect.

Even so, the relative representation of women in many top-level occupations continued to be slight and far below their representation among all employed workers. As a recent volume on women in the labor force has indicated:

In contrast, women workers in European countries have come to be less concentrated in clerical work, and educated women apparently have somewhat better representation in certain professions. For example, women make up 7 percent of the physicians in the United States, whereas in Britain they constitute 16 percent, in France 13 percent, and in Germany 20 percent of the total number. Executive positions, too, have larger proportions of women; only 2 percent of these posts are held by women in this country, in contrast with 4 percent in Britain, 9 percent in France, and 12 percent in Germany (28, p. 48).

Although the increase in the supply of college graduates was rather moderate in the 1950s, when the babies born in the depression of the 1930s were going through college, the number of college graduates entering the labor market rose at an unprecedentedly rapid rate in the 1960s, when those who were born in the high birthrate years of the latter half of the 1940s and early 1950s were in college and enrollment rates were rising rapidly. Yet college graduates found attractive jobs with relative ease during the greater part of the 1960s. We have mentioned the pronounced rise in R&D expenditures and in aerospace employment as important factors in increasing the demand for scientists and engineers. Another major factor in the buoyant demand for college graduates was the extraordinarily favorable job market for elementary and secondary school teachers, which was attributable primarily to a sharp rise in the birthrate in the early postwar years and a persistently high rate (though somewhat below the 1947 peak) throughout the 1950s. As the war and postwar babies grew older, they created first an increased demand for elementary teachers, then for secondary teachers, and eventually for college teachers.

Apart from these special developments affecting the demand for scientists and engineers and for teachers at all levels of education, the demand for college-educated workers in a variety of occupations was maintained at a relatively high level by the generally rapid growth of the economy and by a tendency for the percentage of the gross national product expended on such social needs as health and welfare to rise.

In fact, an important consideration in relation to changes in the demand for college graduates is that, when classified by industry rather than occupation, they tend to account for a considerably larger proportion of all workers in the rapidly growing services sector of the economy—especially in "finance, insurance, and real estate," professional services, and federal and state government agencies—than in goods-producing industries (Appendix A, Table A-7). During the 1950s, the most rapid increases in employment were in the finance group, services, and government, while in the 1960s percentage increases in employment in services and government were especially pronounced, and the percentage increase in the finance group exceeded that in total employment (Appendix A, Table A-8). These trends are expected to continue. BLS projections suggest an increase of only about 8 percent between 1968 and 1980 in employment in goods-producing industries, as contrasted with an increase of about 30 percent in service industries (26, p. 17).

EMPLOYMENT PATTERNS OF PERSONS WITH ONE TO THREE YEARS OF COLLEGE

Thus far, our discussion has focused on college graduates. But, a large and rapidly growing segment of the labor force consists of persons who have had some college education but have not completed a four-year program. Some of them have dropped out of a four-year program, but an increasing number are graduates of two-year colleges. By 1970, enrollment in two-year colleges represented about 28 percent of total enrollment in higher education, and this proportion is expected to rise (29, pp. 131–137). Public community colleges have largely been responsible for this growth, accounting for 94 percent of all enrollment in two-year colleges in 1970. Enrollment in private two-year colleges has tended to decline in recent years. Unfortunately, most available employment data from the Census Bureau and other sources do not permit us to distinguish, within the group with one to three years of college, between those who completed a two-year college program and did not go on to a four-year college and those who dropped out of either a two-year or four-year college.

The pronounced tendency for increasing levels of educational attainment to be associated with employment in professional and technical occupations may be seen in Appendix A, Tables A-9 and A-10, which are based on 1960 census data. The tendency is even more marked among women than among men, largely reflecting the high degree of concentration of women holding bachelor's and more advanced degrees in elementary and secondary school teaching.

Within the professional and technical occupation group, moreover, patterns of employment differ substantially among those with some college, four years of college, and five or more years of college. Men with one to three years of college were likely to be employed as engineers, accountants and auditors, draftsmen, or technicians, and were weakly represented in other professional occupations. However, nearly as large a proportion of men with one to three years of college as with four years of college were in managerial occupations (about one-fifth).

Clerical and sales occupations accounted for about one-fourth of the men with one to three years of college, while a sizable 29 percent were employed in manual and service occupations. These proportions declined markedly with higher educational attainment, although nearly 30 percent of the men with four years of college were in the clerical, sales, or blue-collar groups.

There is a decided tendency for men with a college education to shift into managerial positions as they grow older. This is indicated by the National Bureau of Economic Research (NBER)–Thorndike data presented in Appendix. A, Table A-11.

Turning to women with some college education but with less than a bachelor's degree in 1960 (Appendix A, Table A-10), we find that teachers and nurses (including student nurses) each accounted for slightly more than 10 percent of those in the labor force and together represented about 70 percent of those employed in professional and technical occupations. However, the great majority of the teachers were employed in elementary schools.

The proportion of women with "some college" who were employed in the managerial occupation group, though small, was somewhat above the average for all women and also somewhat higher than among women with four or more years of college. More than two-fifths of the women with some college were employed as clerical workers, while about 6 percent were in the sales group and about 12 percent were in manual and service occupations.

Thus, we find that men and women with one to three years of college were considerably more widely dispersed among the major occupation groups than were those with four or more years of college. They were also represented in substantial proportions in occupations for which training is provided in two-year colleges— e.g., technical training and nursing.

From 1959 to 1971, employed persons with one to three years of college increased from 9.4 to 14.0 percent of the total labor force. Patterns of occupational change for this group were similar in certain respects to those of college graduates, but quite different in other respects:

Employed men with one to three years of college, by major occupation group, 1959, 1968, and 1971	1959	1968	1971
All men with one to three years of college	100.0	100.0	100.0
Professional, technical, and kindred workers	18.3	20.0	18.5
Managers, officials, and proprietors, except farm	24.4	22.1	22.1
Salaried managerial workers	14.4	17.1	17.9
Self-employed managerial workers	10.0	5.0	4.2
Clerical and kindred workers	12.5	12.6	11.0
Sales workers	12.6	15.6	11.7
All other occupation groups	32.2	29.7	36.7

SOURCE: U.S. Bureau of Labor Statistics (18).

From 1959 to 1968, the proportions of these men employed as professional and technical, salaried managerial, and sales workers rose, while the percentages employed as self-employed managerial workers and in "all other" occupation groups (farmers, manual, and service workers) fell. On net balance, the changes appeared to represent occupational upgrading. However, from 1968 to 1971, there was in large part a reverse movement. The only shift that appeared to represent occupational upgrading was a slight rise in the percentage of salaried managerial workers. There were declines in the proportions employed as professional and technical, self-employed managerial, clerical, and sales workers, while the proportion in "all other" occupation groups rose sharply. Thus, on the basis of these rather broad and general data, men with one to three years of college were faring considerably less well in the labor market, in terms of occupational changes, than male college graduates in the late 1960s and early 1970s.

For women with some college, but lacking a college degree, the shifts were less favorable than for their male counterparts:

Employed women with one to three years of college, by major occupation group, 1959, 1968, and 1971	1959	1968	1971
All women with one to three years of college	100.0	100.0	100.0
Professional, technical, and kindred workers	31.9	24.4	21.7
Managers, officials, and proprietors, except farm	6.9	5.4	6.5
Salaried managerial workers	4.4	4.0	5.0
Self-employed managerial workers	2.5	1.4	1.5
Clerical and kindred workers	40.7	48.4	46.6
Sales workers	7.3	6.0	7.2
All other occupation groups	13.2	15.8	18.0

SOURCE: U.S. Bureau of Labor Statistics (18).

There was a pronounced decline over the entire period in the proportion of these women employed in professional and technical occupations. More detailed data show that this was in large part attributable to a sharp decline in the percentage employed as teachers—from 13.1 percent in 1959 to 5.0 percent in 1970. This is not surprising. When the demand for teachers rose markedly in the 1950s, school districts were in many cases forced to hire teachers who lacked certificates, especially as substitutes. Later, as the supply of certificated teachers began to catch up with demand, the employment of noncertificated teachers became relatively less prevalent. Meanwhile, pronounced increases occurred in the proportion of women with one to three years of college employed as clerical workers and in "all other" occupation groups, although there was something of a reversal in the case of clerical workers between 1968 and 1971.

Information on the recent rapid growth of associate's degrees and other awards in occupational programs at the technical or semiprofessional level (chiefly in two-year colleges), and on changes in the distribution of these awards by field, is provided in Appendix A, Table A-13. There have been increases in the relative importance of these awards in health professions and in "other nonscience and nonengineering" fields, especially police technology and law enforcement. On the other hand, probably reflecting changes in the job market, there were significant declines in the proportion of awards in engineering-related programs and in business- and commerce-related programs.

We believe that the labor market conditions of the 1970s are likely to encourage an acceleration of the rise in the relative importance of enrollment in occupational programs in two-year colleges that occurred in the 1960s (29 and 30). In fact, enrollment data for 1971 and 1972, to be discussed in the next section, show that this is occurring. Continued shortages of health workers will be a factor, as well as the prospect of favorable job market conditions for graduates of other technical occupational programs available in two-year colleges. But the dropout from either a two-year or a four-year college program may well be forced to accept, on the average, a job that is lower in the occupational ladder than would have been obtained by his counterpart in the mid-1960s.

A recent study indicates that the proportion of students who drop out of either a two-year or four-year college program is lower than some earlier reports had suggested (31). True, only about 47 percent of students who had entered a sample of four-year colleges and universities in 1966 had received a bachelor's degree four years later, but about 59 percent had either received a degree or were still enrolled for a degree, while as many as 81 percent had received a degree, were still enrolled, *or* had requested that a transcript of grades be sent to another institution. Drop-out rates were higher at two-year colleges than at four-year colleges, as earlier studies had indicated. This is consistent with the fact that two-year colleges are less selective than four-year colleges and that, in general, the more selective a college, the lower its drop-out rate is.

However, when we are considering the relationship between decisions to drop out of college and labor market conditions, it is important to take account of reasons for dropping out. To what extent, for example, do students drop out because they have taken a job or because they want to take a job? Do relatively more students drop out for this reason when labor market conditions are favorable than when they are unfavorable? Existing data on reasons reported for dropping out do not indicate that a desire to take a job is an important motivation, but they show that "changed career plans" and "wanted time to reconsider interests and goals" are relatively important (Appendix A, Table A-12). "Tired of being a student" could also be considered a reason related to changing interests and goals, although we have grouped it under "academic and related reasons." In any case, especially for men, reasons related to changes in career plans, reconsideration of interests and goals, dissatisfaction with the college environment, and unsatisfactory academic records are predominant among reasons for dropping out.

Financial reasons were relatively less important, but nevertheless significant. The data suggest that improved access to student aid would not reduce the incidence of dropouts dramatically, but nevertheless would have an appreciable effect in preventing dropouts. Thirty-seven percent of the women included in this study gave marriage or pregnancy as the major reason for dropping out. In the case of men who gave marriage or their wives' pregnancies as a reason, the considerations were probably to a considerable extent financial and might in some cases be affected by liberalized student aid.

To the extent that dropping out is related to uncertainty about career goals, we believe that improved counseling programs would help in many cases, but that often the student might be better off to stop out of college for a while and perhaps return later when his career goals are more certain. On the other hand, dropping out because the student, for example, has been exposed to poor teaching or because insufficient student aid is available is a phenomenon that may well be preventable in many cases.[4]

Although the data on employment patterns of college graduates are far from ideal, the dearth of good data on graduates of community colleges and on dropouts is far more serious. In our search for relevant information, we have found that a few community colleges or community college systems have conducted follow-up studies of their former students, but in none of the studies available to us was information collected on the occupations that employ these former students.

Recommendation 3: Federal government agencies should develop more adequate data on occupational and industrial employment patterns of graduates of two-year colleges and of dropouts from institutions of higher education. In addition, community college districts should conduct follow-up studies that would provide information on employment patterns of their former students by occupation and industry.

[4] For some relevant recommendations, see Appendix B.

Throughout the last hundred years, and to some degree even earlier, the average level of educational attainment of the American labor force has steadily risen. And, for many professional and managerial occupations that are a primary concern of this report, educational requirements imposed by employers, state licensing agencies, and professional certifying boards have tended to call for increasingly extended periods of higher education.[5] The advancement of knowledge and technology has been a powerful force in inducing this upgrading on the demand side of the labor market. The extension of opportunities for free elementary and secondary education and the growth of the number of student places in higher education, especially in relatively low-cost public institutions, have been major factors on the supply side.

Increasingly, however, the tendency of employers to require a higher level of educational attainment than may actually be needed in many entry positions has become a matter of controversy. We shall consider this issue more extensively in Section 9, but for the moment we are concerned with what has actually happened in recent decades. To what extent has the increased employment of college graduates been attributable to the expansion of employment opportunities in occupations traditionally employing college graduates and to what extent has it been attributable to educational upgrading, that is, to a rise in the proportion of college graduates in specific occupations?

Appendix A, Tables A-2 and A-3 indicate that, between 1950 and 1960, the percentage of workers with four or more years of college in most occupations increased modestly and in some occupations or major occupation groups actually declined. This was especially true for women. If we compute, for each occupation shown in these tables, the number of college graduates who would have been in the labor force in 1960 if the percentage of workers in the occupation who were college graduates had remained at its 1950 level—the "constant college component"—we may obtain an estimate of the relative extent to which the increase in the number of college graduates in the labor force was attributable to occupational growth requirements rather than to educational upgrading within occupations. The results indicate that about three-fifths of the increase in employment of male college graduates and slightly more than 100 percent of the increase in the employment of female college

---

[5] As Samuel Haber (32) and others have pointed out, there was a reversal of this tendency in leading professions in the Jacksonian era.

graduates during the 1950s were attributable to occupational growth requirements rather than to educational upgrading.[6]

The result for women may seem odd, but it should be noted that the percentage who were college graduates declined in a number of occupations, including the important occupation of nursing, as well as among clerical workers, sales workers, and "all other" occupation groups.

With the pronounced increase in the rate of college graduation in the 1960s, it is not surprising to find that the percentages of workers who were college graduates rose during the decade. For both men and women, the most pronounced increases were in the managerial group. All in all, approximately 70 percent of the increase in employment of college graduates, for both sexes combined, between 1959 and 1968 was attributable to occupational growth requirements and, from 1968 to 1971, 60 percent was attributable to occupational growth requirements. However, these are rough estimates based on major occupation groups and are not precisely comparable with the estimates for changes between 1950 and 1960, which were based on detailed occupations.

There has also been a distinct tendency for the proportions of employed professional workers holding master's and doctor's degrees to rise. We shall consider this tendency later in connection with discussions of particular professions.

RELATIVE INCOMES OF COLLEGE GRADUATES Also providing evidence that the job market for college-educated workers was relatively favorable in the 1950s and 1960s was the behavior of their incomes relative to those of less educated workers. Ratios of median income of college graduates to median income of high school graduates and of all persons aged 25 and over rose for both sexes between 1949 and 1959. In the next ten years these ratios continued to rise in relation to high school graduates but fell somewhat in relation to all persons.

Historically, black college graduates have fared less well in the job market than have white college graduates. Becker's study of returns to investment in education, based on 1939 and 1949 income data, showed that in 1939 nonwhite male college graduates received a considerably lower rate of return on their investment in higher education than did their white counterparts (36, pp. 94–100). The rate of return was even lower for nonwhite male grad-

---

[6] According to Folger and Nam (1, p. 172), 54 percent of the increased employment of white male college graduates aged 35 to 54 during the decade was attributable to occupational growth requirements.

		Men		Women	
Ratios of median income of college graduates to median income of all persons and of high school graduates, by sex, 1949 to 1969		*All men*	*High school graduates*	*All women*	*High school graduates*
	1949	1.63	1.34	2.13	1.47
	1959	1.66	1.41	2.45	1.72
	1969	1.62	1.45	2.38	1.80

NOTE: The data relate to persons 25 years of age and older with income. The data for 1949 and 1959, which are from decennial censuses, may not be precisely comparable with data for 1969, which are from the Census Bureau's *Current Population Survey.*
SOURCES: U.S. Bureau of the Census (33, p. 128; 34, pp. 38 and 112; and 35, p. 101).

uates in the North than in the South. In the Southern states, Becker speculates, there were more opportunities for blacks in certain professions — doctors, dentists, clergymen, teachers, or lawyers — to cater to a segregated labor market.

There is considerable evidence that the relative position of black college graduates in the labor market improved in the 1950s and 1960s — for black women throughout the period and for black men to a greater extent in the 1960s than in the 1950s (Chart 10). (The ratios in the chart for 1949 and 1959 relate median income of non-whites, rather than of blacks, to median income of all persons, but since blacks comprise more than 90 percent of all nonwhites, the ratios closely approximate those of blacks to all persons.)

Interestingly, in 1949, the relative median income of male non-whites to that of all males varied inversely with level of education. The relatively low median income of nonwhite male college graduates is at least partly explained by their comparatively heavy concentration in such low-paid professional occupations as elementary and secondary school teaching and the ministry. On the other hand, they were strikingly underrepresented, as compared with white male graduates, in such fields as engineering, the law, and managerial positions. Freeman's recent studies show that during the latter part of the 1960s black males began, at least in the black colleges, to shift out of teacher education and into such fields as engineering and business administration, while corporations expanded their recruiting activities at the black colleges to a very pronounced extent (37 and 38). By 1971, 63 percent of all employed nonwhite males with college degrees were in professional and technical occupations, as compared with about 52 percent in 1950, while 15 percent were employed in managerial occupations, as con-

CHART 10 *Ratios of median income of nonwhites* to all persons aged 25 and over, by educational attainment and sex, 1949, 1959, and 1969*

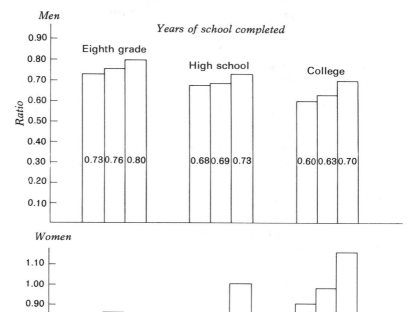

* Data for 1969 relate to blacks only; for earlier years, to nonwhites.
SOURCE: U.S. Bureau of the Census (see references 33, 34, and 35).

trasted with only about 7 percent in 1950 (17, pp. 107–122, and 39, p. A-16).

For nonwhite women, the situation was quite different. Nonwhite college graduates fared better, incomewise, relative to all women with similar educational attainment in 1949, than did nonwhite women with an eighth grade education, and *very* much better than female high school graduates. By 1969, among both high school graduates and college graduates, the relative income position of nonwhite women had improved substantially, but it had slipped back somewhat in the 1960s for nonwhite women with an eighth grade education. Strikingly, median income of nonwhite women who were college graduates was well above that of all female college graduates by 1969. On the other hand, nonwhite male college graduates had a median income that was still far below that of all male college graduates.

The fact that black women with college degrees were earning more, on the average, than their white counterparts in 1969 was apparently explained in large part by their greater tendency to be year-round full-time workers. For all female professional workers, the ratio of black to white median income was 1.17, but, if we consider only those who were year-round full-time workers, the black-white ratio was 0.95 (35, p. 113).[7] Similarly, in the case of female elementary and secondary school teachers, the ratio of black to white median income was 1.09, but among year-round full-time workers, the ratio was 0.96.[8] However, let us not suppose that the favorable relative income position of nonwhite women who were college graduates suggested affluence. Their median income was $6,747 in 1969, compared with $5,817 for all college educated women. The corresponding medians for men were $8,567 for non-whites and $12,255 for all male college graduates.

One would expect beginning salaries of college graduates to be more sensitive to changing currents in the job market than average income of all adult college graduates, and here again the evidence suggests a favorable job market for college-educated workers during the greater part of the 1950s and 1960s.

Series of data available on the ratios of starting salaries in business and industry to average compensation of employees in all industries from 1950 to 1971 for male holders of bachelor's degrees in four occupations show certain characteristics in common and certain significant differences (Chart 11). All four series display an upward trend throughout the greater part of the period, with the most pronounced rise occurring from 1951 to 1957. The timing of this rise suggests that the sharp increase in the percentage of GNP expended on research and development in this period affected industrial demand not only for engineers and scientists, but also for college graduates with other types of training. In varying degrees,

---

[7] Data on incomes of year-round full-time workers are available by major occupation group but not by educational attainment.

[8] Probably many of the teachers who reported themselves as year-round full-time workers held other types of jobs during the summer.

CHART 11 *Ratio of average starting salary for male college graduates in selected occupations to average compensation of employees in all industries, 1950 to 1971*

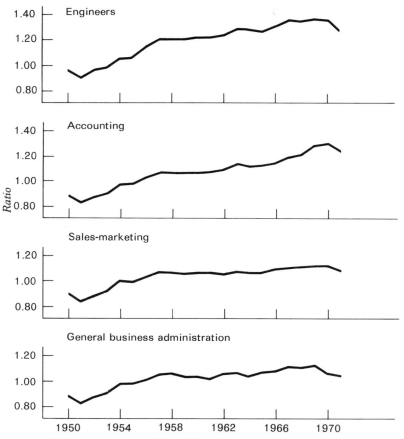

NOTE: Data relate to men with bachelor's degrees.

SOURCES: Endicott (40); National Education Association (41, p. 72); and *Economic Report of the President* (22, pp. 209 and 226).

the ratios leveled off or declined from about 1958 to 1961 or 1962 —a period of relatively high unemployment rates—suggesting that during a period of depressed business, when firms are not likely to be hiring on a substantial scale, beginning salaries of college graduates do not tend to rise in relation to general wage and salary levels. After about 1962, the behavior of the four series differed somewhat. The steadiest advance, until 1971, was in accounting, which is consistent with reports that this is one field in which the demand for college graduates has remained brisk. Engineers' beginning salaries in relation to average employee compensation rose irregularly until about 1967 and then tended to level off; sales-marketing salaries rose very moderately relative to average employee compensation until 1970; and beginning salaries in general business administration rose gently relative to average compensation until 1969 and then declined sharply.

Additional ratios for men and women are presented in Chart 12. Here again, the relatively favorable behavior of beginning salaries in accounting in relation to the general wage and salary level shows up, in this case for both men and women. Several of the other series show a tendency to level off after 1967 — in some cases, less so for women than for men. However, of interest are the consistently

CHART 12 *Ratio of average starting salary for college graduates with bachelor's degrees in selected occupations to average compensation of employees in all industries, 1964 to 1971*

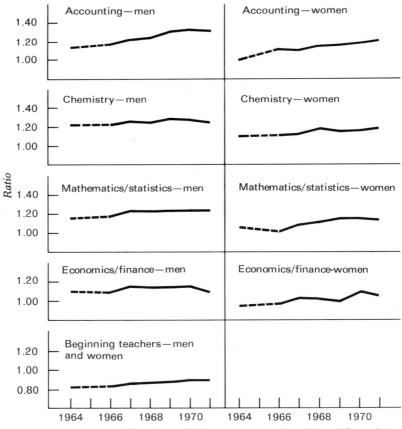

SOURCES: Endicott (40); National Education Association (41, p. 72); and *Economic Report of the President* (22, pp. 209 and 226).

lower average starting salaries for women, occupation by occupation. In general, the lower incomes of female than of male college graduates can be explained in considerable part by the relatively greater prevalence of part-time work among women and by the less favorable occupational mix in terms of salary levels for female college graduates. But here we have evidence that, even *within* rather narrowly defined occupational fields, female college graduates tend to start at lower salaries than do male college graduates. However, this is a tendency that may well change decisively in the future.

There is substantial evidence of a long-run trend toward greater equality of income and toward a narrowing of both occupational and educational earnings differentials in developed countries.[9] This is scarcely surprising, in view of the trend toward increasing equality of opportunity at all levels of education as industrialization proceeds. Even so, the secular tendency toward a decline in the ratio of the income of college graduates to incomes of those with less education may be interrupted by spurts in demand for persons with advanced levels of training, as clearly happened during parts of the postwar period in the United States, and the behavior of income in various professions may differ considerably because of variations in particular demand and supply situations.

Colin Clark has assembled data for the United States over the period 1890 to 1951, showing a pronounced decline in the ratios of earnings of federal civil service workers, post office workers, and clergy to average earnings of unskilled workers.[10] The ratio of earnings of teachers to unskilled workers rose from 1890 to 1926 and then declined until 1951 — the rise probably reflecting in part the sharp increase in high school enrollment rates, especially in the 1920s. And, as we have seen, relative incomes of teachers rose again in the 1950s and 1960s, reflecting the impact of the pronounced rise in the elementary and secondary school population.[11]

[9] As Kuznets has shown, there is likely to be a trend toward increased *inequality* of income in the early stages of economic development, followed by a reversal of the trend later on (42).

[10] In the case of the first two groups, the decline was probably partly attributable to an increase in the proportion of clerical and manual workers among employees in the federal civil service and the Post Office Department over this period.

[11] Clark also gives some figures from a French study, showing a long-term decline — though not always a continuous decline — in the real salaries of top civil service workers and school and university teachers in France from 1815 to 1948 (43, pp. 541–543).

CHART 13 *Ratios of average annual earnings of selected professional workers to average annual earnings per full-time-equivalent employee in all industries, selected years, 1929–1970*

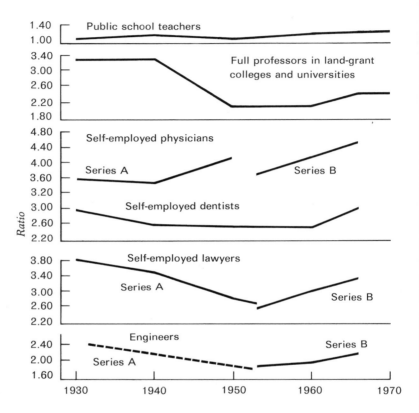

SOURCE: Gordon (46). In the cases of physicians, lawyers, and engineers, series A and B are not precisely comparable.

In Chart 13, several series have been assembled showing changes in ratios of earnings in six professions to annual average earnings of full-time-equivalent employees in all industries. With the exception of physicians, all these professions experienced a decline in earnings relative to the general salary level from 1929 or 1930 to the early 1950s, but all experienced a gain relative to average wages and salaries between the early 1950s and 1966 or 1970. The data support the general theme of this section—that the 1950s and 1960s were a period of exceptional increases in demand as well as in supply in the job market for college graduates and holders of professional and advanced degrees. The improvement in the relative income position of these highly educated workers during this period appears to be contrary to the secular trend and may be reversed under the less favorable job market conditions in prospect for the 1970s, at least for some of these professions.[12]

---

[12] Evidence of a long-run tendency for ratios of salaries of college professors and teachers to average wages in manufacturing to decline is provided by data assembled by Keat for the period 1904–1953 (44, p. 590). In a multivariate analysis, Chiswick and Mincer (45) have shown that inequality of personal income of adult males in the United States declined between 1939 and the early postwar years but subsequently remained unchanged. Their analysis indicates that changes in the income distribution were affected mainly by changes in distributions of schooling, age, and employment. However, in the 1949–1969 period, changes in the level and inequality of age and in the inequality of schooling were small. The business cycle was a more important influence through its effects on the dispersion of weeks of employment.

4. The Outlook for the 1970s — College Graduates in General

Despite reports early in 1973 that the job prospects of college graduates were considerably more favorable than in the several preceding years, most predictions indicate that they are unlikely to return to anything resembling the situation that prevailed during a large part of the 1960s, when recruiters were besieging college placement offices and prospective graduates could pick and choose among attractive job offers. According to the *Manpower Report of the President, 1972* (2, p. 114), the "unique conjunction of demand and supply factors" that produced the shortage situation of the recent past "will not recur in the foreseeable future (short of a major war or other national catastrophe involving full mobilization of the country's resources)." On the basis of analyses by the U.S. Bureau of Labor Statistics, the report estimates that 9.8 million college-educated persons will enter the labor force during the 1970s and that the demand for college-educated workers will amount to 9.6 million—of which 3.3 million will be attributable to employment expansion, 2.6 million to educational upgrading, and 3.7 million to replacement needs.

Educational upgrading refers to an expected increase in the proportion of college graduates in major occupation groups—chiefly in the professional, managerial, and sales occupation groups. The expected changes for the period from 1970 to 1980 are indicated in Table 1. The total estimated demand of 9.6 million for college graduates includes replacement demand as well as the expansion of employment shown in the table.

The increase of 2.6 million attributable to educational upgrading from 1970 to 1980 represents 27 percent of the 9.6 million increase in demand for college-educated workers over the course of the decade. This differs very little from our estimate (based on Appendix A, Tables A-2 and A-3) of a 28 percent increase attributable to

	1970		
Occupational group	*Total employment* (thousands)*	*College graduates† (thousands)*	*Percentage of graduates to total*
All occupational groups	78,626	10,030	12.8
Professional and technical	11,140	6,662	59.8
Managers, officials, and proprietors	8,289	1,666	20.1
Sales	4,854	573	11.8
Clerical	13,714	645	4.7
All other	40,629	484	1.2

* 16 years of age and over.

† Data include persons 18 years of age and over having four years of college or more.

SOURCE:Unpublished data produced by U.S. Bureau of Labor Statistics.

educational upgrading for both sexes combined in the 1950s and our rough estimate of 30 percent for the period from 1959 to 1968. It would represent considerably less educational upgrading, relatively, than our estimate of 40 percent for the relatively unfavorable job market period from 1968 to 1971. Thus, the BLS projection does not suggest a relatively greater role for educational upgrading than in the 1950s and from 1959 to 1968. However, all the estimates cited are crude in the sense that they refer to all college graduates and do not differentiate between holders of bachelor's and of more advanced degrees. Given the relatively unfavorable outlook for Ph.D.'s, to be discussed in Section 8, it seems probable that holders of bachelor's degrees will be adversely affected, to a relatively greater extent than in the 1950s and in most of the 1960s, by a tendency for holders of more advanced degrees to accept positions that would previously have gone to bachelor's recipients.

How serious was the downturn in the job market for college graduates in the recent recession? The first suggestions of trouble came from the College Placement Council early in 1970, when it was reported that job offers to bachelor's degree candidates were down 20 percent, and those to master's degree candidates were down 24 percent, from the previous year (47). During that same first quarter of 1970, the national unemployment rate averaged 4.1 percent, as compared with 3.4 percent in the first quarter of 1969 (48, p. 223). By the spring of 1971 the national unemployment rate was fluctuating around 6 percent (22, p. B-22), and spokesmen for the College Placement Service were characterizing the job market

| | 1980 | |
Total employment* (thousands)	College graduates† (thousands)	Percentage of graduates to total
95,100	15,907	16.7
15,500	10,540	68.0
9,500	2,926	30.8
6,000	996	16.6
17,300	865	5.0
46,800	580	1.2

for college seniors as the "toughest in 20 years" (49). Because the aerospace industries were suffering especially severely from the recession, the situation was reported to be more serious for graduates in engineering and scientific fields than in other fields. However, black students were said to be less affected by the scarcity of jobs than were white students.

By the first half of 1972, recovery from the recession was well under way, but the unemployment rate had been slow to fall, reaching 5.8 percent in the first quarter and 5.7 percent in the second quarter (50, p. 97). The behavior of the job market for college graduates appeared to be consistent with the behavior of the overall unemployment rate. By July, the College Placement Council was reporting that job openings were more numerous than in 1971 but still far below the number available two years earlier.

In early 1973, the job market for college graduates was clearly recovering from the effects of the recession. The College Placement Council was reporting that job prospects were the "best in four years." The council predicted that there would be an average increase of 20 percent in the hiring of Ph.D. holders, 22 percent for master's degree holders, and 15 percent for bachelor's degree holders, as compared with the previous year. The outlook was reported to be particularly favorable for women and members of minority groups. Moreover, prospects for engineering graduates, which had been reported to be improving a year earlier, appeared to be especially favorable, whereas the market was least favorable for liberal arts graduates (51). And it was clear that the impact of pronounced changes in demand-supply relationships, especially for school and college teachers, would continue to affect the job market unfavorably as the economy recovered from the recession.

The extent of actual unemployment among 1970 and 1971 graduates was indicated by special BLS data for October 1971 (52). Among 1970 and 1971 recipients of bachelor's and more advanced degrees, 7.4 percent were unemployed, at a time when the overall unemployment rate (not seasonally adjusted) was 5.4 percent. Women were considerably more likely to be unemployed (9.6 percent) than men (5.8 percent), unemployment rates were higher for younger than for older degree recipients, and holders of bachelor's degrees were more likely to be unemployed than recipients of master's degrees. Among fields of study, those who had received degrees in humanities (13.0 percent) and in social sciences (9.2 percent) were hardest hit by unemployment, whereas unemployment rates for those with degrees in business administration, education, and "all other fields" were below average.

Among the degree recipients who were employed in October 1971, the proportion in professional and technical occupations was higher for men and about the same for women, as compared with proportions for all college graduates in March 1971 (18 and 52):

Occupation group of employed 1970 and 1971 degree recipients, October 1971, and of all college graduates, March 1971

	Men		Women	
	All graduates, March	*Recent degree recipients, October*	*All graduates, March*	*Recent degree recipients, October*
TOTAL	100.0	100.0	100.0	100.0*
Professional, technical and kindred workers	57.6	66.2	74.9	74.1
Managers and administrators, except farm	25.3	3.2	3.5	1.7
Clerical and kindred workers	3.8	7.1	12.3	18.2
Sales workers	7.3	11.3	2.0	1.7
All other occupation groups	6.0	12.2	7.3	4.4

*Items add to slightly more than total because of rounding.

However, the proportions employed in managerial jobs were very small, while the proportions employed in clerical occupations (for both sexes), sales occupations (among the men), and "all other occupation groups" (again among the men) were relatively high.

Not only were corporations reported not to be hiring for managerial positions in 1971, but men who eventually become employed in managerial positions often begin lower on the occupational ladder or in certain professional occupations, such as engineering.[1]

Also of special interest, 20.8 percent of the male 1970 and 1971 degree recipients and 49.9 percent of the women were employed as "teachers, except college." Despite the reports of trouble in the market for schoolteachers, these percentages were actually higher for men and approximately the same for women as the proportions of all college graduates employed as schoolteachers in 1960 (Appendix A, Tables A-9 and A-10).

Furthermore, the majority of these recent graduates (52 percent of those with bachelor's degrees and 77 percent of those with other degrees) had obtained jobs directly related to their major fields of study. In this respect, however, variations by fields were very great, ranging from 80 percent in education, for example, to only 35 percent in the social sciences.

The United States is not the only advanced industrial country that has recently been experiencing a difficult job market for college graduates. British students who graduated in 1971 had considerable difficulty in obtaining jobs, but a recent article expressed an optimistic view about the long-term outlook there (53). In France, where liberalized admission requirements were at least partially responsible for an increase of more than 50 percent in enrollment in higher education in the five years from 1965–66 to 1970–71, students are complaining that "the reformed system gives them diplomas but not jobs" (54, p. 264). Unemployment of college graduates is an old story in India and certain other underdeveloped countries, and deficient demand for professional workers and rather rigid attitudes of college graduates about the kinds of jobs they will consider accepting perpetuate the problem.

Long-term manpower forecasting, along with other types of economic forecasting, is a hazardous business. It seems doubtful that anyone, in the years immediately after World War II, could have predicted the pronounced upsurge in research and development expenditures that began in the United States early in the

---

[1] See the data, previously discussed, in Appendix A, Table A-11. Moreover, the October 1971 data are not necessarily inconsistent with our earlier finding in Section 3 that the proportion of managerial workers who had had five or more years of college had increased substantially between 1970 and 1971. That change occurred between March 1970 and March 1971, probably reflecting, chiefly, hiring of June 1970 graduates.

1950s and that played an important role, as we have seen, in stimulating the demand for engineers and scientists. Nor could the dimensions of the future demand for elementary and secondary school teachers have been predicted with any accuracy, because it was not at all clear how long the high birthrates of the early post-war years would last.

Looking ahead in the 1970s, we cannot be certain whether or not some new development—not anticipated at present—might provide a new stimulus to the demand for college graduates that would restore the generally favorable conditions of the 1960s. On the other hand, the increase in demand could be below that indicated by BLS projections if the rate of increase in real GNP were to fall below the rate assumed in the estimates (4.3 percent per year).

A few years ago, because of such uncertainties, most forecasters would probably have said that the course of future demand for college-educated manpower was far more difficult to predict than the supply of college graduates, which could be predicted with a fair degree of reliability on the basis of past trends. Now this is not so certain. Unusual shifts in patterns of enrollment, to be discussed at a later stage, are occurring, and there are some indications that the less favorable job market for college graduates may be playing a role, along with other factors, in discouraging some high school graduates from entering college.

Past experience does not provide a very reliable guide to the impact of a relatively unfavorable job market for college graduates on the propensity to enroll in college. To be sure, the enrollment rate declined in the worst years of the Great Depression of the 1930s, but this probably occurred primarily because many young people could not afford to go to college rather than because the job market for college graduates was poor. In fact, the lack of jobs for high school graduates probably induced some students to go on to college who might not have done so in a more favorable labor market situation.

Postwar data from the *Current Population Survey* of the Census Bureau suggest that there may be some tendency, though not an altogether consistent one, for enrollment rates to fall or level off during recessions (46), but the evidence is not very conclusive as yet. And again, the data do not tell us whether reluctance to enroll in a recession is related to the job market or to the difficulty of financing a college education for many young people when there is substantial unemployment.

However, in the fall of 1971, evidence began to develop suggesting that the poor job market outlook for college graduates might be affecting enrollment patterns. There were news reports that unusual shifts were occurring in college enrollment patterns, including an accelerated shift away from traditional academic programs and into vocational programs of all types, whether in community colleges, apprenticeships, or under other auspices. Not only were high school graduates reported to be enrolling in vocational programs in greatly increased numbers, but also students were said to be shifting from academic programs in four-year colleges to occupational programs in two-year community colleges, while returning veterans were also reported to be flocking into the latter type of program.

The Carnegie Commission's fall 1971 enrollment survey tended to confirm these reports about enrollment shifts (55).[2] Perhaps the most significant result was a decline in first-time freshman enrollment in four-year colleges and universities.

By July 1972, there were indications that these shifts in enrollment patterns were continuing. The National Association of Admissions Counselors, citing 300,000 to 500,000 unfilled student places, predicted that there would continue to be openings in September for 175,000 freshmen and 125,000 transfer students (56). Admissions officers were reporting a number of reasons for the unusually large number of openings: (1) the increasingly high cost of attending college, (2) changes in the draft law that make it no longer necessary to attend college in order to avoid military service, (3) the unfavorable job market for college graduates, and (4) the increasing tendency for students to "stop out" of college for a period and return later — a tendency that was being encouraged by liberalized policies of a number of colleges and universities permitting deferred admission of freshmen and guaranteed readmission of students in upper classes who had stopped out.

Also of interest is the fact that applications to eight Ivy League colleges rose quite sharply after having declined in the previous

[2] Mailed questionnaires, seeking detailed information on enrollment, including enrollment by field of study, were sent to all institutions of higher education in the United States. The response rate was only 48 percent, but the sample of respondents was quite representative by type and control of institution and by region. We had anticipated a response rate of not more than about 50 percent, because of the detailed work required of administrators in supplying all the data sought by the questionnaire.

year, whereas state universities were reported to be experiencing the lowest growth in freshman applications in 19 years (57). These conflicting trends were interpreted as indicating that well-to-do families could afford the $5,000 or so annual cost of attendance by a son or daughter at an Ivy League college but that the annual cost of about $2,000 for a student living away from home at a state university was "out of reach for many middle-income families." Another indication that rising costs were a factor in shifting enrollment patterns was a sharp drop in the number of out-of-state applications to state universities—tuition charges tend to be considerably higher for out-of-state students and have been rising rapidly in recent years.[3]

The results of earlier unofficial surveys were in large part confirmed when U.S. Office of Education data on fall 1971 and fall 1972 enrollments became available. Total enrollment increased about 6 percent in the fall of 1971—in line with Carnegie Commission projections—but prebaccalaureate degree-credit enrollment in four-year institutions actually declined, and the overall increase would have fallen below Commission projections had it not been for the sharp upsurge in occupational enrollment in two-year institutions (Chart 14). Between the fall of 1971 and the fall of 1972, total enrollment increased only 2 percent, or well below the Commission's projected rate of increase of 6 percent.[4] The shifts that had been suggested by 1971 data were continuing. Prebaccalaureate degree-credit enrollment in four-year institutions declined again, while in two-year institutions it rose considerably less than our projection based on past trends would have indicated. Meanwhile, occupational enrollment in two-year institutions once more showed a substantial gain, reaching about 835,000, or about 75,000 more than our projected 760,000.

Also significant was the fact that the total first-time degree-credit enrollment (not shown in Chart 14) tended to level off, falling well below projected amounts.

[3] However, court decisions limiting the period of time required for legal residence in a state to not more than 30 days, along with the recent acquisition of adulthood by 18- to 20-year-olds, are likely to mean that out-of-state students will in practice pay the same tuition as state residents in the near future.

[4] The projected rates of increase for fall 1971 and fall 1972 are based on the lowest of three projections that have been developed by the Commission. For a description of the differing assumptions used in these projections, see Carnegie Commission on Higher Education (29, p. 43).

CHART 14 *Enrollment in higher education—total, prebaccalaureate degree-credit in two-year and four-year institutions, and non-degree-credit in two-year institutions—actual, 1959 or 1960 to 1972, and projections based on past trends, 1971 and 1972 (in thousands)*

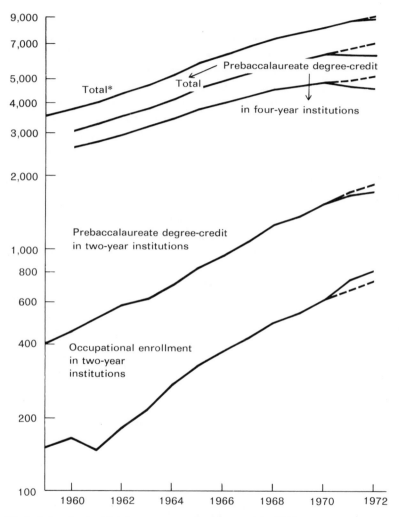

*Projected and actual totals were approximately equal in 1971.
SOURCE: U.S. Office of Education data, adjusted by Carnegie Commission staff; projections by Carnegie Commission staff.

Although other factors mentioned above were clearly playing a role in explaining these shifts, it seems highly likely that changes in the job market were influential in inducing the sharp increase in occupational enrollment in two-year institutions.[5]

The results of the Carnegie Commission's fall 1971 enrollment survey (55), as well as other data, suggested that declines in first-time enrollment in four-year colleges were occurring among white males, while very modest increases were occurring among white females; enrollment of blacks and members of other minority groups was increasing sharply, continuing the marked upward trend that began in the mid-1960s.

It is too early to predict whether these recent enrollment shifts will persist and eventually require substantial revision of enrollment projections prepared by the Carnegie Commission and other agencies, but the shifts certainly introduce a far more important element of uncertainty about the future behavior of enrollment than was thought to exist a few years ago. Meanwhile, other developments are likely to affect the future supply of college graduates, beyond those already mentioned. The indications that increasing numbers of colleges and universities are adopting or seriously considering a three-year B.A. program, or are placing increased emphasis on opportunities for advanced standing of entering freshmen, or are offering opportunities for high school seniors to enroll in college suggest that the number of B.A.'s awarded might rise above the number projected on the basis of past trends as students move through the undergraduate pipeline more rapidly.

[5] The unpublished tables that we have received from the U.S. Office of Education providing data on 1971 and 1972 enrollment do not include a non-degree-credit category but rather a category called "resident and extension nonbachelor's degree-credit students (in vocational and technical programs of less than 4 years, not normally leading to bachelor's degree)," but this category of enrollment appears to be comparable to the non-degree-credit category used in earlier OE published data. We have used the term occupational enrollment to describe it. There are also some indications that enrollment in proprietary schools has been increasing, but data on these schools are very incomplete.

5. The Outlook for the 1970s — Teachers

The occupations in which surpluses of college-educated jobseekers are likely to be most serious in the 1970s are elementary and secondary school teaching and college-level instruction. In each of these occupations the reasons for the current and future surpluses are primarily demographic.

The children entering elementary school in the fall of 1971 were born in 1965 or 1966, when the number of live births was declining significantly. Instead of facing a situation in which elementary and secondary school enrollment was rapidly increasing, as had been the case in the 1950s and the early 1960s, the college graduate or the holder of a master's degree in education seeking a teaching position in the public schools faced a situation in which the rate of increase in enrollment was falling off and would eventually be replaced by a period of absolute decline. There were indications of a surplus of persons seeking teaching jobs in a number of states beginning about the fall of 1969. By 1971, an oversupply of qualified applicants "for a diminished number of openings in elementary and secondary schools was reported in all sections of the country" (2, p. 118). According to the National Education Association, a record 338,000 persons completed teacher training between September 1971 and August 1972, but only 197,000 new teachers were needed in the fall of 1972 (58).

Because total employment in elementary and secondary school-teaching is so much larger than in college teaching, the impact of the unfavorable market for schoolteachers on the market for college graduates in general is likely to be more serious than the impact of the poor market for college faculty members, particularly in the case of women. In 1970 there were about 2.3 million teachers in public elementary and secondary education (27, p. 60). Whereas employment of elementary and secondary schoolteachers increased

69

by more than 700,000 between 1960 and 1970, the number employed is expected to rise by only about 40,000 in the 1970s (2, p. 118). The main demand for new teachers in the 1970s will be for replacement.

In the past, the number required to replace those who retire, die, or leave for other reasons has far exceeded the number required to fill newly added positions even in the years of rapid expansion in the professions. In the present decade replacement requirements are likely to be greater than ever before (simply because of the increased size of the profession). But altogether, the demand for teachers, both as replacements and to fill the projected small numbers of new positions, is estimated at well under 200,000 per year throughout the 1970s (ibid., pp. 118–119).

The percentage of college graduates required to fill the demand for new teachers has declined from 1963 on, and is expected to decline substantially more in the 1970s (Table 2).

It will be imperative for colleges to counsel an appropriate proportion of the students who express a preference for teaching to train for other fields. The impact on women will be particularly impor-

TABLE 2
Actual and projected demand for new elementary and secondary school teachers compared with number of college graduates, selected years, 1963–1980 (numbers in thousands)

Year	Total teachers employed	Number required for growth and replacement	New teachers required*	Total number of college graduates†	New teachers required as percent of graduates
1963	1,806	209	157	444	35
1966	2,028	228	171	551	31
1968	2,162	230	173	667	26
1970	2,312	231	173	827	21
1972	2,326	180	135–180	903	15–20
1974	2,323	175	131–175	990	13–18
1976	2,311	177	133–177	1,100	12–16
1978	2,317	181	136–181	1,207	11–15
1980	2,349	200	150–200	1,300	12–15

* Figures for 1963–1970 represent 75 percent of the total number required for growth and replacement, with a conservative allowance for the numbers of teachers who returned to the profession. Since the return flow of experienced teachers may possibly decline during the 1970s, the ranges shown indicate the numbers and percents of new teachers that would be required with a return flow ranging from 0 to 25 percent.

† Includes bachelor's and first-professional degrees awarded.

SOURCE: U.S. Department of Labor (2, p. 119).

tant, because, as we have seen, about one-half of all employed female college graduates have been engaged in teaching. To some degree, women will doubtless choose other careers without counseling, as the changing market conditions for teachers become widely known. But, significantly, the BLS points out:

Over the 1968–80 period, the number of women graduates is expected to increase two-thirds or twice the rate for men. Traditional "women's" fields will not be able to absorb this increase because about 2 out of every 5 women in professional jobs are elementary or secondary school teachers.[1] Through proper counseling, women can be made aware of this expected sharp decline in the proportion of new graduates who will be needed in teaching. Some may enter social work, chemistry, engineering, or other shortage areas to help achieve a supply-demand balance and improve their own employment prospects. Unless women enlarge the range of occupations, strong competition for jobs may develop (25, p. 4).

Nevertheless, it is important to recognize that "teaching opportunities for both men and women will be very favorable in urban ghettos, rural districts, and other areas offering unfavorable working and living conditions" (ibid., p. 14). There will also be increased demands for teachers of mentally retarded or physically handicapped children, for teachers in vocational and technical schools, and for teachers in two-year colleges. Despite the widespread reports of surpluses of teachers in 1971, about half of the states reported shortages in particular fields, such as "industrial arts, special education, mathematics, trades, industrial and vocational subjects, remedial reading, speech correction, and distributive education" (2, p. 118). There are likely also to be increased demands for teachers in kindergarten and nursery schools, as well as in day-care centers, while local school districts may increase their faculty-student ratios under conditions of an excess supply of teachers.

In fact, the prospects for an excess supply of teachers suggest that school districts should seize the opportunity to expand and improve intensive programs of compensatory education for disadvantaged youngsters. Not only will teachers be available, but reduced enrollment and the reduced rate of increase in teachers'

---

[1] It should be noted that the statement in the preceding paragraph about the proportion of women engaged in teaching applies to *college graduates*, not to all professional women.

salaries that will be likely in a looser labor market for teachers should mean a considerably reduced rate of increase in overall public school costs. That reduction would facilitate meeting the special costs associated with compensatory programs. The effectiveness of increased school resources in improving educational progress in ghetto schools is, of course, a matter of controversy. Both the Coleman Report (59) and the more recent study by Jencks and others (60) provide evidence suggesting that differences in expenditures per pupil and other measures of school resources have little effect on educational results, once adjustments have been made for differences in family background and ability of students. Bowles (61) has criticized these findings of the Coleman Report on several methodological grounds and has found, on the basis of reanalysis of the Coleman data, that school resources have a significant relation to scholastic achievement, particularly for Negro children. Perl (62) has arrived at similar conclusions. Some of the methodological criticisms of the Coleman Report would also apply to the Jencks volume. Moreover, Jencks and his coauthors (60, chap. 2) strongly advocate increased federal aid to bring about greater equality of school expenditures per pupil among the states.[2]

A detailed analysis of this controversy would be beyond the scope of the present report.[3] But we believe that the criticisms of the Coleman findings must be taken seriously and that a great deal of additional research bearing on the issues involved is needed. Meanwhile, we do not believe that the Coleman and Jencks results should be used as a basis for ceasing to strive for reduced student-faculty ratios and for other ways of enriching the education of disadvantaged young persons. In fact, the Coleman Report itself points out that "school factors are more important in affecting the achievement of minority group students [than of white students]" (59, vol. 1, p. 297).

Closely related to this controversy is the debate over the impacts of school desegregation. Recently, Armor has reviewed the results of several studies of communities that have had busing programs, and has reached the general conclusion that "over the period of two or three years, busing does *not* lead to significant measurable gains

---

[2] Although they question the efficacy of increased expenditures in appreciably improving educational results, they believe that teachers and children should not have to endure crowded and inferior school environments.

[3] A more detailed discussion will be included as part of a forthcoming Commission report, *The Purposes and Performance of Higher Education in the United States.*

in student achievement or interracial harmony (although it does lead to the channeling of black students to better colleges)" (63, p. 115). Pettigrew and three associates have prepared a critique of the Armor article, in which they maintain that Armor's choice of studies to be reviewed was "selective" and omitted a number of studies with more positive results on the favorable effects of busing and school integration programs. They also charge that Armor set an impossible criterion for the success of school desegregation — that it must lead "in one year — to increased achievement, aspirations, self-esteem, interracial tolerance, and life opportunities for black children" (64, p. 1). Moreover, busing was considered a failure by Armor if achievement gains by blacks were not significantly greater statistically than gains by whites. An additional criticism was inadequate use of the data from the studies selected for review.

We believe that an important aspect of this entire controversy is the tendency of some analysts and commentators to concentrate on the impact of school desegregation on academic achievement alone. More basic issues involve the severe difficulties, so well described by Conant in his book entitled *Slums and Suburbs* (65), in relying on the schools alone to overcome the invidious impacts of slum environments on the development of children, and the whole question of whether we want to aim at a segregated or desegregated society.

In an earlier report, the Commission recommended that the "first priority in the nation's commitment to equal educational opportunity be placed on the increased effectiveness of our preelementary, elementary, and secondary school programs" (66, p. 5). We continue to adhere strongly to that position.

As was indicated in Section 3, BLS data on the employment of teachers reveal a considerably larger increase in recent years than OE data:

Employment of teachers, except college (in thousands)

	OE		BLS		Difference
Fall 1965	1,951	March 1966	2,148		197
Fall 1966	2,032	March 1967	2,230		207
Fall 1967	2,087	March 1968	2,476		389
Fall 1968	2,162	March 1969	2,493		331
Fall 1969	2,241	March 1970	2,701		460
Fall 1970*	2,340	March 1971	2,894		554

*Estimated.

SOURCES: U.S. Office of Education (27, p. 60, and 66, p. 6) and U.S. Bureau of Labor Statistics (18).

The BLS data report all "teachers, except college," whereas the OE data relate only to teachers in kindergarten through twelfth grade. We have compared OE fall 1965 data with BLS March 1966 data, for example, because they relate to the same school year.[4] In addition to the probable influences of increased enrollment in day-care centers, enrollment in Head Start programs probably also played a role. There has been growing support for substantially increased federal expenditures for day-care centers and other programs contributing to childhood development, but the outlook for sizable increases in these expenditures in the near future is uncertain.[5]

Data from the 1970 census (Appendix A, Table A-4) tend to confirm that OE data understate the increase that has occurred in the number of teachers. The total number of elementary and secondary schoolteachers in the census data (2.4 million) is somewhat larger than the OE figure for 1970. The number of teachers in other settings (326,500) is somewhat smaller than the difference between BLS and OE totals for 1970, but the census data also suggest a rapid growth in the 1960s of the number of teachers in settings other than elementary and secondary schools.

Another consideration that suggests that official projections of the future demand for teachers may be overly pessimistic is that school enrollment may expand in rapidly growing suburban areas, while it levels off or contracts in most other school districts. Because an increasing proportion of teachers will have tenure in districts in which enrollment levels off or declines, new hires in districts with increasing enrollment may well exceed layoffs in districts with declining enrollment.

If there is uncertainty about predictions of the demand for teachers in the 1970s, there is even greater uncertainty about the outlook

---

[4] It should also be noted that the BLS data are subject to sampling variability. Nevertheless, the almost steadily widening margin of difference between the two series is certainly significant. Annual average BLS data on the employment of teachers do not show quite as pronounced an increase, but the annual averages are held down by the drop in employment of teachers in the summer. We believe the March data shown here, drawn from those issues of the *Special Labor Force Report* that are concerned with educational attainment, provide a more reliable index of the employment of teachers during the school year than do annual averages.

[5] A bill providing for greatly expanded early childhood development programs was vetoed by the President toward the end of 1971, but revised legislation calling for expenditures of $1.2 billion for such programs was passed by the Senate in 1972. No action was taken in the House. Expenditures for Head Start rose from $5 million in 1964–65 to $331 million in 1969–70 and were expected to continue to increase at a modest rate.

for the 1980s. Children who will be entering elementary school in that decade have not yet been born. Moreover, past predictions of changes in the birthrate have been strikingly unreliable. Many of us remember the predictions of continuing stagnation of the birthrate in the late 1930s and the accompanying discussions of the implications of a steady aging of the population for future economic and political developments. At present we have a situation in which not only the crude birthrate but also the *absolute number* of births in the United States has been declining for some years. And in the last few years this has occurred in the face of a sizable growth in the number of young people who reach typical ages for marriage and childbearing. For example, those reaching the age of 25 in 1972 were born in 1947, when the birthrate reached its postwar peak. Earlier predictions of a population explosion when the postwar babies reached childbearing age have not been borne out, and as yet we do not know enough about the relative roles of the "pill," the zero-population-growth movement, women's lib, liberalized abortion laws, and other influences in accounting for this.[6] However, there now appears to be a possibility that the birthrate will remain relatively low and that there will not be an appreciable rise in the number of children entering elementary school in the 1980s.

Thus far, the impact of changing enrollment trends on the financial status of local school districts has frequently been unfavorable. State aid and some types of federal aid tend to be based on enrollment or average daily attendance (ADA) figures and to be restricted or cut back as enrollment becomes stationary or declines. Quite apart from the impact of ADA formulas, fiscal pressure in some states has limited appropriations for aid to local school districts in recent years. However, there is some support for a major increase in federal aid in elementary and secondary education, while the decision of the California Supreme Court in Serrano *v.* Priest[7] and similar decisions in a few other states have led to intensive

[6] There have been some recent analyses in states with liberalized abortion laws suggesting that abortions have been an important factor.

[7] In this case, the California Supreme Court decided (August 30, 1971) that heavy reliance on local property taxes for the support of public schools was unconstitutional because families living in impoverished school districts were denied "equal protection of the law" as compared with families in wealthier school districts. In other words, in districts with high-assessed-property valuation, a relatively low school tax rate would make possible large expenditures per school child, whereas, for families living in districts with low-assessed valuation, the same tax rate would yield much lower expenditures per child.

consideration of proposals at the state level to limit the contribution of local property taxes to the support of public schools and to increase the state's share of financial support. These developments appear almost certain to lead in the near future to increases in the federal and state, relative to the local, shares in the support of elementary and secondary education.

Meanwhile, institutions of higher education that have been heavily involved in the training of teachers are facing difficult decisions. Should they limit admissions into their schools of education in the light of deteriorating job prospects for teachers? Early in 1972 it was reported that such leading institutions as Michigan State University, Ohio State University, the University of Colorado, Pennsylvania State University, the University of Illinois, and the University of Iowa were taking steps to curb teacher training (67). Such decisions are likely to have less significant repercussions on the institution as a whole in these large state universities, with their highly diversified educational programs, than they would in comprehensive universities and colleges[8] in which a large proportion of all students train as teachers and in many liberal arts colleges that play an important role in the education of teachers. The problem is likely also to be of concern for black colleges—the colleges founded for Negroes—with their historic mission of training the teachers for the formerly completely segregated schools for black children in the South. Conflicting forces are at work here—on the one hand, a probable increase in demand for black teachers in ghetto areas in the North and the West, and, on the other hand, an adverse impact of school desegregation on job opportunities for black teachers in the South. But the changing market for teachers is another reason for diversification of the programs of black colleges that we recommended in an earlier report (see Appendix B).

A large proportion of students training for teaching do not now receive a bachelor of education degree, as was common in earlier years, but rather, major in English, history, mathematics, or other subjects that are taught in elementary and secondary schools. As we have seen, many liberal arts colleges are heavily involved in the training of teachers, and in 1966 public comprehensive colleges and universities prepared 47 percent of those eligible for initial certification as teachers (68, p. 119). Many of these public comprehensive

[8] We refer here to comprehensive universities and colleges as classified by the Commission, and as distinguished from doctoral-granting universities. See the description of the Commission's classification of institutions of higher education in its report *New Students and New Places* (1971, Appendix A).

colleges and universities originated as normal schools, later became state teachers colleges, and then in many cases broadened their curricula to provide liberal arts majors and professional programs, such as engineering, business administration, and nursing.

The answer for many of the state colleges that are not now very diversified will be to attempt to broaden their programs along the lines of those of the more comprehensive of these institutions. However, this will be more readily accomplished by state colleges that are located in, or adjacent to, large urban communities than by colleges in relatively rural areas. In urban areas, professional and vocational programs can benefit from proximity to business enterprises, hospitals, and other institutions that will employ their graduates, and that will, in some cases, provide clinical or other work experience. Particularly difficult will be the adjustment problems of public colleges in such states as North and South Dakota, which have concentrated heavily on teacher training and are located in relatively small communities.[9] It will be especially important for such states to develop plans involving a division of labor among state colleges as they add occupational programs. For each state college in a system to become broadly diversified will not be feasible, and in some situations a merger of two such colleges into one location may be the only practical solution.

However, the Commission believes that there is a danger of overreaction to the changing job market for teachers. As we have suggested earlier, declining enrollment in the public schools should create an opportunity for school districts to devote more of their resources to compensatory education, and more generally to raising faculty-student ratios. And projections may underestimate the impact of increasing enrollments in day-care centers and in other programs for young children.

There was also an acceleration of the rate of increase in the number of degrees awarded in the field of education at all levels in the latter half of the 1960s (Chart 15).[10] In fact, the appearance of a surplus of teachers in all parts of the country by 1971 was

[9] The two-year county teachers colleges in Wisconsin, many of them located in very small communities, are being phased out.

[10] A semilogarithmic scale has been used in Chart 15, so that an increase in the upward slope of any of the series represents a rise in the percentage rate of increase. In the preparation of this chart and subsequent charts, we have been greatly assisted by access to the extensive tables providing adjusted data on degrees by field, prepared by Douglas L. Adkins of the faculty of the Graduate School of Business Administration, New York University.

CHART 15 *Degrees awarded in education, by level and sex, 1947–1970 (logarithmic scale numbers of degrees in thousands)*

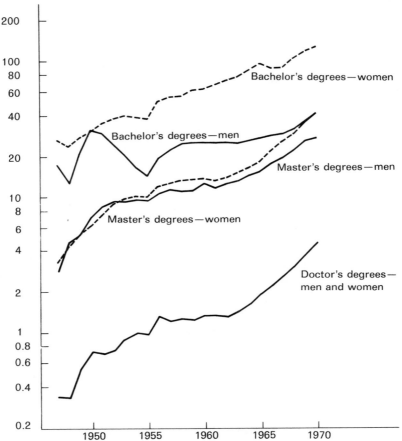

SOURCE: U.S. Office of Education (27); data on numbers of degrees awarded have been adapted by D. L. Adkins.

undoubtedly at least as much a result of a large increase in supply as of a slackening of demand. In this connection, it must be kept in mind that many students receiving degrees in arts and sciences were also expecting to teach. The Carnegie Commission's fall 1971 enrollment survey showed a 9.4 percent decline, as compared with 1970, in undergraduate enrollment in the field of education, but an 8.1 percent increase in graduate enrollment in education (55, p. 14). Probably many recent college graduates who had failed to get teaching jobs were returning for master's degrees in the hope of improving their employment prospects. But eventually the declining demand for elementary and secondary schoolteachers is likely to result in a reduction in enrollment for master's degrees in education, if the percentage of undergraduates training for teaching continues to decline, as it almost certainly will. American Council on Education data on career choices of entering college freshmen show a pronounced decline from 1968 in the percentages planning a career in teaching, for both men and women (Appendix A, Table A-14).

Another consideration is the deficient quality of teacher education in many institutions. In some former state teachers colleges that have been experiencing rapid growth and have broadened their programs, younger members of the faculty are far more interested in efforts to develop the college along the lines of the more prestigious universities, adding research and, eventually, doctoral programs, than in improving the quality of teacher education (68 and 69). If there is a widespread movement to restrict teacher training on an institution-by-institution basis, we believe there will be a serious danger of neglecting efforts to improve quality and to introduce innovations in the education of teachers. This could interfere with the greatly needed expansion of emphasis on methods of stimulating deprived youngsters in ghetto schools, along the lines of the successful work of some particularly gifted teachers, through use of the new electronic technology, and in other ways.

Recommendation 4: State planning agencies should give very high priority in the next few years to careful adaptation of teacher education to the changing needs of a period of shrinking job opportunities for elementary and secondary school teachers. We believe that consolidation of teacher education into a more limited number of institutions that can offer high quality training would be generally preferable to a cutting back of teacher education on an across-the-board basis. States should encourage the participation of private as well as public colleges and universities in such planning. We also recognize that many state colleges that have largely concentrated on teacher education will need to develop more comprehensive programs if they are to serve students effectively, and that in sparsely populated states this will require division of labor among such state colleges in adding new fields or in some cases a merger of two or more such state colleges into a single location.

Recommendation 5: High priority should be given to adaptation of teacher-training programs to changing needs. There should be increased emphasis on specialized training to prepare teachers for service in ghetto schools, in programs for mentally retarded or physically handicapped children, in early child development programs and day-care centers, and in vocational education programs.

Recommendation 6: The U.S. Bureau of Labor Statistics and the U.S. Office of Education should develop revised estimates of the future demand for teachers that take account, as existing projections do not, of the growing demand for teachers in pre-elementary education and in such other settings as adult education programs. There is also a need for revised estimates of supply that take account of the declining enrollment in undergraduate education programs and of a possible future decline in enrollment in master's degree in education programs.

Although many students considering preparation for teaching should be counseled to prepare instead for other occupations, we urge counselors not to neglect the need to encourage promising students to prepare themselves for specialized fields in which the demand for teachers is likely to rise.

Critical problems of school financing must be solved if our society is to meet the challenge of overcoming severe problems of inequality of opportunity in elementary and secondary education. We believe that greatly increased federal and state aid to local school districts will be required if these problems are to be overcome. We also believe that there is a strong case for lowering the age of permissible entrance into the public schools, so that four-year-olds will be encouraged to attend.

Recommendation 7: States should give careful consideration to the adoption of policies encouraging a lower age of entrance into the public schools, specifically at the age of four.

We also believe that a surplus of teachers is likely to result in increased tendencies for local school districts to prefer or require possession of a master's degree on the part of applicants for employment, in line with the long-run trend toward increased emphasis on length of training. We urge that major emphasis be placed instead on careful selection, especially in view of the need for teachers who are qualified to meet the special needs of disadvantaged young persons.[11] This is not to suggest that preference should be given to holders of bachelor's degrees over those with more advanced degrees but simply to state that possession of an advanced degree should not be the governing criterion.

There are indications that institutions of higher education and relevant state agencies need to give attention to improvement of master's degree programs in education in many instances. Probably the most significant finding of a recent study of master's degree programs in public and private institutions in New York State concerned the influence of state teacher certification requirements on enrollment in master's degree programs, especially in liberal arts colleges (70, pp. 62–63):

Most graduate students in these institutions are seeking permanent certification as teachers, whether they are enrolled in arts and science programs or in teacher education programs. Without the support given by the mandate that thirty credits beyond the baccalaureate are necessary to qualify for such certification, it is not likely that many liberal arts colleges would be in the business of awarding graduate degrees — there simply would not be a sufficiently large market. The lack of such a mandate would even affect doctoral study. The guaranteed large-scale demand for high-tuition of first-year graduate students — instruction often given at a lower level and in sizeable classes rather than in seminars and tutorials — is admittedly one means of subsidizing some of the small, high-cost doctoral programs in the multiversities.

Although the situation in New York State may differ in some respects from that in other states, there is reason to believe that much the same problems exist elsewhere. On the other hand, there is evidence that some of the experimental innovations in master's degree programs that were developed in the 1950s and 1960s have had very promising results. In particular, a study evaluating the Breakthrough Programs sponsored by the Ford Foundation beginning in 1958 indicated substantial progress as a result of a number of these projects (71). For the most part, relatively prestigious institutions were selected for the experiments. The majority of the projects involved either a master of arts in teaching program or a five-year combined undergraduate and graduate program, while six of the projects were exclusively undergraduate. But there is much

---

[11] This point was also emphasized in the staff report of the Commission on Human Resources and Advanced Education (4, p. 114).

evidence from the New York State master's degree study as well as from other sources that there is room for a great deal of improvement in both undergraduate and graduate education programs. The decline in enrollment in undergraduate majors in education and the probable future decline in master's degree programs should create an opportunity for major efforts to improve quality, as well as to consolidate education programs in a smaller number of institutions.

6. The Outlook for the 1970s—
Health Professions

The most serious shortages of professional personnel are in the health field. There is little question that the Medicare and Medicaid programs, adopted in 1965, tended to exacerbate these shortages by channeling substantially increased funds into the health care system without embodying appropriate and decisive policies for accompanying increases in the supply of health manpower and facilities. Certainly the rise in the medical care component of the consumer price index occurred at a substantially accelerated rate after 1965. Adoption of a comprehensive national health insurance system—an eventuality that seems likely in the not-too-distant future—could have a similar effect in increasing the demand for health care services and enhancing existing shortages of health manpower. Whether and to what extent it would have such an effect depends on which of the widely differing measures now before Congress is adopted and how far we manage to overcome current shortages of health manpower before legislation becomes effective. Possibly a more immediate prospect is the enactment of legislation to stimulate the development of Health Maintenance Organizations (HMOs)—prepaid group practice plans—for which there is considerable support.

MEDICINE AND DENTISTRY Although there is general agreement about the existence of serious shortages of nurses and allied health workers, a few medical economists maintain that there is no need for expansion of the capacity of medical schools to train M.D.'s. Those who oppose the expansion of medical schools contend that the real problem is the maldistribution and inefficient use of physicians. They also argue that (1) the ratio of other health workers to doctors is increasing rapidly, (2) the work of the health care team will soon be far more effectively coordinated than at present, and (3) physician's associates and assistants with less prolonged training than the fully certified doctor now receives will increasingly take over some of the physician's duties so that his time will be released for the use of his highest skills.

In an earlier report, the Commission carefully considered these arguments but concluded that there was a need for approximately a 50 percent increase in the number of medical school entrant places in the 1970s, to be accomplished partly through expansion of the number and size of schools and partly through acceleration of medical education.[1] While agreeing that the changes mentioned above were occurring, the Commission expressed doubt that they would take place rapidly enough to rule out the probability of continuing shortages of physicians throughout this decade.

Recognizing that the evidence of a shortage of dentists was not quite as clear as in the case of physicians—dentists, for example, average about 43 hours of work per week as compared with about 60 hours for physicians—the Commission recommended an increase of approximately 20 percent in the number of dental school entrant places in the 1970s. We realize, however, that this may turn out to be an underestimate of the need, especially if the trend toward inclusion of dental care in private health insurance plans continues and if dental care is eventually covered under a national health insurance program.[2] As we noted in our earlier report, there is a critical need for continuous analyses of changing demand and supply relationships in all the health professions.

In the last few years, at least in part as a result of the appearance of an unfavorable job market for Ph.D.'s, there has been a sharp upsurge in the number of applications to some of the professional schools, especially law and medical schools. This has given rise to speculation whether such shifts are likely to lead eventually to surpluses in the affected professions. We shall consider the case of law schools at a later point. So far as the medical schools are concerned, the difficulty and high cost of increasing the number of student places are well known. The number of medical school entrant places

[1] See Carnegie Commission on Higher Education, *Higher Education and the Nation's Health: Policies for Medical and Dental Education,* McGraw-Hill Book Company, New York, 1970. Many of the recommendations in that report were incorporated in the Comprehensive Health Manpower Training Act of 1971.

[2] The Commission's estimate of the increased need for dental school places was based largely on a projection developed by the Council on Dental Education of the American Dental Association.

has increased substantially in recent years, but largely in response to earlier plans to expand capacity rather than in response to the recent upsurge in applications. Between the fall of 1968 and the fall of 1972, the number of medical school entrants increased from 9,863 to an estimated 12,900, or 31 percent, while the number of applicants increased from 21,118 to an estimated 35,000, or 66 percent. Clearly, also, prospective medical students were applying to more schools, because the total number of applications increased from 112,000 to 245,000 or 119 percent. It was also reported that many of the applicants for fall 1972 were holders of master's degrees or doctorates in science who could not find steady employment (72). Meanwhile, many disappointed applicants to United States medical schools have been entering foreign medical schools.

Nevertheless, we believe that the expansion of medical and dental school capacity will need to be assessed continuously to guard against the eventual development of a surplus of physicians and dentists. The BLS now estimates that, on the basis of the lower of two estimates of increased demand, the shortage of physicians will be overcome by about 1977, and that, even on the basis of a considerably higher estimate of increased demand, the shortage will be overcome by 1980. These estimates, however, assume that "large numbers of graduates of foreign medical schools will continue to enter practice in this country each year" (2, p. 131). On the other hand, projections of the supply of physicians developed for the Carnegie Commission by Blumberg adopted the assumption, admittedly somewhat arbitrarily, that the influx of FMGs would cease in the late 1970s (73). Even though that assumption was arbitrary, it does seem reasonable to suppose that, as the supply of United States medical graduates increases, the demand for FMGs will eventually begin to slacken. This is just one illustration, among a number that we shall have occasion to mention in later parts of this report, of projection techniques used by government agencies that fail to take account of interactions between demand and supply. We shall return to a discussion of the "brain drain" of foreign medical graduates in Section 9.

NURSING   The 1970 census indicated that there were nearly 830,000 registered nurses, the great majority of whom were women (Appendix A, Table A-4). This was 130,000 more than had been estimated as recently as in early 1972, before detailed occupational data from the 1970 census were available. Thus the rate of increase during the

1960s was about 50 percent, as compared with the 27 percent suggested by the earlier estimate of 700,000 for 1970. Along with other evidence to be discussed later, this indication that the supply of nurses increased very rapidly in the 1960s suggests that the shortage of nurses that has been chronic throughout the postwar period may be disappearing in many parts of the country, although there are still pronounced geographic imbalances—as there are in the supply of physicians and other health personnel.

In the past, a number of experts have suggested that the shortage of nurses could be largely overcome if the substantial numbers of registered nurses who have dropped out of the labor force could be induced to seek reemployment by a sharp increase in nurses' salaries, which historically have been relatively low. A 1970 report indicated that almost half of all graduate nurses were not employed in nursing, and half of these retained licenses (74, p. 132). In the years since 1966—clearly stimulated by Medicare and Medicaid— the rate of increase in nurses' salaries has greatly accelerated, and there are beginning to be indications that this has induced a substantial increase in the supply of nurses. For example, the median annual salary of supervising nurses employed in nonofficial agencies rose at an annual average rate of 4.4 percent from 1960 to 1966, as compared with an annual average rate of 11.1 percent from 1966 to 1970 (75, p. 52). Corresponding rates of increase of annual average compensation of employees in all industries were 3.6 percent in 1960 to 1966 and 5.5 percent in 1966 to 1970. However, the rate of increase in nurses' salaries slowed down somewhat between 1970 and 1971, and there continue to be complaints that nurses' salaries compare unfavorably with those of teachers.[3]

In a recent study of supply and demand for nurses, Altman cites data showing that the vacancy rate (vacancies as a percentage of

---

[3] Despite the generally rapid rise in recent years, nurses' salaries on a 12-month basis—with monthly medians of about $665 to $705 for staff nurses in official and unofficial agencies in 1970 (75, p. 798)—continued to compare unfavorably with 9-month teachers' salaries. In 1970–71, the median minimum monthly salary for teachers with bachelor's degrees was about $760 (dividing the annual salary by nine), and the median maximum was about $1,100 (76, pp. 8-9). Teachers with higher degrees tended to earn somewhat more. However, for those teachers who do not obtain employment during the summer and must live year-round on their annual teaching salary, the comparison with nurses is considerably less favorable. Yet the relative salary position of nurses has been improving. Earnings of registered nurses employed as general duty nurses in hospitals rose from 60 percent of salaries of public school teachers in 1956 to 83 percent in 1969, on the basis of data for 13 large cities (77, p. 80).

positions offered) in nonfederal hospitals was 20.7 percent in 1962, as compared with a vacancy rate of 7.9 percent revealed by a 1969 study (77, pp. 8 and 13).[4] He attributes the decline primarily to (1) a rapid increase in the number of practicing nurses, (2) the rising salaries paid to professional nurses, and (3) the collective bargaining activities of the American Nurses' Association.

However, as in the case of physicians, though not to the same relative extent, the increase in the supply of nurses has been explained in part by an inflow of professional nurses trained in foreign countries. The annual inflow of foreign graduates into employment as nurses in the United States rose from 2.6 percent of the number of United States nursing graduates in 1950 to 12.0 percent in 1967 (ibid., p. 144).

Altman's study also suggests that simple comparisons of average salaries, for example, of teachers and nurses obscure the fact that young women entering teaching can look forward to relatively greater salary increases with advancing age than can a woman choosing nursing as a career. Whereas, in 1959, average full-time earnings of teachers aged 55 were 49 percent higher than those of teachers aged 21, 55-year-old nurses were earning, on the average, only 26 percent more than 21-year-old nurses (ibid., p. 55). Although age-earnings profiles for a given year do not provide a reliable guide to age-earnings expectations in later years, this comparison strongly suggests that salary schedules for professional nurses are considerably more compressed than those for teachers.

As in the case of physicians and dentists, there are exceedingly wide geographic variations in ratios of nurses to population. Among the states the ratio ranged in 1966 from a low of 133 per 100,000 population in Arkansas to 536 per 100,000 in Connecticut (2, p. 133). Along with the pronounced regional variations in supply, there are wide regional differences in the compensation of nurses.[5]

Moreover, although the number of nurses covered by collective bargaining agreements has increased markedly in the last decade or so, in 1968 there were only eighteen states in which any nurses

---

[4] The methods used in the two surveys on which the data are based were not precisely comparable, he notes, but he concludes that "it is clear that a substantial decline has occurred in the reported shortage of hospital nurses" (ibid., p. 13).

[5] In April 1971, median salaries of nurses in local official health agencies varied from a low of $7,673 in the Southern states to a high of $10,313 in the Western states (78, p. 799).

were covered and only five states in which 10 percent or more of registered nurses were covered. These five, in order of relative extent of coverage, were Washington, Minnesota, Hawaii, California, and Massachusetts (77, p. 17).

Until recently, also, there were indications that nursing had become a relatively less attractive profession for women over the years. Admissions to professional nursing schools as a percentage of female high school graduates declined more or less steadily from 7 percent in 1956 to 4.4 percent in 1966, but then began to increase slowly, reaching 4.8 percent in 1969 (ibid., p. 87). Between 1968–69 and 1969–70, admissions to nursing school rose 10 percent, or more rapidly than in preceding years (2, p. 134). Moreover, American Council on Education (ACE) data show that the proportion of freshman women designating nursing as a career choice rose steadily from 5.3 percent in 1966 to 8.6 percent in 1971 (Appendix A, Table A-14). A particularly sharp rise occurred between 1969 and 1970, when there was also a sharp drop, as we have seen, in the percentage indicating elementary or secondary school teaching as a career choice, suggesting that women entering college were becoming aware of the weakening demand for teachers as compared with nurses. The Carnegie Commission's fall 1971 enrollment survey showed an increase of 18.8 percent in the number of new students enrolled in undergraduate nursing programs and of 26.7 percent in the number enrolled in graduate nursing programs in four-year colleges and universities. There was also a sharp increase in the number enrolled in health service programs (including dental care, nutrition, nursing, pharmacy, etc.) in two-year colleges (55, pp. 14, 28–29).

The BLS has estimated that the demand for registered nurses would reach 1 million by 1980, or 52 percent more than the 660,000 estimated to be employed in 1968 at the time their projection was developed (26, p. 58). Altman has estimated that the supply is likely to range from 864,000 to 924,000 in 1980 (77, p. 5). In the light of the evidence that the supply of nurses has increased very rapidly in recent years, both of these projections now seem somewhat obsolete. Clearly, there is a need for new analyses that will take account, not only of the unexpectedly large number of nurses revealed by the 1970 census, but also of the sizable recent increases in enrollment in nurse-training programs. On the other hand, proposed budgetary cuts in federal support of nurse-training programs could discourage increasing enrollment.

What accounts for the discrepancy between the 1970 census figure and the lower numbers used by federal agencies? The data used by the Bureau of Health Manpower Education were based on the inventory of active registered nurses maintained by the American Nurses' Association. The 1970 estimate was obtained from the Interagency Conference on Nursing Statistics. It seems probable that these sources provide more reliable data on nurses employed in hospitals and public agencies than on those employed in small nursing homes, convalescent centers, and private homes. It may well be that some married nurses returning to the labor force and obtaining employment in these latter settings are not included in the inventory of registered nurses. In any event, the 1970 census indicates a considerably more pronounced increase in the supply of active nurses during the decade of the 1960s than do the data used by the Bureau of Health Manpower Education.

As in the case of physicians and dentists, it is very difficult to determine what will be an adequate ratio of nurses to population in the late 1970s and early 1980s. Enactment of a comprehensive national health insurance bill would almost certainly result in an accelerated increase in demand, for a time, particularly because such a demand would tend to increase the capacity of residents of low-income states, where ratios of nurses to population are relatively low.

In connection with his projections of supply, Altman concluded:

Whether this supply will be adequate to meet all demands for nursing services in the years ahead is somewhat of a moot question. What is clear, is that this increased number of health professionals will provide a larger pool of trained manpower to give the medical care industry increased flexibility to meet expected future demands (77, p. 5).

The development of such professions as pediatric nurse's assistants and associates, as well as the growing interest in community medicine programs, in which nurses are playing a key and responsible role in health teams serving the poor,[6] suggests that there will be many more challenging positions opening up for nurses in the years to come. Other developments in a similar direction are (1) the advance of technology, requiring skill in the use of complex equipment in such facilities as intensive care units for heart cases,

[6] An example of such a program is at the Martin Luther King, Jr., Health Center in the Bronx, New York.

and (2) the growing involvement of nurses holding bachelor's or advanced degrees in nursing education, as the training of nurses increasingly moves out of hospital nursing schools and into comprehensive colleges and community colleges.

Nurses were formerly trained almost exclusively in nurse's diploma programs in hospitals, but during the postwar period there was a rapid increase in the number of nurses trained in baccalaureate degree programs in colleges and universities, and in associate's degree programs in two-year colleges. Although the majority of those enrolled in nursing programs in the past were in hospital diploma programs, the number of enrollees in these programs is declining, and, if present trends continue, they will become a minority of all enrollees in nurse's training before long. By 1969, 24 percent of admissions in nurse's training were in baccalaureate degree programs, 35 percent in associate's degree programs, and 42 percent in diploma programs (77, p. 89).[7]

Another significant development in nursing education is training at the master's and even at the Ph.D. level. The number of nurses awarded master's or higher degrees increased from 728 in 1957 to 1,560 in 1970. However, in the latter year, only 11 of the degrees awarded were doctorates. Holders of advanced degrees in nursing are chiefly engaged in teaching, supervision, administration, and research. In this growing field, the need for advanced training is certain to increase, and the number of nurses enrolled in graduate programs can be expected to rise rapidly. This will be especially true in view of the shift in nursing education to two-year and four-year colleges, where nurses with advanced degrees will be needed as teachers.

Along with these changes in nursing education, there are a number of serious and controversial problems in the training of nurses and in the utilization of nurses that are of particular concern to nurses' associations and nurse educators. Among the more important of these are:

1 The weakness of career-ladder opportunities in nursing education, although these problems are closely related to the need for more carefully developed career-ladder opportunities in education for the health professions generally, and are not greatly different from similar needs in education for other professions.

---

[7] For an illuminating discussion of the factors underlying these shifts, see Altman (77).

2   The failure of some states to develop strong occupational programs, including training programs for nurses and allied health workers, in their state colleges and/or community colleges.

3   The fear in the nursing profession that, as the use of physician's assistants develops and expands, the nurse will be increasingly separated both from the physician and the patient.

4   A more general concern about the role of nurses in relation to other members of the health team. One concern is that, with the growing use of licensed practical nurses and nurse's aides, registered nurses often find themselves involved in administrative and supervisory roles, with little contact with patients. Some progress is being made in overcoming this problem in some large hospitals that have achieved decentralization of services, and that in some cases are utilizing nurse clinicians and clinical practitioners (79, p. 483). Another concern has to do with the ambiguity of the nurse's role in relation to the physician. As the National Commission for the Study of Nursing and Nursing Education put it:

> As clinical specialization increases in nursing, there will be a host of ques-
> tions raised about authority and judgment. The resolution will have pro-
> found effects on the profession of nursing — and of medicine. Law and tradi-
> tion hold that nurses do not make diagnoses. Aside from what a nurse must
> and will do when no doctor is available for a patient in critical need, there
> is evidence in the work of a cardiopulmonary specialist or in the decision-
> making of a pediatric nurse clinician that diagnoses are being made, on
> some plane and to some degree, and that these practices cannot be ignored
> (74, p. 41).

5   Growing concern about variations in licensing practices and requirements from state to state.

6   Uncertainty about the types of doctoral education most suitable in nursing.

We believe that some of these problems can be resolved as they become more widely recognized. Some of them are related to the more general problem that, despite the enormous increase in the ratio of nurses and allied health workers to physicians, we are still far from having developed a health care system in which health service personnel function as a well-integrated team. Within nurse education circles there is a tendency to question the widespread acceptance of the concept of the physician as the leader and supervisor of the health care team (79, p. 491; and 80). In fact, these nursing spokesmen believe that the concept of a health team in which the members of the various disciplines develop cooperative relationships rather than simply accept the notion that the functioning of the team must be supervised by the physician would contribute to a more effective health care system. They argue that physicians and nurses cooperate more effectively in some European countries that have achieved high standards of health care.

As a commission concerned with higher education, the Carnegie Commission is not in a position to recommend changes in the system of health care delivery, but we can heartily endorse the concept stressed by many nurse educators that education in the health professions needs to place much greater emphasis on training members of the various health disciplines to work together. We believe, also, that careful comparative studies of how the health team functions in European countries that have achieved lower infant mortality rates and higher life expectancy rates with lower physician-population ratios than the United States are long overdue.

In our report on medical and dental education, we strongly recommended the development of physician's assistant training programs in university health science centers. We believe the problems of the relationship of nurses, on the one hand, and physician's assistants, on the other, to physicians and patients can be satisfactorily worked out as the use of physician's assistants gradually becomes more prevalent. Moreover, as the pioneering programs at the University of Colorado School of Medicine and at the University of Rochester have demonstrated, nurses can be successfully trained to assume increased responsibility as pediatric nurse practitioners and pediatrics associates. There is no reason why they cannot also be trained to serve more generally as physician's assistants and associates, although thus far the medical schools that have developed such programs have tended to recruit their students largely from the ranks of military ex-corpsmen.

The future demand for, and utilization of, nurses will be greatly affected by how vigorously and rapidly we take steps to develop a more effective system of health care delivery in the United States. Many developments are getting under way: community and neighborhood health centers, area health education centers, the National Health Service Corps, and the prospect of legislation to stimulate the development of HMOs — quite apart from the prospect of national health insurance — which are bound to have an effect on the future utilization of nurses. Among other things, these developments are likely to involve nurses to a relatively greater extent in the care of ambulatory patients and to reduce gradually what many leaders in the profession regard as overconcentration of nurses in hospitals, where about two-thirds of all nurses have been employed in recent years.[8] These trends may well also lead to a greater degree of responsibility and independence in the performance of nursing functions.

We believe, also, that the concept of training in the health sciences, with emphasis on human biology, which can lead on to a variety of careers in health services, education, or research, will increasingly become part of the undergraduate curriculum. Exemplifying a number of aspects of such a program is the new Center for Allied Health Careers at the Johns Hopkins School of Medicine, which will develop plans for a School of Health Services offering baccalaureate and graduate programs in several allied health disciplines (81). We believe that such a curriculum will contribute to the development of career-ladder opportunities for nurses and allied health workers.

We believe that nursing schools should not be maintained as entirely separate entities but should become parts of broader centers for the training of health care personnel. Our entrance into a period in which the shortage of nurses is less acute than it has been since World War II should create an opportunity for increased attention to innovations in the training of nurses and of other health care personnel. Specific recommendations will be presented after we have discussed allied health workers.

ALLIED HEALTH PROFESSIONS The proliferation of allied health professions has been one of the most striking occupational developments of the postwar period, associated clearly with the advance of technology in health care. It has been estimated that there are more than 125 specialties in the health manpower field. These occupations are expected to be a major source of increased employment in the 1970s.

The most recent estimates by the U.S. Bureau of Health Manpower Education of increases in the supply in allied health professions include only graduates of approved programs in selected professions in their projections of additions to supply, and thus do

---

[8] As suggested earlier, however, this proportion may have declined by 1970 as employment of nurses in nursing homes and other settings increased.

not shed much light on the overall increase in either demand or supply in these fields. It is apparent that many persons are currently employed in allied health occupations who are not graduates of approved programs. Earlier estimates of the total increase in employment in allied health professions between 1967 and 1980 provide a more adequate indication of the probable increase in employment. They do not, however, indicate the increase in total demand because they take no account of replacement needs. They suggest an overall increase in employment of more than 400,000 in these professions during the 13-year period:

	1967	1980	Increase, 1967–1980
Allied health— at least baccalaureate	229,500	410,000	180,500
Allied health— less than baccalaureate	424,000	656,000	232,000
TOTAL	653,500	1,066,000	412,500

SOURCE: U.S. Public Health Service (82, p. 34).

The Allied Health Professions Personnel Training Act of 1966, which was amended in 1970, provided federal funds for the support of education in these fields, but appropriations have been considerably below authorized funding.[9] Another obstacle to adequate expansion of training has been the failure of many states to develop occupational programs, including programs for training allied health workers, in state colleges and community colleges. There were enormous state-by-state variations in enrollment in occupational programs as a percentage of undergraduate enrollment in 1968. In 12 states—Rhode Island, California, Washington, South Carolina, Delaware, Hawaii, Oregon, North Carolina, Michigan, Virginia, Florida, and Arizona—occupational programs accounted for 10 percent or more of undergraduate enrollment, with proportions ranging downward from Rhode Island's 23 percent to Arizona's 10 percent. At the other end of the spectrum were eight

[9] Grupenhoff and Strickland (83) have prepared a useful summary of federal health legislation. Data on authorizations and appropriations under the Allied Health Professions Training Grants program may be found on page 86 of the summary. See, also, Greenfield (84) for an analysis of the development of allied health professions.

states with less than 3 percent of undergraduate enrollment in occupational programs — Kansas, Kentucky, Georgia, Arkansas, Alaska, Louisiana, Nebraska, and South Dakota.[10]

However, enrollment in allied health programs in both two-year and four-year colleges has been expanding rapidly (83, p. 88). There has also been pronounced expansion of enrollments in training programs for such occupations as licensed practical nurse, nurse's aide, and hospital orderly under the Manpower Development and Training Act (ibid., p. 89), while the training of health workers has been encouraged as well under other federal legislation, such as the Economic Opportunity Act.

The rapid development of the allied health professions has led to complex problems in relation to accreditation and licensing standards. Licensing standards vary from state to state, and it has been suggested that "too rigid standards may . . . prevent some of the more successful experiments in training disadvantaged persons for other-than-menial jobs in the health field from being replicated in other areas" (2, p. 136). A two-year moratorium on the establishment of new categories of health personnel by state legislation, to allow time for the development of uniform national standards, was recommended by the U.S. Department of Health, Education and Welfare in a June 1971 report to the Congress. This report also recommended the use of national examinations for licensing of health personnel, where these had been developed (ibid., p. 137).

The indications of recent increases in supply of personnel and of shifts in enrollment into nursing and allied health training programs suggest that we may be moving out of a period of chronic general shortages in these fields, even though problems of geographic maldistribution are likely to continue. Projections of demand and supply clearly need to be continuously reviewed, so that students can be given the best possible advice about employment opportunities in the health professions. Whereas the disappearance of shortages among physicians and dentists, who are predominantly self-employed, would not lead to unemployment of these highly educated professionals but rather to a reduction in their *relative* incomes, a shift in the job market for nurses and allied health workers could

[10] Only 1.2 percent of undergraduates in New York were classified as enrolled in occupational programs, but this is misleading, because New York has reclassified most of its non-degree-credit programs (roughly equivalent to occupational programs) to degree-credit status. Actually, New York is one of the states with relatively well-developed occupational programs.

lead to unemployment, at least for temporary periods, in these professions.

Recommendation 8: Vigorous efforts should be made at the state level to develop training programs in nursing and allied health professions in state colleges and community colleges in those states that have lagged in the past.

Despite the evidence of rapidly increasing enrollments in these fields, opportunities for training are not well distributed geographically.

Recommendation 9: There should be increased emphasis on basic programs of education in the health sciences—in curricula leading to associate's, bachelor's, and master's degrees—to provide a uniform core of training for nurses, allied health workers, physicians, dentists, and persons preparing themselves for administrative, educational, and research careers in the health field.

Recommendation 10: There should be increased emphasis in educational programs on providing experience in working with other health care personnel as a team.

Recommendation 11: Federal government agencies involved in studies of health manpower should continuously review projections of supply and demand during the 1970s. Meanwhile, as long as shortages continue, federal funds to support the training of health personnel should not be cut back, as under the proposed federal budget for 1973–74.

Recommendation 12: University health science centers and area health education centers should provide leadership in encouraging the development and expansion of continuing education programs for nurses and allied health workers in appropriate educational institutions.[11]

[11] For a discussion of the functions of area health education centers, see Carnegie Commission on Higher Education (85, pp. 55–57). In the last few years, a number of area health education centers have been established, but many more are needed to provide the extensive geographic coverage recommended by the Commission.

Recommendation 13: There should be increased emphasis on encouraging research on alternative ways of utilizing health manpower. There is a need for studies evaluating innovations in health care delivery, and there is also a need for comparative studies on differing patterns of utilization of health manpower in selected countries, especially with a view to determining how a number of other industrial countries have achieved lower infant mortality rates and higher life expectancy rates than the United States, despite lower physician-population ratios.

7. The Outlook for the 1970s— Other Selected Professions

In this section we shall consider the outlook for employment opportunities in some leading professions, other than teaching and the health professions, which employ large numbers of college graduates and holders of advanced degrees.

LAW   As in the case of medical schools, law schools have been experiencing a sharp rise in applications for admission in the last few years. Also as in the case of medical schools, the appearance of a less favorable market for Ph.D.'s has played a role in increased applications. But interest of students in careers that would contribute to the solution of society's problems has been an additional important factor. In the summer of 1971, the Association of American Law Schools reported that there were two applicants for each student place that would be available in the fall. The most selective schools — Yale, Harvard, Stanford, Boalt Hall (University of California, Berkeley), Columbia, and Chicago were reporting more than 10 applicants for each place, while schools that had never before reached capacity were finding that their applications had doubled or even tripled during a two-year period.

This pronounced rise in interest in a legal education, along with a job market for lawyers that has been somewhat depressed in the last few years, has led to speculation about a growing surplus of lawyers in the coming years. Although law school enrollments have increased, they have not increased nearly as much as applications, as has already been indicated. Significantly, also, the number of entrants has increased no more than was indicated by the lower of two projections prepared some four years ago by the Commission on Human Resources and Advanced Education (CHRAE).[1] The actual number of entrants fell below the low projection from 1967 through 1969 but approximated the low projection in 1970 and 1971 (86; and 4, p. 80):

	Law school entrants	Low projection	High projection
1965	26,508	26,100	26,100
1966	26,552	26,550	27,140
1967	26,716	28,260	29,516
1968	25,959	32,490	34,560
1969	30,719	35,820	39,004
1970	37,003	37,620	41,800
1971	37,538	37,980	43,044

The failure of enrollment to rise above the low projection occurred despite the fact that the number of male bachelor's recipients has increased somewhat more rapidly than indicated by the projection used by the staff of the Commission on Human Resources and despite the fact that law schools have been admitting larger ratios of women and minority group students in recent years. After remaining at less than 3 percent of total law school enrollment for decades, enrollment of women increased to about 5 percent in 1968 and to about 9 percent in 1971 (87). The rise in relative representation of minority-group students has apparently been less pronounced. Despite an increase in recent years, the number of nonwhite law students was estimated at no more than 2 percent of the total in 1969 (ibid.). Chart 16 shows a pronounced rise in the number of degrees awarded to women in law during the 1960s, following a decline in the 1950s. However, in law, as in many of the other fields that we shall consider, the number of degrees awarded was particularly high in the late 1940s and early 1950s, reflecting, in part, a "bunching" of degrees awarded to persons who had received some of their higher education before entering military service and, in part, a tendency of veterans to be strongly oriented toward pro-

---

[1] This lower projection was based on the assumption that law school entrants as a percentage of male bachelor's degree recipients would remain constant at 9 percent, while the higher projection assumed that the number of entrants as a percentage of male bachelor's recipients would rise by two-tenths of a percentage point per year—from 9.0 percent in 1965 to 11.4 percent in 1977.

fessional programs. Thus, comparisons of the distribution of degrees awarded between 1948 and 1970 do not provide an adequate indication of long-run trends in many respects (Appendix A, Table A-15). Moreover, in the case of law, unlike in other fields, we have had to combine degrees at all levels in Chart 16, because the J.D. was classified as a doctor's degree in 1948 but was later classified as a first-professional degree, as it gradually came to replace the LL.B. as the typical first degree in law.

As in the case of medical schools, a major problem facing law schools seeking to expand minority-group enrollment has been the lack of adequate funds for student aid. But, unlike medical schools,

CHART 16 *Degrees awarded in law, by sex, 1948–1970 (includes LL.B., J.D., B.A., M.A., and Ph.D. degrees; logarithmic scale, in thousands)*

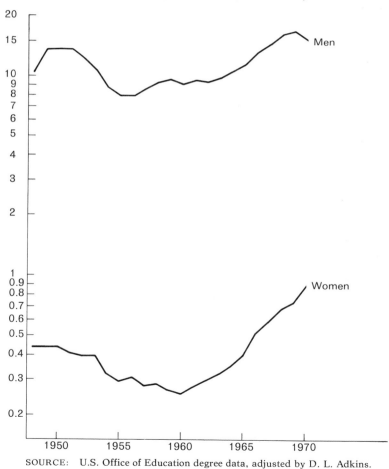

SOURCE: U.S. Office of Education degree data, adjusted by D. L. Adkins.

law schools have not been included in any of the federal programs under which training grants and student aid are provided for professional and other postbaccalaureate students.

The rising trend in the number of law school entrants was reversed, perhaps temporarily, in the fall of 1972. The American Bar Association (ABA) reported that total freshman enrollment in the nation's law schools was down 3 percent from the previous year, and the decrease was attributed to admission cutbacks that were forced on the schools as a result of movement into the upper classes of the two large entrant classes of the preceding two years (88). This development tends to reinforce other evidence that law schools are cautious about increasing the number of student places in response to the recent upsurge in enrollments. However, budgetary stringency, as well as concern over the possibility of creating a surplus supply of lawyers, are contributing factors.

The conclusions of the staff report of the Commission on Human Resources and Advanced Education were optimistic about the future demand for lawyers. In addition to the two projections of enrollment and of the future supply of lawyers based on student-demand assumptions, their report also included a somewhat lower projection of supply based on past trends in the rate of increase of law school capacity. The report concluded that it was likely that by 1980 total law school enrollment would fall short of the lower student-demand projection by about 10,000. In addition, "the demand for persons with legal training is likely to be sufficient to absorb all the graduates the law schools can produce."

Student demand for legal education will be at least as great and perhaps considerably greater than the capacity of law schools to accommodate the applicants. The task of the legal profession is twofold: first, to improve the quality of the poorer schools that still remain, and second, to expand the number of opportunities for legal education at a faster rate in the next decade. Unless both quantity and quality of legal education can be increased, there will be unmet student demand for legal education, and unmet societal demands for legal services (4, p. 84).

Underlying the commission's conclusions were several important considerations relating to the probable future behavior of the demand for lawyers. In the first place, there has been a tendency for the percentage of lawyers engaged in private practice to decline, while the percentages employed by business enterprises and by government agencies have increased. In other words, the sources of demand for legal services have become more diversified. The commission predicted that the proportion of all lawyers in private practice would decline from about 75 percent in 1963 to about 60 percent in 1980, while the percentage working for business and industry would double—from 11 to 22 percent—and that there would be a "modest increase from 14 to 18 percent in government legal employment." These shifts continued between 1963 and 1970, but at a slower rate than the commission's predictions suggested. In 1970, 72.7 percent of employed lawyers were in private practice, while 12.4 percent were in business and industry, and 14.3 percent were in government service (89).

Secondly, the commission considered the behavior of the ratio of lawyers to population. Before examining these ratios, however, we need to take account of the fact that for recent decades the commission used data on the number of lawyers that more closely approximate American Bar Foundation (ABF) figures,[2] based on directory listings, than census-BLS data, based on the decennial censuses:

	CHRAE-ABF	Census-BLS
1900	107,592	107,592
1920	122,519	122,519
1940	180,483	180,483
1950	205,539	171,480
1960	250,132	208,696
1970	324,818	272,400
1980	457,000	335,000

Total number of lawyers, selected years, actual, 1900–1970, and projected, 1980

SOURCE: Appendix A, Table A-4; 4, p. 77; 89, p. 5; 19, pp. 111 and 178; and 90, pp. 153–154.

The fact that the American Bar Foundation figures are consistently higher than the census-BLS data is primarily attributable to the classification of all lawyers, regardless of their type of employment, as *lawyers* in the ABF series, whereas in the census-BLS data a lawyer who had assumed managerial responsibilities would be classified as a *manager*.[3]

[2] The American Bar Foundation also publishes another, somewhat higher series, which is designed to adjust for unlisted lawyers and for multiple listings.

[3] There may be other reasons as well for differences between the two series, comparable perhaps to differences between employment data collected on an establishment basis and those collected on a household survey basis.

Ratios of lawyers to 100,000 population, based on the two series provided above and using U.S. Bureau of the Census projections D and E for the population in 1980, are as follows:

	CHRAE-ABF	Census-BLS
1900	141	141
1920	115	115
1940	137	137
1950	135	113
1960	138	116
1970	160	133
1980		
Series D	201	147
Series E	203	149

Ratios of lawyers to 100,000 population, actual, 1900–1970, and projected, 1980

The first point to be noted about these comparisons is that, according to American Bar Foundation figures, the number of lawyers increased more rapidly between 1960 and 1970 than the commission had estimated. The second point is that the commission, as was customary at the time its work was conducted, used a population projection more closely approximating census series B than the lower series D and E projections, which are now more commonly used and which reflect recent birthrate trends. The CHRAE-ABF series of ratios of lawyers-to-population reflects an increase of 16 percent between 1960 and 1970 and of 26 to 27 percent from 1970 to 1980. The census-BLS series, on the other hand, reflects an increase of 15 percent from 1960 to 1970 and of 11 to 12 percent from 1970 to 1980. In light of the behavior of the ratio in the last few decades, an acceleration of the rate of increase from 1970 to 1980 appears to be reasonable, but the commission's projection may be on the high side, whereas the BLS projection seems low.

However, significant changes are occurring in the market for lawyers. Some of the changes are likely to have a very positive effect on demand, while others are likely to have a negative effect. A development likely to have a positive effect was the U.S. Supreme Court decision of June 12, 1972 in the case of Argersinger *v.* Hanlin, under which an accused indigent must be provided with counsel for any offense, felony, or misdemeanor, whether or not a jury trial is required. Another set of developments likely to increase the demand for lawyers is the heightened interest in the last few years, accompanied by considerable legislative action at both federal and state levels, in legislation to protect the environment and to protect the consumer. Lawyers will be needed on both sides of actions brought under such legislation. Less recently adopted, but continuing to have a positive impact on the demand for lawyers, has been the program of legal services for the poor, which has been under the U.S. Office of Economic Opportunity and is likely to be continued, perhaps in a different form and under other auspices. Another very recent development has been the formation in a few areas of private legal insurance groups, along the lines of private health insurance groups. This movement is so new that its future impact is impossible to assess.

On the other hand, the spread of no-fault automobile insurance and of simplified divorce procedures beyond the few states that have already adopted legislation on such matters could have a significantly negative effect on the demand for legal services.

Meanwhile, proposed reforms in legal education could also have important effects on both the supply and demand sides of the market for lawyers. These reforms have been proposed by a curriculum study committee (the Carrington Committee) of the Association of American Law Schools, but have not been adopted. The criticisms of traditional legal education that have led to these proposals for change are discussed at length in two studies recently prepared for the Carnegie Commission (87 and 91) and will be touched on only briefly here.[4] Many of the proposed reforms resemble changes that have taken place or are taking place in medical education.

In the first place, although specialization has become very common in legal practice, especially in large cities, it has never been as formally recognized in legal licensing or certifying procedures as it has under the numerous medical specialty boards. The underlying principle of legal education, strongly influenced by the pattern established by Christopher Columbus Langdell at the Harvard Law School in the latter part of the nineteenth century, is that of a three-year curriculum designed to provide broad preparation in all the important branches of the law and to train a generalist rather than a specialist. There is little variation among American law schools in the first two years of the curriculum, although recently there

---

[4] The full text of the Carrington Report has been published as Appendix A to the Packer and Ehrlich volume (91).

has been a trend toward introducing increased variety and flexibility into the third year.

Secondly, paralegal specialties, comparable to paramedical specialties (allied health occupations), have barely begun to develop in any formal way, and there have been few educational programs specifically designed to train such workers. Yet, in practice, some of the functions once performed by lawyers have gradually been taken over by a variety of occupational groups, including claims adjusters, bail bond brokers, realtors, and accountants. Legal secretaries also frequently become very adept at processing a wide variety of legal forms, but they learn through experience rather than through formal training.

A third characteristic that has been largely absent from academic legal education until very recently, but is now being introduced here and there, especially for third-year law students, is clinical training, somewhat comparable to the clinical training that characterizes the last two years of education for the M.D. Some experts on legal education prefer the term *operational* training to *clinical* training. The law student must find his clinical training in a variety of community settings, among which programs of legal services for the poor have played a significant role in recent years. Along with the trend toward introducing clinical training, some of the more innovative law schools have begun to introduce courses concerned with nontraditional aspects of the law, such as consumer advocacy and the analysis of legal paths to protection of the environment.

Packer and Ehrlich are skeptical about clinical education as "the only way" of providing skills training. Changes in curricula and methods, they argue (91, p. 43), "may do just as well." They point out that exposure to the problems of the poor may not lead to understanding, but merely to strong feelings, unless there is also an opportunity "to discuss the interesting means/ends problems of changing the structural characteristics of society with students who have become emotionally sensitized to the problems of the poor through participation in clinical programs" (ibid.).

Unlike the situation in Europe, American legal education is almost entirely absent from the undergraduate curriculum in American colleges and universities, except for an occasional specialized course in constitutional law (usually in the political science department) or a course in commercial or business law in the school of business administration.

Very briefly, the Carrington Report recommended:

1 Shortening by as much as two years the time from a student's freshman year in college until his graduation from law school. Only three years of undergraduate study would be required for admission to law school, and as little as two years in law school would be required for the J.D. degree.

2 Development of undergraduate majors in law, with suggestions about the types of courses and seminars to be included.

3 Creation of a new master of arts in law degree to be awarded after one year of graduate study.

4 For students who wished to go on for a third year of law school, that a variety of courses be available to prepare an individual for specialized law practice.

5 Training students for new "allied legal professions" to provide counseling and advocacy services in such fields as family, welfare, labor, and taxation law (91, Appendix A).

Packer and Ehrlich, while generally sympathetic to many of the recommendations in the Carrington Report, fear that its proposals for the curriculum of the first two years might make it "more rigid than it is at present" (ibid., p. 80). The main thrust of their proposals for reform is expressed as follows:

In this study of new directions in legal education, our major recommendation for the future can be summed up in one word: *diversity.* We are convinced that over the next generation our nation's law schools will increasingly diversify. Legal education has, for too long, been in the grip of a single model. The process of remodeling is well under way—not by discarding the old patterns completely but rather by building on those patterns where new development is called for. We expect that some schools with limited financial resources will concentrate the expenditure of those resources in a few areas in order to maintain the highest standards of educational excellence in those areas. Other more well-endowed schools may continue their past practices of broad curricular coverage. But even these schools, we suspect, will try different approaches and different techniques in legal education (ibid., p. 84).

Both the Carrington Committee recommendations and the Packer-Ehrlich proposals are being intensely debated in legal education circles. Precisely what the outcome will be is not clear, but changes in the general direction indicated are almost certain to occur, just as they are occurring in other professions.

The graduation of students with master's degrees in law, as well as of persons trained in allied legal professions, would increase the complexity of predicting the future demand for full-fledged lawyers, just as similar developments have complicated the problem of predicting the future demand for physicians and dentists. Yet it seems clear that the skills of fully trained lawyers could be used more effectively if assistants with less prolonged legal training were available to do research on prior decisions relevant to particular cases, conduct preliminary interviews with clients, study and summarize documents involved in cases, and the like.

In view of the conflicting trends that are likely to affect the future supply and demand for lawyers, the Carnegie Commission believes that the law schools should move cautiously, as they appear to be doing, in expanding their capacity. We agree with the staff report of the Commission on Human Resources and Advanced Education that the American Association of Law Schools (AALS), the American Bar Association, state planning agencies, and individual colleges and universities should devote major attention to strengthening the weaker law schools, which, in any case, appear to be absorbing much of the current increase in enrollment.

Recently a special task force of the American Bar Association also came to the conclusion that law schools should neither restrict capacity to guard against an impending surplus of lawyers nor undertake pronounced expansion at the present time. According to the chairman of the task force:

This is not the time to hit the panic button and seek immediately either to limit or increase access to the study of law or to the profession (92).

This comment applied only to the issue of the number of student places provided in law schools and did not in any way relate to the issue of reform in legal education. There is little question about the need for reform, but we shall defer recommendations to the end of this section, because many of the changes needed in legal education parallel changes needed in other professions as well.

BUSINESS ADMINISTRATION The managerial occupation group includes persons with a wide variety of educational backgrounds, ranging from self-employed managers with very little formal education to top-salaried managers holding advanced degrees in business administration, engineering, law, and other fields. However, the long-run trend, as we have seen, is toward a pronounced increase in the relative importance of salaried managers, and, within that group, toward those with a bachelor's or more advanced degree. And, although managerial occupations are classified separately from professional occupations by the U.S. Bureau of the Census and the BLS, salaried managers are frequently regarded as belonging to the "management profession." In fact, a recent study of professional education prepared for the Carnegie Commission classified management as a profession but characterized it as conforming least among the professions to the author's criteria for identifying professional occupations (93, pp. 10–11). In any event, schools of business administration are generally regarded as professional schools preparing their students for managerial professions.

In the late 1950s, the Carnegie Corporation of New York and the Ford Foundation each sponsored a thorough study of higher education in business. The two studies came to similar conclusions that were very critical of education in most business schools at the time (94 and 95). They were especially critical of the tendency, in all but a few of the schools, toward training students for narrow specialties, such as particular branches of retailing, instead of placing their major emphasis on training for analytical decision making in a rapidly changing economic environment. Their recommendations were influential in leading to major changes in business school curricula.

There is little doubt but what the two studies had an important and serious impact upon individual schools of business and the American Association of Collegiate Schools of Business. . . . The A.A.C.S.B. accepted the challenge contained in the Carnegie and Ford Reports and, during the sixties, directed its principal efforts towards upgrading the quality of education for business careers at both undergraduate and graduate levels (96, p. 5).

There is little question that the AACSB did make substantial progress in raising standards, but some experts on business school education believe that the major factor in upgrading quality was the influence of innovative efforts in some of the leading business schools.

Business schools have been among the relatively rapidly developing sectors of higher education, especially in the 1960s. Their pronounced growth has been in considerable part a response to the marked increase in the number of salaried managers, which we discussed in Section 3. In addition, it must be kept in mind that business schools also provide much of the training for such occupational specialists as accountants and industrial relations specialists, who are classified in the professional rather than in the management major occupation group (see Appendix A, Tables A-2, A-3, and A-4).

Degrees in business administration and other management specialties rose significantly as a proportion of all degrees awarded to men after World War II—from 16.3 percent in 1948 to 18.4 percent in 1970 (Appendix A, Table A-15)—but declined as a percentage of all degrees awarded to women (Appendix A, Table A-16). As we have seen, conclusions drawn from comparisons between the late 1940s and 1970 are somewhat misleading, for there was a tendency during the immediate postwar years, when large numbers of veterans were enrolled in higher education, for men to receive degrees in unusually high numbers in such fields as education (Chart 15), law (Chart 16), business administration (Chart 17), and engineering (Chart 18). The same tendency was evident in medicine.[5]

If we look back over a somewhat longer period, we find that business degrees accounted for only 3.2 percent of all degrees awarded (at all levels) in 1920 and had risen to 9.1 percent by 1940 (95, p. 21). Then there was a sharp increase between 1940 and the late 1940s. Not only was the number of degrees awarded to men higher in the late 1940s and (in the case of master's and doctor's degrees) the early 1950s than for some time thereafter, but this was also true for women. The master's and doctor's series peaked later than the bachelor's series in this early postwar period, indicating that many of those who received bachelor's degrees returned for master's degrees and some for doctorates. The postwar flood of degree recipients satisfied a backlog of demand that had been building up during the 1940s, and by the mid-1950s the market for graduates of schools of business administration, at least in some specialties, was not particularly favorable. However, employment of salaried managers rose substantially from 1957 to 1965 and even more sharply in the late 1960s. (Annual data are not available for years before 1957.) The acceleration in the rate of increase of all business degree series in the latter half of the 1960s undoubtedly occurred, at least in part, as a response to the increase

[5] See the useful table compiled for the Pierson study (95, p. 711). See also the data in Appendix A, Tables A-5 and A-6.

CHART 17 *Degrees awarded in business administration and other management specialties, by level and sex, 1936–1940 and 1947–1970 (logarithmic scale, in thousands)*

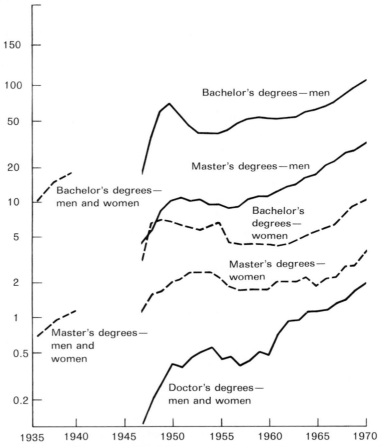

SOURCES: Degrees, U.S. Office of Education, prewar, compiled for Gordon-Howell study (94), and postwar, adapted by D. L. Adkins.

in demand. Moreover, employment of accountants, for whom demand was very favorable in the latter half of the 1960s, is not included in the data on employment of salaried managerial workers.

Clearly another important influence, and perhaps the dominant one, was a growing demand of employers for persons trained specifically for managerial positions. We shall discuss the major factors underlying this trend later.

For men, the increase in the number of master's and doctor's degrees awarded since World War II has been more pronounced than the increase of bachelor's degrees. This change undoubtedly reflected not only the influence of changing patterns of demand, but also the impact of the strong recommendations of the Carnegie and Ford studies for the strengthening of graduate programs in business administration. The trend is also consistent with the relatively sharp rise in graduate enrollment in many fields and with the tendency, in field after field, for the proportion of master's and doctor's degrees to rise in relation to all degrees awarded.

The recent increases in the numbers of bachelor's and master's degrees awarded to women began somewhat later than in the case of men. In the late 1950s, the job market for teachers was especially favorable, and this was undoubtedly a factor in inducing many women to enroll either in education or in arts and science fields, rather than in a field like business administration. However, as we observed in Section 3, employment of female salaried managers has increased rapidly in recent years, and the increase in the number of degrees awarded to women in business administration appears to have occurred at least partly in response to the increasing demand.[6]

Despite the increase in the number of salaried managers in 1970 and 1971, and the rise in the proportion with five or more years of college (Charts 4 and 8), the job market for graduates of schools of business administration was reported to be somewhat depressed in the 1970–71 recession, though less so than the market for graduates in most other fields. In this connection, it is important to keep in mind that the annual data presented in Charts 4 and 8 are collected in March, and that data for March 1971 do not reflect the depressed job market that confronted June graduates in that year.

Total enrollment in schools of business administration rose by a considerably smaller percentage between the fall of 1969 and the fall of 1970 than it had the previous year, but enrollment in master's programs came close to repeating the sharp increase of the pre-

---

[6] We have not shown the number of doctor's degrees awarded by sex in Chart 17, because the number awarded to women has been very small. Although there was an upward trend in the number of doctor's degrees awarded to both men and women in the 1960s, it was more pronounced for men than for women, and there was a tendency for the proportion of doctor's degrees awarded to women to decline—from about 8 percent in 1960 to 5 percent in 1970.

ceding year (97). The Carnegie Commission's fall 1971 enrollment survey revealed relatively modest increases in new enrollment in the field of business administration in four-year colleges and universities at both the undergraduate and graduate levels, as compared with the increases of the 1960s (55, p. 14). In addition, unlike the situation in such fields as law and medicine, the survey showed that applications to schools of business administration increased only 0.3 percent between 1970 and 1971 (ibid., p. 20).[7] The substantial improvement in the job market for business administration graduates in the spring of 1972, especially for holders of M.B.A. degrees, may bring about another reversal in enrollment trends.

What is the long-run outlook for graduates of business schools? In Section 3, we called attention to the increased use of computers in the analysis of managerial decision-making problems as tending to increase the demand for trained managers, but this is only one factor among many tending to raise the demand for trained managers in the long run. Among those identified in the Gordon-Howell study are the following (94, pp. 13–15):

1   As business firms have grown in size, increasing emphasis is being placed on organizational problems. . . .

2   With the separation of ownership and management in the large firm, business leadership has largely been taken over by salaried executives. Capital or family connection is no longer necessary for a top position in business. . . .

3   The accelerating tempo of scientific and technological change is having a profound effect upon the practice of management. Businessmen increasingly need some technical background so that they can communicate with scientists and engineers. Long-range planning becomes more difficult but at the same time more essential. . . .

4   There is growing need for highly trained staff specialists, as well as for administrators to coordinate the work of such specialists. . . .

5   The increasing complexity of the firm's external environment has steadily added to the difficulties of the businessman's task.

---

[7] AACSB data show that undergraduate applications for admission fell somewhat between the fall of 1967 and the fall of 1968 but increased in the following year. However, in the fall of 1969, they were only 1.6 percent higher than in 1967, and the percentage of applications accepted rose from 64 to 68 percent in the two-year period (98).

A recent article on the outlook for graduates of schools of business administration in the 1970s expresses much the same point of view (99, p. 11):

It is anticipated that the demand for salaried managers and officials will expand rapidly—propelled by the increasing reliance of both the business and government sectors on highly trained management specialists. In turn, this increased dependence on managerial technicians will be necessitated by the continued trend toward larger firms and the accelerated application of sophisticated technological advances to the solution of management problems.

During the latter half of the 1960s, a number of large corporations, impressed with the growing importance of operations research and the use of sophisticated tools in decision making, stepped up their hiring of M.B.A.'s.[8] The results were not always satisfactory. The M.B.A.'s had been trained in the analysis of top-level problems of managerial decision making and expected to be put to work on the analysis of such problems immediately. But some of the corporations expected newly hired young executives to learn the business from the "ground up," and a number of corporations had not developed careful plans for using the expertise of their newly hired M.B.A.'s. The result, in many cases, was dissatisfaction from the point of view of both management and the M.B.A.

In the spring of 1972, it was reported that "corporations are favoring the MBA with some kind of experience as their number one candidate for employment today" (100, p. 54). The preference for M.B.A.'s with previous work experience was apparently less pronounced as recently as 1967–68; but in the last few years the M.B.A. with two to four years of experience prior to business school has been able to command an annual starting salary some $1,500 higher than an M.B.A. with no previous work experience (101, p. 60). Perhaps partly in recognition of this trend, a recent article

---

[8] Some of our information on recent trends in the market for graduates of business schools and on trends in business school programs is based on helpful interviews with Jesse M. Smith, Jr., managing director, and Ronald R. Slone, assistant director, American Association of Collegiate Schools of Business; Professor G. Leland Bach, Graduate School of Business, Stanford University; Associate Dean George Strauss, School of Business Administration, University of California, Berkeley; and Earl F. Cheit of the Ford Foundation, who is conducting a study of business and other professional schools for the Carnegie Commission.

on probable future developments in graduate business school programs predicted that the advantages of work experience prior to enrollment in the graduate program would be recognized to an increasing extent, and that the vast majority of students admitted would have been out of college for several years. In addition, the "better graduate programs in business administration will give admission preference to applicants with undergraduate preparation in fields other than business administration" (96, p. 8).[9]

By late 1972, along with more general reports of an improvement in the job market for all college graduates, the market for M.B.A.'s was reported to be showing a pronounced upsurge; there were also the first appreciable increases in starting salaries since 1970 (102). Some business school educators were pointing out that employers would not be able to recruit as many M.B.A.'s with previous work experience as the number of returning veterans declined.

Although salaried managerial positions constitute the chief source of employment for business school graduates, corporations do not by any means confine their recruiting to business school graduates. Nor are the positions for which they recruit exclusively managerial. A 1956 survey indicated that 43 percent of the inexperienced college men hired by a sample of 192 companies were in engineering positions, 16 percent were in other professional positions (chiefly accountants, chemists, and physicists), and 12 percent were in sales positions (94, p. 119).

Nevertheless, estimates of the future increase in employment of salaried managers probably provide the best general indication of the rate of growth of future demand for graduates of business schools. The BLS estimates that total employment of managers, officials, and proprietors (other than farm) will reach 9.5 million by 1980, while a more recent estimate prepared for the President's Commission on School Finance (CSF) projects total managerial employment at 10.2 percent in 1980 (103). On the assumption that the number of salaried managers will rise from 72.7 percent of all managers in 1970 to about 85 percent in 1980,[10] the BLS pro-

---

[9] In this connection, Gordon and Howell commented more than a decade ago that "it is helpful . . . if two or more years of work experience, or at least military service, intervene between the undergraduate years and graduate business training" (94, p. 129).

[10] The estimate of 85 percent was developed by the Carnegie Commission staff but was later concurred in by BLS officials concerned with analyses of the market for college graduates. The BLS has not published a projection of the number of salaried managers.

jection would indicate 8,075,000 salaried managers by 1980, and the Commission on School Finance projection, 8,627,000 salaried managers. The BLS projection, then, would imply an increase of about 54 percent in the number of salaried managers in the 1970s, while the CSF projection would imply an increase of nearly 65 percent.[11]

If the rise in the proportion of all managers in the salaried category should continue in line with trends of the 1950s and 1960s, the salaried contingent would come to represent nearly 100 percent, rather than 85 percent, of all managers. This appears unlikely. A recent article by Andrew F. Brimmer, Member of the Board of Governors of the Federal Reserve System, suggests that the factors making for relatively rapid growth of large-scale industry will continue to have an adverse effect on opportunities for self-employment, but comments that "the major part of the structural shift from small-scale proprietor-owned retail stores to large enterprises appears to have occurred. Consequently, it is anticipated that the decline in the number of proprietors during the present decade will be somewhat slower than it was during the 1960s" (99, p. 11).

Another trend which appears likely to slow down the decline in self-employment is the recent upsurge of college graduates' interest in starting small business enterprises, to be discussed more fully in Section 9. It has been reported that graduates of leading business schools have been moving into their own small business enterprises. Whether this trend will survive the recent improvement in the job market for college graduates is not clear, but it may persist to some degree because of the philosophical aversion among many young people to becoming involved in large-scale corporate enterprises.

In any event, the rising demand for salaried managers is likely to be a major factor in continued growth in the employment of M.B.A.'s and holders of other appropriate degrees in the 1970s.

During the 1960s there was rapid growth in the demand for graduates with advanced degrees in computer sciences, and this trend probably will continue in the 1970s. Specialized programs in computer sciences are frequently found in departments of industrial

---

[11] It should be noted that both projections were developed before detailed occupational data from the 1970 census became available and thus may need some revision on the basis of those data. The total number of managers shown in Appendix A, Table A-4 (both sexes combined), is considerably smaller than the total shown in Table 1 for 1970 (see p. 60). The number shown in Table 1 was evidently estimated before the 1970 census data were available.

engineering or as entirely separate departments rather than in schools of business administration. But business school students receive training in the use of computers. Cooperation between business schools and other schools and departments utilizing computers is especially needed in this rapidly developing field to avoid costly duplication of effort.

Another important relatively recent development has been the growth of programs designed to train managers for the public and nonprofit sectors of the economy. Increasingly, government agencies, hospitals, universities, and other large service organizations have come to recognize their need for administrators who have received training in the analysis of complex managerial problems. Here again, the patterns of response have varied. One pattern, exemplified by Berkeley and Harvard, has been to establish a school or institute of public affairs. Another response has been the expansion of programs in schools of business administration to provide appropriate training for managers in the public sector. By 1971–72, among the 153 schools accredited by the AACSB, 13 had names suggesting that their programs had been broadened in this manner — for example, the School of Management at Case Western Reserve, the Graduate School of Business and Public Administration at Cornell, and the College of Administrative Science at Ohio State. In other instances, schools have expanded their programs without changing their names. A leader in this movement was the Graduate School of Industrial Administration at Carnegie-Mellon University.

One of the most recent significant steps was the establishment of a program in urban management at the Graduate School of Business, Stanford University. In announcing the new program, the school called attention to the highly complex and crisis-oriented responsibilities of a city manager in a sizable city today (104).

Whether a separate school of public affairs or a broadened business school program is the appropriate answer may depend on circumstances in particular institutions, although we believe, in general, that the preferable solution lies in broadening the business school curriculum to encompass both types of managerial problems. Much of the training in managerial decision making and in such specialized fields as personnel relations is appropriate for both the private and public sectors of the economy. Even if a separate school of public affairs is established, there should be close cooperation with the business school to avoid duplication of effort. Probably some duplication is inevitable.

Although blacks are clearly entering business administration programs in response to improved opportunities for managerial jobs, data on the extent of their enrollment in collegiate business schools are sparse. In the spring of 1970, a survey was conducted of black enrollment and of black representation on the faculty in the 81 graduate schools of business whose M.B.A. programs were officially accredited by the AACSB. Among the 62 respondent schools, 2.7 percent of the students enrolled in graduate programs were black. Blacks also represented 2.7 percent of enrollment in the undergraduate programs of responding schools. There were only 41 blacks enrolled in doctoral programs, and only 28 black faculty members in all the respondent schools (105, pp. 27–28).

Some leading business schools have developed active programs designed to recruit black students. The Graduate School of Business at the University of Chicago was a pioneer in this effort.

Business schools, along with other segments of higher education, are striving to increase the number of blacks on their faculties, but this will not be accomplished easily. A black graduating from an M.B.A. program could, in 1972, obtain a good job paying from $14,000 to $16,000 a year. Often he had family obligations—for younger siblings if not for a wife and children of his own—and could not afford to go on for a doctorate. Even if he completed the doctorate, his beginning salary as a faculty member in a business school would be only about $12,500, although salaries in schools of business administration tend to be higher than the average salaries elsewhere on campuses.

In 1970–71, there were 493,000 students enrolled in business programs in the 386 institutions reporting enrollment to the AACSB (97). This represented about 14 percent of total enrollment in these colleges and universities. Nearly one-fifth of the reported enrollment was in evening programs. It would appear that enrollment in business administration will at least hold its own, and perhaps increase, as a percentage of total enrollment during the remainder of the 1970s. But all the evidence suggests that enrollment in graduate programs will rise considerably more rapidly than enrollment in undergraduate programs, in line with the trend of the 1960s. Increases in enrollment will also probably occur more rapidly in those schools that are broadening their programs to include specific training for management in the public and nonprofit sectors. In addition, business administration programs are likely to be especially attractive to students taking advantage of new opportunities to study for external degrees or otherwise participate in part-time study programs designed for working adults.

During the last two decades, as already suggested, impressive progress has been made in improving standards in higher education for business and in the development of more broadly conceived and analytical training programs. But there is a noticeable lack of careful studies of patterns of employment of students who have earned degrees in business administration or of probable changes in demand-supply relationships in the future. The AACSB is aware of this lack and is initiating steps to overcome it. In BLS analyses of supply and demand for college graduates, there is a similar absence of careful study of the probable future behavior of employment of salaried managerial workers, though there are useful projections of employment of such professional specialties as accounting and public relations specialists. And yet all the data we have examined suggest that the behavior of the salaried managerial component in the employment of college graduates will be an exceedingly important determinant of the overall demand for holders of bachelor's and more advanced degrees in the coming years.

ENGINEERING Engineering has been an almost exclusively male occupation, and it accounts for more male professional workers by a considerable margin than any other professional occupation. In 1970, there were 1.2 million employed engineers, of whom only about 20,000 were women. Moreover, from 1900 to 1960 engineering was a leading "growth" occupation for male professional workers—accounting for about 6 percent of male professional and technical workers in 1900, about 13 percent in 1930, nearly 18 percent in 1950, and 19 percent in 1960. During the 1960s, however, other professional occupations—especially those affected by the rapid increase in the number of college faculty members (Chart 7)—experienced comparatively more rapid growth, and engineering lost relative ground within the major occupation group of male professional and technical workers.

Another leading characteristic of engineering is that the growth of employment of engineers has been very irregular, reflecting fluctuations in the demand for engineers in the economy. Sizable proportions of engineers are employed in durable goods manufacturing and in construction—two industry groups that are especially affected by cyclical fluctuations. And, as we have seen, during the last two decades the demand for engineers has been strongly influenced by research and development expenditures and employment in the aerospace industries.

There is substantial evidence, also, that enrollment in engineering programs in colleges and universities is highly sensitive to shifts in the job market for engineers. In fact, as Freeman (106, chap. 4) and others have shown, there is clearly a *cobweb effect* (in the economist's terms) at work.[12] When the demand for engineers increases sharply, students flock into undergraduate engineering majors, and before very long the increased supply of engineers begins to overtake the increase in demand; starting salaries for engineers level off; jobs in engineering become more difficult to find, and the flow of students into engineering schools declines. Sooner or later, depending on the behavior of the demand for engineers, this decline in engineering enrollment is followed by the reappearance of a shortage of engineers, and the cycle repeats itself.

In 1970–71, there was concern over unemployment among engineers and scientists, resulting mainly from cutbacks in employment in the aerospace industries, but also reflecting (especially for the scientists) the appearance of an unfavorable market for Ph.D.'s. The unemployment rate for engineers rose from 0.7 percent in 1968 to 2.9 percent in 1971. In the latter year it was equal to the unemployment rate for professional and technical workers, but well below the 5.9 percent for the civilian labor force as a whole (107, p. 16). But the 30,000 engineers who were unemployed tended to be concentrated in the areas in which aerospace industries were located. A special survey conducted in June-July 1971 by the Engineers Joint Council for the National Science Foundation (ibid., pp. 16–21) indicated that 32 percent of the unemployed engineers were either aeronautical or electrical and electronics engineers; that unemployment rates among engineers were well above the national average in such areas as Seattle, Los Angeles, and Wichita, Kansas; and that unemployment rates were relatively high (4.4 percent) for engineers with less than a bachelor's and for those with a master's degree (3.2 percent).

By the spring of 1972, the job market for engineering graduates was improving, but new reports about the extent of continuing unemployment among previously employed engineers were mixed.[13]

[12] Folk (20) has also conducted an extensive analysis of the supply of engineers.

[13] However, we have been informed by BLS officials that unpublished data have shown a decline in the percentage of unemployed engineers.

Special placement efforts by the federal government had apparently had some success, but a number of the retraining programs designed for engineers had disappointing results, particularly those intended to train unemployed engineers to deal with environmental problems.[14] Despite the enactment, within the last few years, of legislation designed to protect the environment, the number of jobs available for environmental specialists is still quite limited.

Meanwhile, in contrast with the relatively poor prospects for engineering graduates reported in 1971, by early 1972, the College Placement Council was reporting that engineering graduates had "the best" job prospects, along with students trained in business and accounting (110). Moreover, a placement officer at one of the large university campuses on the West Coast was reported as commenting that employers were showing preferences for inexperienced engineering graduates over unemployed aerospace engineers because of the substantially lower salaries at which the new graduates could be hired. By the fall of 1972, there were reports of shortages in some engineering specialties.

As Chart 18 suggests, there was a very sharp rise in the number of bachelor's degrees in engineering awarded to men immediately after World War II, followed by an increase in the number of master's and doctor's degrees awarded. Data reported by Folk (20, p. 95) indicate that enrollment rates of veterans in engineering programs were higher than those of nonveterans, not only in the late 1940s, but throughout the period from 1948 to 1963. In 1948, for example, 15.4 percent of male veteran students in higher education were enrolled in engineering, as compared with 9.9 percent of nonveteran male students. Because of this very sharp influx into engineering in the late 1940s, data showing a decline in the proportion of male bachelor's degree recipients getting degrees in engineering in the postwar period are somewhat misleading (Appendix A, Table A-15). However, there has in fact been a long-term decline in the percentage of male bachelor's degrees awarded in engineering. Bachelor's and first-professional degrees awarded in engineering

[14] In August 1971 (108) it was reported that the heaviest emphasis and expenditure has been devoted to preparing retrainees for some branch of ecological management, and that only very small percentages of the graduates of retraining programs had been placed. This experience may have been influential in the development of more varied retraining programs, which were reported by the Manpower Administration in September 1972 (109). Success in placing the retrainees, even before their training periods had been completed, was also reported, but the total number enrolled in the retraining projects was only 315.

represented 13.6 percent of all male bachelor's and first-profession-al degrees awarded in 1924 and 13.9 percent of those awarded in 1934 (95, p. 711 and 111, p. 211), whereas by 1970 they repre-sented only 9.1 percent (Appendix A, Table A-15).[15] One of the fac-tors in this decline is that attrition among engineering students is slightly higher than the average for all college students. Apparently at least partly because of tightening standards in engineering under-graduate programs, the percentage of entering engineering students who received a degree in engineering declined from about 63 in 1950 to 49 in 1959 (4, p. 95). There is also evidence that, at least in the 1960s, the proportion of the relevant age group graduating in science and engineering was remarkably stable.[16]

The data in Chart 18 suggest that the number of bachelor's degrees in engineering awarded to men followed, with a lag of sev-eral years, changes in the job market for engineers, but Freeman's sophisticated analysis provides more convincing evidence on this point (106). Shifts in the number of degrees awarded in various engineering specialties also appeared to be sensitive to market trends. The upward trend in the number of master's and doctor's degrees awarded in engineering over the postwar period as a whole has been pronounced, and in terms of these advanced degrees engi-neering has gained ground relative to all degrees awarded to men (Appendix A, Table A-10). Although the number of degrees awarded to women in engineering has been extremely small, there has been a rather sharp upsurge in recent years.

The BLS has estimated that the number of engineers will rise from 1.1 million in 1968 to 1.5 million in 1980. This would repre-sent an annual average rate of growth of 2.9 percent from 1968 to 1980, as compared with 3.7 percent from 1960 to 1968 (25, p. 5). Although new graduates are the primary source of new engi-neers, significant numbers come from transfers from other occupa-tions, including upgraded technicians, persons re-entering the labor force, veterans, immigrants, and new graduates who did not major in engineering. After allowing for these sources of employed engi-

---

[15] The data on the number of bachelor's and first-professional degrees awarded in engineering in 1924 and 1934 include awards to both sexes, but it can be assumed that the numbers awarded to women were so small that they would not appreciably affect the percentages we have cited.

[16] Brode (112) found that the percentage of all 22-year-olds graduating in science and engineering remained essentially constant at 3.7 to 3.8 percent during the 1960s.

neers, the BLS estimates that the number of engineers graduating annually is likely to fall slightly below the number required to achieve the estimated need for employment of engineers by 1980—

CHART 18 *Degrees awarded in engineering, by level and sex, 1948–1970 (in thousands)*

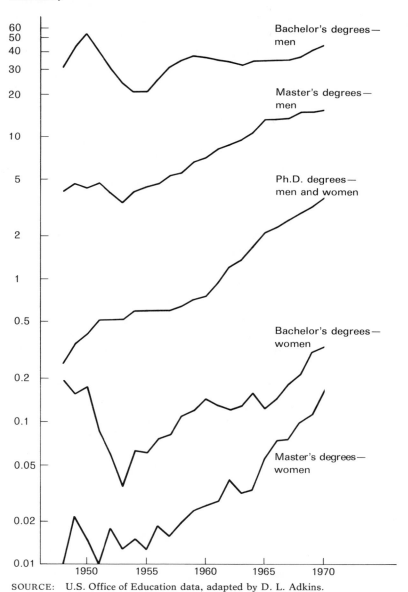

SOURCE: U.S. Office of Education data, adapted by D. L. Adkins.

that is, that a shortage of engineers is likely to reappear by the latter part of the 1970s.

Confining its attention to Ph.D.'s, the National Science Foundation (NSF) has recently predicted a sizable surplus of engineering doctorates by 1980 (113, p. 6). However, it does not appear that allowance has been made for such factors as the sensitivity of enrollment patterns to changes in the job market or the likelihood that minimal increases in the last few years in starting salaries of engineers—as compared with the rapid advances of the early 1960s—will induce employers to hire relatively more engineers with advanced degrees.

Engineering enrollments have been falling in the last few years in the manner suggested by the "cobweb" theorem. To begin with, the ACE data on career choices of entering college freshmen indicated a steady decline in the percentage of entering men choosing engineering from 1966 to 1970 and an acceleration of the rate of decline between 1970 and 1971 (Appendix A, Table A-14). The NSF reported a decline of 1.9 percent in graduate enrollment in doctoral-granting departments of engineering in 1969 (114). The Carnegie Commission's fall 1971 enrollment survey showed a decline of about 15 percent in new undergraduate enrollment and of about 12 percent in new graduate enrollment in engineering between 1970 and 1971 (55, p. 14).[17] There was also a modest percentage decline in enrollment in engineering-related programs in public two-year colleges and a sharp decline in private two-year colleges. According to a preliminary report by the Engineering Manpower Commission of the Engineers Joint Council, enrollment in engineering continued to decline between 1971 and 1972, although the decreases were not quite as pronounced as in the preceding year. Freshman enrollment in engineering was down about 14 percent; total undergraduate enrollment in engineering, about 9 percent; and graduate enrollment in the field, nearly 5 percent (116).

These pronounced declines in enrollment, along with the indications of improvement in the job prospects of engineering graduates in the spring of 1972, suggest that there may well be a reappearance of a shortage of engineers before many more years have passed. In

[17] These results are generally consistent with those reported by the Engineering Manpower Commission of the Engineers Joint Council, which indicated that freshman enrollment in engineering was down 18 percent; sophomore enrollment, 10 percent; upper-division enrollment, 2 percent; and advanced degree enrollment, 16 percent (115).

1970, there were nearly 44,800 bachelor's degrees awarded in engineering, about the number the BLS estimates will be needed annually in the 1970s. But the downward trend in new undergraduate enrollment in engineering in the last few years will mean that the number of bachelor's degrees awarded is likely to fall well below 45,000 in the mid-1970s. The Engineering Manpower Commission has recently estimated that the number of bachelor's degrees awarded in engineering will be down to 29,000 by 1976 (116). For the next few years, we can expect employers to be hiring relatively more engineering graduates with advanced degrees than has been their pattern in the past, but a situation may well emerge in the latter part of the 1970s in which they will once more be hiring persons with less than a bachelor's degree for some of their engineering openings.

In view of these probabilities, the recommendation of the staff report of the Commission on Human Resources and Advanced Education to the effect that engineering schools should analyze closely the factors affecting retention of students in their programs continues to be pertinent. We also believe that engineering schools should encourage the recent upward trend in the enrollment of women, even though it will be many years before the number of women graduates makes an appreciable contribution to the supply of engineers.

In the past, disadvantaged minority groups have been very underrepresented in the field of engineering. Freeman (37) has shown that men in black colleges have been shifting into engineering as a major field of study. But the shift was not comparable in dimensions to that into business administration, which enrolled 21 percent of black males in his sample of black colleges in 1972, as compared with 4 percent in engineering. A recent report on the Economic Opportunity Program at the University of California—a program under which disadvantaged students, chiefly blacks and Chicanos, who cannot meet normal admission standards, are enrolled and given special financial and other kinds of assistance—indicated that the undergraduate majors most frequently chosen by students in the program were political science, sociology, history, engineering, and psychology. On a nationwide basis, however, the number of blacks receiving bachelor's degrees in engineering continues to be a very small proportion of the total number of bachelor's degrees awarded—only 0.9 percent in each of the years 1970 and 1971 (117, p. 433; and 118, p. 804). There are indications that black students tend to perceive the engineering curriculum "as a difficult one for which they do not feel adequately prepared" and have "an image of engineering as a 'white' profession in which they might not be welcome" (119, p. 794). Before there is a sizable increase in the representation of blacks in the engineering profession, there would need to be more programs, like that at the Newark College of Engineering, especially designed to interest black high school students in engineering and to enroll them in a prefreshman summer program that is specifically designed to overcome inadequacies in their preparation (ibid., pp. 794–798).

As we have seen, fluctuations in federal expenditures for research and development and for aerospace procurement have been in large part responsible for the pronounced shifts in the job market for engineers in the last several decades. We believe that a more stable policy in support of research and development is needed and that, with careful advanced planning, greater stability could be achieved in aerospace procurement, especially in other projects not directly related to national defense.

Meanwhile, schools of engineering have had to adjust to sharp fluctuations in enrollment. We believe that they should seek to adapt their resources to long-run trends in the demand for engineers, insofar as these can be determined from the various available projections. This implies utilizing temporary faculty personnel to some extent in periods of sharp enrollment increases in order to guard against having a surplus of tenured faculty members in periods when enrollment falls off. Long-range planning of this type will be particularly important during the remainder of the 1970s, as higher education approaches the relatively stationary enrollment period projected for the 1980s.

As Jencks and Riesman have pointed out (120, p. 229), until relatively recently the study of engineering began in the freshman year and ended four years later with a B.A. However, as we have seen, the proportion of engineering students going on to do graduate work has been rising. This has encouraged some of the engineering schools to adopt a policy of delaying the start of an engineering major until the junior year, so that prospective engineering students can benefit from a general education program during the first two years of college. One means of accomplishing this has been through the five-year B.S. in engineering, with the first two years devoted to general education and the last three years to technical education. We believe that in engineering, as in other fields, efforts should be made to resist continuation of the trend toward prolongation of the period of training, and that careful consideration should be given to possibilities for integrating work for the bachelor's and for the master's degree. But the case for adequate time devoted to general education for engineering students is strong, whether or not general education precedes the technical portion of the curriculum. In view of the fact that engineers frequently move into managerial positions as they gain in maturity and experience, the arguments for a good general education background are very similar to those relating to the field of business administration.

SCIENCE   In 1970, natural scientists comprised 4.5 percent and social scientists represented 1.2 percent of all professional and technical workers. Both groups had experienced very pronounced percentage increases in employment in the 1960s but were expected to experience less rapid growth in the 1970s (Chart 7).

Toward the end of the 1960s, as our discussion in Section 3 indicated, the job market became considerably less favorable for scientists in most disciplines. A special survey conducted by the National Science Foundation in the spring of 1971 indicated an unemployment rate of 2.6 percent among scientists, but, as in the case of engineers, some groups of scientists were affected more severely than others (121). Unemployment rates were highest in much the same metropolitan areas that were experiencing relatively severe unemployment of engineers; scientists with doctorates had a comparatively low unemployment rate, while higher rates were found among holders of master's degrees, bachelor's degrees, and less than a bachelor's degree; young scientists were more likely to be unemployed than older scientists; women were more likely to be unemployed than men; noncitizens were considerably more likely to be unemployed than citizens; and about 45 percent of the unemployed scientists reported that their last science-related employment was supported to some degree by federal government funds.

As in the case of engineers, the fact that those with master's degrees were more likely to be unemployed than those with bachelor's degrees is probably explained by the younger average age of those with master's degrees, reflecting the relatively rapid growth in the number of master's degrees awarded in the 1960s. Ph.D.'s were also likely to be relatively young for the same reason, but employers were undoubtedly less inclined to lay off young Ph.D.'s than holders of master's degrees.

Of special interest were the variations in unemployment rates by field:

TOTAL	2.6%
Chemistry	3.0
Earth and marine science	2.7
Atmospheric and space science	2.8
Physics	3.9
Mathematics	2.6
Computer sciences	3.6
Agricultural sciences	0.9
Biological sciences	1.7
Psychology	1.6
Statistics	2.2
Economics	1.6
Sociology	3.8
Political science	3.4
Anthropology	1.3
Linguistics	4.5

Unemployment rates of scientists, by field, spring 1971

SOURCE: National Science Foundation (121).

The highest rates were not only among those groups of scientists who were most likely to be employed in the aerospace industries, but also among other groups—especially those in sociology, political science, and linguistics—whose employment opportunities were in large part confined to academic institutions.

When we consider the various projections that have been developed of demand-supply relationships in 1980 (Table 3) we find, also, that shortages are most likely to re-emerge in those fields in which there are substantial employment opportunities in government and industry. (The projections are not sufficiently detailed, however, to tell us anything about variations within the broad group of social sciences.)

Let us look, then, at some of the available data on patterns of employment of scientists. The National Roster of Scientific and Technical Personnel for 1970 showed that 63 percent of all social scientists and 60 percent of all biological scientists were employed in educational institutions, whereas percentages so employed were considerably smaller in the physical sciences, mathematics and related fields, and agricultural science (Appendix A, Table A-17).

		National	
	U.S. Bureau	Science	
	of Labor	Foundation	R. B. Freeman
Field	Statistics	(Ph.D.'s)	(Ph.D.'s)
Physical sciences		Surplus or shortage*	Shortage
Chemists	Significant shortage		
Geologists and geophysicists	Slight shortage		
Physicists	Significant shortage		Shortage
Life sciences	Significant surplus	Surplus	
Mathematicians	Significant surplus	Surplus	
Social sciences		Surplus	

TABLE 3 *Projections of shortages and surpluses in the natural sciences and social sciences, by 1980*

*The NSF high utilization assumption would result in a shortage; the low utilization assumption would result in a surplus.

SOURCES: U.S. Bureau of Labor Statistics (25); National Science Foundation (113); and R. B. Freeman (122).

However, within the physical sciences, physicists were considerably more likely to be employed in educational institutions than chemists, earth and marine scientists, and atmospheric and space sciences. Within mathematics and related fields, mathematicians were very much more likely to be employed in educational institutions than statisticians or computer scientists. Alternative employment opportunities outside of academia were relatively more important for psychologists and economists than for sociologists, political scientists, or anthropologists.

Nearly three-fifths of the scientists employed in educational institutions held Ph.D. degrees. The proportion of Ph.D.'s was also relatively high in nonprofit organizations. On the other hand, the percentages holding only bachelor's degrees were comparatively high in business and industry and in the federal government (Appendix A, Table A-18).

Relative proportions of holders of Ph.D.'s, master's and bachelor's, and other degrees varied widely among these scientific fields. There was a general tendency for the proportion of Ph.D.'s to be relatively high in those fields in which employment was predominantly within academic institutions. The NSF data also indicate that there was a tendency for the proportions of holders of advanced degrees to increase, relative to holders of bachelor's degrees, during the 1960s. We have presented only the 1970 statistics because of problems relating to the comparability of the data from year to year. However, a gradual increase in the proportions of holders of more advanced degrees would be expected because of the relatively pronounced increases in the number of master's and doctor's degrees awarded during the 1960s.

Freeman has shown that the cobweb adjustment process applies to the supply of doctorates in a number of scientific fields, as well as in engineering. The most important reason for this phenomenon is the lengthy training period. When there are sharp fluctuations in demand, supply adjustments occur with a lag of four to five years, and the job market tends to be in a state of continuous disequilibrium or incomplete adjustment. In an analysis of what has been happening in the market for scientific manpower in the last few years, Freeman finds that the "classic adjustments of a declining sector" are occurring (122). Relative wages are falling, and these comparative wage declines are tending not only to induce additional demand but also to alter the flow of new manpower into the various scientific fields.[18] In addition, unemployed older scientists are being "pushed" into nonscientific jobs. Applying an analytical model incorporating these adjustments, Freeman estimates the supply of holders of doctorates in the physical sciences in 1980 at 74,300, or 7 percent below the NSF "low supply" projection of 80,100 and 12 percent below its "high supply" projection of 84,400 (113, p. 6). This implies a supply slightly below the NSF's "low utilization" projection of 75,600 and well below its "high utilization" projection of 88,100.

In view of the complex process of adjustment in the job market for highly educated manpower, no single supply projection, such as Freeman's, should be regarded as possessing a high degree of reliability. But the value of his analysis lies in calling attention to the

---

[18] It should be noted here that the "additional demand" to which Freeman refers is induced because employer demand, in the economist's terms, is assumed to be "elastic," i.e., a given percentage decline in relative wages for a specific occupational group will induce a more than proportional increase in employer demand, *all other things being equal.* But in the job market of the last few years, all other things have not been equal — demand has been adversely affected by cutbacks in federal funds and by diminishing needs for new faculty, as well as by the recession of 1970–71. Nevertheless, elasticity of employer demand may be operating as a partial offset to these adverse factors. In Section 3, we found evidence that this type of adjustment process was probably operating in the market for salaried managers.

need for incorporating more sophisticated adjustment assumptions in projection models developed by the NSF and other agencies. Folk (20) has criticized the methodology used in BLS projections on similar grounds.

Probably the most detailed data relating to the actual adjustment process occurring in the last few years have been developed in the field of physics. The number of bachelor's degrees awarded to both men and women rose after World War II, declined in the first half of the 1950s, rose sharply in the latter half of the 1950s, and then showed more moderate and irregular gains in the 1960s, with a decline between 1969 and 1970 (Chart 19). There was a pronounced upward trend in the number of master's and doctor's degrees awarded in the 1960s, but, in the case of male master's degrees there was a tendency toward leveling off toward the end of the decade. However, the most illuminating data relate to enrollment. The number of juniors enrolled in undergraduate physics majors reached a peak of 7,822 in 1967 and declined to 6,593, or 16 percent, by 1971. The drop in enrollment of seniors in physics began a year later, as might be expected. First-year graduate enrollment turned downward even earlier and shrank from 4,358 in 1965 to 3,336 in 1971, or 23 percent (123, p. 495).

The Economic Concerns Committee of the American Physical Society has developed data on the fall 1970 employment status of the 750 Ph.D.'s who graduated from 38 physics departments between the fall of 1969 and the fall of 1970. Only 11.5 percent were employed above the instructor level on physics faculties. About 38 percent held postdoctoral research or instructorship appointments, while 21 percent were employed in industry, government, or on nonphysics faculties. This left approximately 28 percent, of whom half (or 14 percent of the total) had left the country. Of these emigrants, half were U.S. citizens. The remaining 14 percent had left physics, or were unemployed, underemployed, in the armed forces, or unknown. Those classified as underemployed had taken high school or junior college positions (124, pp. 741–742). Data were also collected on experienced physicists who had left faculty positions or jobs in research laboratories and on those who had applied to the American Institute of Physics Placement Service in the spring of 1970. Among the three surveyed groups, substantial proportions, though well under half, had left the country or left physics.

In the field of chemistry—the largest field in the physical sciences

CHART 19 *Degrees awarded in physics, by level and sex, 1948–1970 (logarithmic scale, in thousands)*

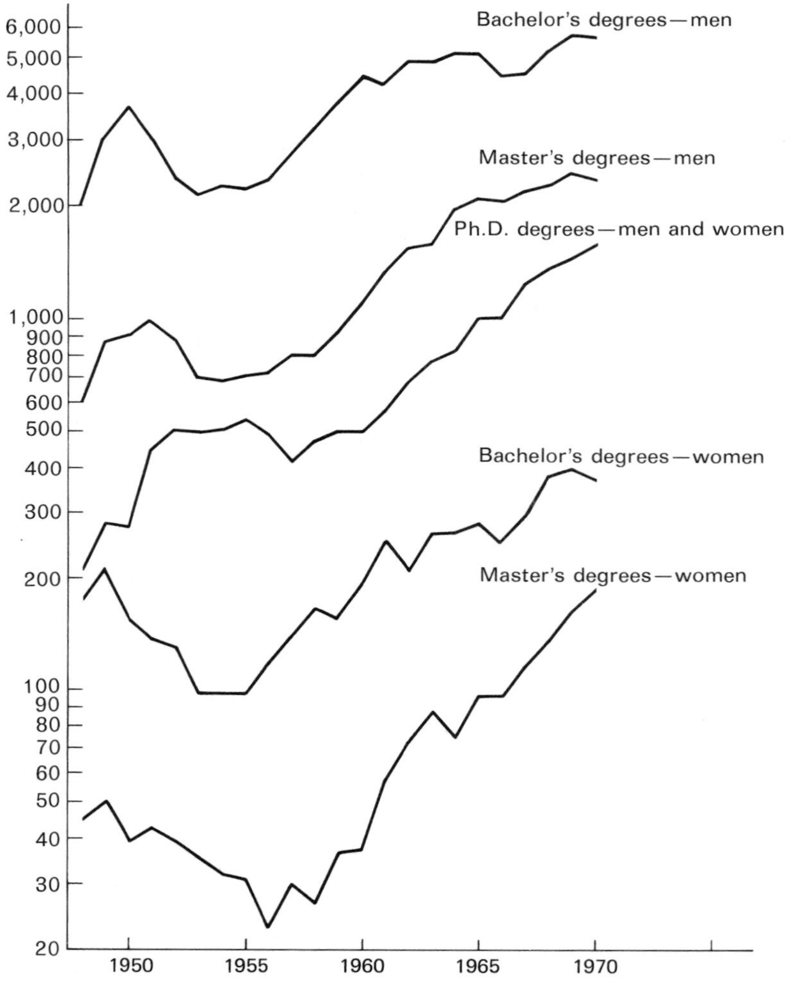

SOURCE: Adapted from U.S. Office of Education data by D. L. Adkins.

in terms of numbers employed and degrees awarded—there was likewise a sharp rise in the number of degrees awarded following World War II and a decline immediately thereafter. By the end of the 1960s, the number of bachelor's degrees awarded to men was barely back to its 1950 level, but was somewhat higher for women (Chart 20). However, there were quite pronounced upward trends in the numbers of more advanced degrees awarded.

CHART 20 *Degrees awarded in chemistry, by level and sex, 1948–1970 (logarithmic scale, in thousands)*

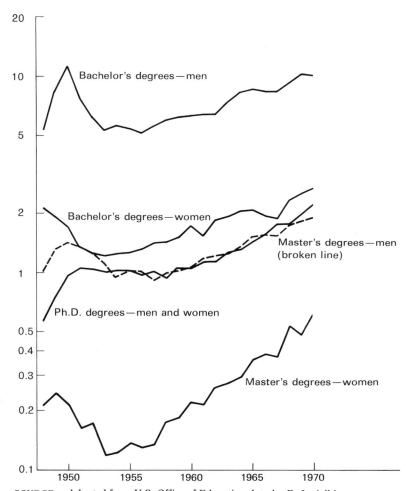

SOURCE: Adapted from U.S. Office of Education data by D. L. Adkins.

In contrast with other sciences, the biological sciences have experienced a relatively steady and pronounced upward trend in the number of degrees awarded at all levels and to both sexes since the mid-1950s (Chart 21). To a large extent this rise has been associated with the increase in expenditures on research concerned with health problems.

Any attempt to develop independent projections in this complex area of scientific employment is beyond the scope of the present

CHART 21 *Degrees awarded in biological sciences, by level and sex, 1948–1970 (logarithmic scale, in thousands)*

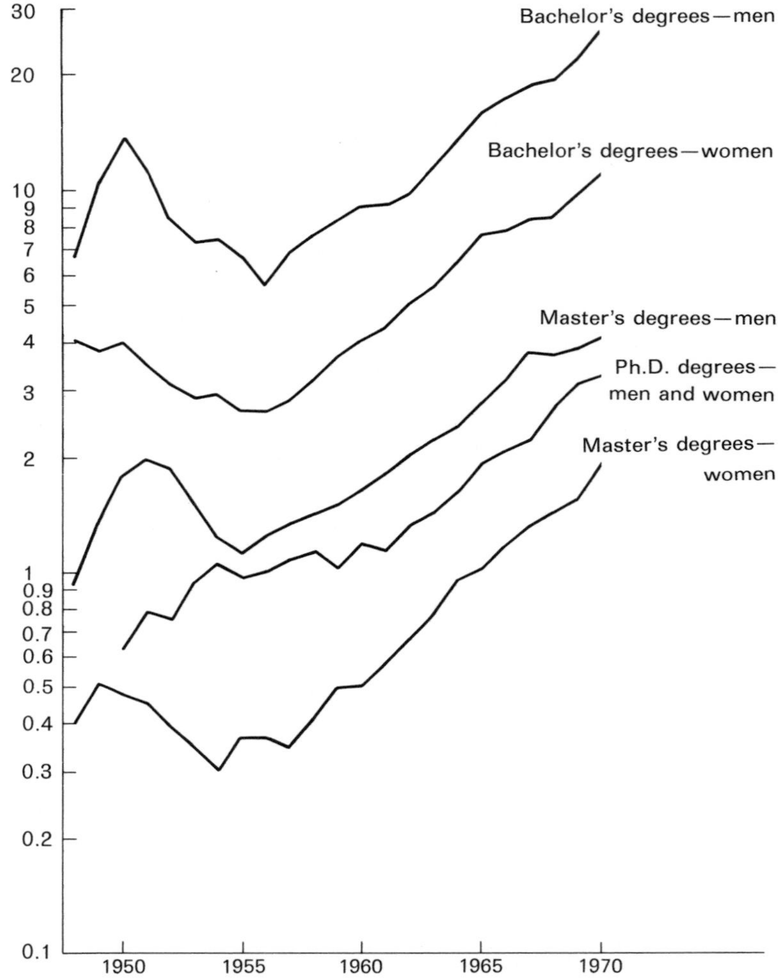

SOURCE: Adapted from U.S. Office of Education data by D. L. Adkins.

report. But there is clearly a need for continuous and sophisticated analyses of demand and supply relationships in scientific fields. Moreover, as Brode has emphasized in his recent papers (for example, 112), the proportion of the relevant age group receiving bachelor's degrees in the physical sciences and engineering remained remarkably constant during the greater part of the 1960s. This evidence, along with other types of evidence, suggests that the proportion of the college-age population with both the ability and motivation to pursue studies in these relatively rigorous fields is limited. Another way of putting the same point is that, as enrollment rates in higher education rose in the 1960s, the physical sciences and engineering lost ground in their shares of enrollment. Large proportions of students were flowing into other fields. The evidence of growing interest by women in these fields is encouraging in terms of long-run supply, but their numbers are still too small, except in the biological sciences, to have a significant effect on supply in the near future.

If the proportion of college-age young people who have the ability and motivation to enter the physical sciences and engineering is actually relatively stable, then shortages in these fields are virtually certain to reappear, because of the long-run upward trend in demand for services of these professionals, associated with the advance of knowledge and technology. How soon such shortages will reappear will probably vary by field.

In view of this probability, and in view of the shifts in the job market situation facing other professional fields, there is clearly a need for increased emphasis on research and data gathering on college-educated manpower. Recently a decision has been made to discontinue the National Roster of Scientific and Technical Personnel. Manpower programs and research in the Department of Labor have been heavily oriented to blue-collar and service workers. Only very recently have there been any special placement and retraining programs for professional workers, and the analysis of supply and demand relationships for professional occupations within the Bureau of Labor Statistics has been relatively limited. The U.S. Office of Education has recently discontinued some of its special series relating to graduate and professional education.

The data relating to the market for Ph.D.'s in physics, collected under the auspices of the American Physical Society, provide a good illustration of the valuable insights that can be gained from this type of meticulous data gathering, which probably could be successfully carried out only by a professional association.

The contribution of highly educated scientific and technical manpower to our economic progress and international competitive position has received widespread recognition in the recent past. It will be no less important in the future, but there appears to be a growing danger that the atrophy of federal government programs designed to encourage the development of highly trained scientific and technical manpower will give us cause for regret within the next decade or so.

The 1960s were years of rapid and steady advances in the number of degrees awarded in the social sciences, for both sexes and at all levels (Chart 22). This increase in the relative popularity of these fields is explained in part by the rise in demand for college faculty and also, to some extent, by increases in the number of students preparing themselves to teach social sciences in secondary schools. In addition, it reflected marked increases in demand for social scientists in nonteaching types of employment, particularly for economists and psychologists, who are relatively more likely than other social scientists to be employed in government and industry. Clinical psychologists are frequently self-employed. But changing student interests were also an important influence. As the report of the Behavioral and Social Sciences Survey Committee (1969) pointed out:

> The record of the 1960's shows that college students in increasing numbers majored in social sciences and also that the number of degrees awarded in these subjects increased at a more rapid rate than in the physical sciences. One likely explanation of this trend is that, currently, the attention of young men and women is being drawn increasingly to the problems of society. They seek to understand why the cities of the nation are in trouble, why there is conflict between racial groups, what the implications of population growth are, and what might be the prospects of control of that growth. They are puzzled by the prevalence of violent crime and curious about the nature and causes of mental illness, suicide, homosexuality, drug addiction, and alcoholism. They want to understand economic development, international tensions, monetary crises, inflation, war, and revolution (125, p. 261).

The rate of increase in numbers of degrees awarded varied considerably among social fields. Over the postwar period as a whole, economics has lost relative ground among the social sciences, while other fields have gained (Appendix A, Tables A-15 and A-16).

CONCLUSIONS AND RECOMMENDA-TIONS Clearly the various professional fields have many problems in common as they face the shifting and uncertain job market trends of the 1970s and as they consider various proposals for innovation and reform in their educational programs. We shall therefore conclude the present section with a group of recommendations that are applicable to all professions in varying degrees:

CHART 22 *Degrees awarded in the social sciences, by level and sex, 1948–1970 (logarithmic scale), in thousands*

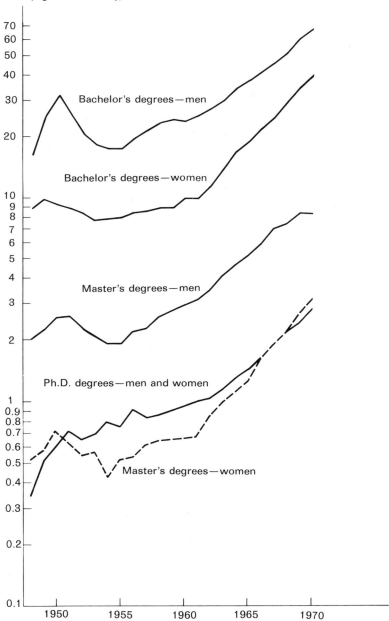

* Social sciences includes anthropology and folklore, economics and agricultural economics, political science, sociology and social psychology, and other social sciences.

SOURCE: Adapted from U.S. Office of Education data by D. L. Adkins.

Recommendation 14: Associations of professional schools and professional societies should undertake the responsibility for careful studies of manpower supply and demand for graduates in their respective fields.

In the recent past, some of the professional associations have been considerably more active than others in undertaking this type of analysis. We believe that student choice should be the primary determinant of changes in the number of student places available in various fields. Such choices can be better made if good information is available to students, and to faculty members and others who provide them with advice.

Although we oppose the creation and assignment of student places in accordance with an overall manpower plan, we recognize that situations exist in which institutions and governmental agencies must plan for the allocation of places and resources on the basis of more than immediate student choices. For the institutional decisions to be made well, field-by-field manpower studies can be helpful. Sudden pronounced increases in applications, as in the case of law and medical schools in recent years, create especially difficult problems for institutional decision making because they may reflect shifts in student choices that are rather temporary. The fluctuations that have been characteristic in engineering also create problems, which we have already discussed. And we do believe that manpower planning is needed in relation to the supply of Ph.D.'s and of physicians and dentists.

Recommendation 15: The federal government should give high priority to the development of more adequate, sophisticated, and coordinated programs of data gathering and analysis relating to highly educated manpower. Because professional associations can be particularly helpful in these efforts, we also believe that federal government agencies should develop programs designed to elicit and support the efforts of these associations.[19]

Recommendation 16: Associations of professional schools should collect annual data on enrollment of women and minority-group students and should stimulate programs designed to encourage

---

[19] More detailed recommendations along these lines have been made recently by the U.S. Department of Labor's Subcommittee on Scientific, Professional, and Technical Manpower, under the chairmanship of Allan M. Cartter (126).

and assist them. Within arts and science fields there should be similar efforts.

Here again, the associations have varied greatly in the extent of their activity.[20] It should be noted, in this connection, that the annual reports of institutions of higher education to the U.S. Civil Rights Commission on the racial composition of enrollment do not provide data by field or separate data for professional schools within general campuses.

Recommendation 17: Professional schools in universities and colleges should undertake the responsibility for cooperating with and providing guidance for comprehensive colleges and community colleges in the development of paraprofessional training programs, as we have earlier recommended in the case of university health science centers.

Such guidance will be especially needed where paraprofessional training has not existed in the past, as in the field of law.

Recommendation 18: Professional schools in universities and colleges should also undertake the responsibility for providing guidance and advice in connection with programs of continuing education for members of their professions, whether these are provided under the auspices of extension divisions, evening school programs of the professional schools, or in other ways.

There is now widespread recognition of the problem of educational obsolescence in all fields as the pace of technological advance quickens and as society's needs for specialized services increase, as in the fields of medicine and law. We anticipate rapid expansion of programs of adult and continuing education in response to these needs in the 1970s.[21]

---

[20] The Association of American Medical Colleges was one of the first associations of professional schools to develop an annual survey of enrollment of the racial composition of students in its member schools. Publication of the results of these surveys probably in itself played a role in stimulating the increases of percentages of students who are women or members of minority groups in the medical schools in recent years.

[21] These problems will be considered more extensively in a forthcoming Commission report.

Recommendation 19: Associations of professional schools, as well as individual professional schools in universities and comprehensive colleges, should undertake leadership and responsibility in more carefully planned integration of preprofessional and professional education.

In the field of medicine, integration of premedical and medical education programs is eliminating overlapping and duplication between premedical and medical education and is shortening the time between high school graduation and receipt of the M.D. degree. Similar developments are now being proposed in law and in other professional fields.

Recommendation 20: In virtually all professional fields, increased attention should be devoted to providing students with opportunities to proceed along carefully planned and at the same time flexible career training ladders.

We have discussed examples of this type of development in the health professions, for instance.

Recommendation 21: In all professional fields, careful and sustained attention needs to be given to adaptation of educational programs to the advancement of knowledge and technological change, and to society's changing problems and needs.

This is so widely recognized in some fields that it may seem obvious, but it has not been universally recognized. For example, in the field of law, we have noted the persistence of a uniform program of instruction, especially in the first two years, despite the feeling of a number of experts that there is a growing need for diversified training in a profession that has long since become highly specialized in practice. Another manifestation of this problem that has not as yet received the recognition it deserves is the need to encourage faculty members to engage in periodic retraining or retooling efforts in response to shifting needs for particular specialties.[22]

Recommendation 22: All programs of professional education involving human services should seek to incorporate clinical or opera-

---

[22] See Appendix B for some relevant recommendations.

tional experience in the student's training, but we would also warn that successful clinical training requires careful planning, evaluation, and adaptation to changing needs.

Such training may also require increased faculty-student ratios, as some law schools are discovering.

Recommendation 23: Most professional schools and academic departments should be actively involved, along with their institutions, in developing policies that encourage students to stop out between high school and college, or after several years of undergraduate education, or between undergraduate and graduate work, and that assist those students to gain relevant work experience during periods away from school. Of equal importance are policies that facilitate part-time study for the working student.

However, there are exceptions to this general principle. Stopping out is probably least desirable for the medical student, whose training is very prolonged and whose clinical education involves a great deal of work experience. On the other hand, as our discussion of the job market for M.B.A.'s has indicated, stopping out is especially desirable in the field of business administration.

In recent years, there has been a trend toward the development of joint degrees between professional schools and departments — for example, law and sociology or law and city planning. This trend has been associated with the emergence of societal problems that are essentially interdisciplinary in character, for example, urban and environmental problems. The need for such developments has been stressed by Edgar Schein in his study of professional education (93).

Recommendation 24: Professional schools and academic departments should cooperate in the development of joint degree programs in response to emerging societal problems and in response to the advancement of knowledge or technological change.

However, such programs are more likely to be successful if the student receives thorough training in the basic principles and analytical methods involved in at least one of the two disciplines, and preferably in both, than if his training in one or both of the fields is superficial. It has been found, for example, that students can receive adequate training for a joint degree in law and business administration in a four-year program. But one of the weaknesses sometimes found in interdisciplinary programs is that the student may take a sampling of courses in several fields and escape exposure to rigorous training in analytical methods in any field.

Recommendation 25: The federal government should not only stabilize its support of graduate training and research, but should attempt to stabilize the scope of activities, like the space program, that have in the past involved sudden and sharp shifts in the demand for scientists and engineers.

8. The Changing Market for Ph.D.'s and Its Implications

Whereas the market for Ph.D.'s was exceptionally favorable during the greater part of the 1950s and 1960s — until 1968 or 1969 — there is substantial agreement that it is likely to be increasingly unfavorable during the 1970s. Numerous estimates of the supply and demand for holders of doctor's degrees have been made in the last few years, and there are some wide differences among them, especially on the supply side. But they all lead to essentially the same conclusions — there is likely to be a large and growing surplus of Ph.D.'s in the 1970s, a surplus that will reach sizable proportions by 1980, at least in relation to any reasonable projection of demand based on past patterns of employment of Ph.D.'s.[1] The severity of the surplus, as our discussion in the previous section has suggested, will vary from field to field and is expected to be most serious in fields such as the humanities, where the great majority of Ph.D.'s are employed in academic institutions. On the other hand, we may well witness the reappearance of shortages in engineering and in some of the physical sciences before long.

The underlying causes of the growing overall imbalance in the market for Ph.D.'s are on both the supply and demand sides of the job market. If undergraduate enrollment in higher education in the United States has been increasing at an extraordinary rate, graduate enrollment has been increasing even more rapidly. Between 1950 and 1970, undergraduate degree-credit enrollment increased from 2.1 to 6.8 million, or 3.2 times, while graduate resident enrollment increased from 220,000 to 940,000, or 4.3 times. By far the greater part of this increase occurred in the 1960s.

Not only has the propensity of American college graduates to go

---

[1] A most useful summary of various projections has been prepared by Wolfle and Kidd (127 and 128).

on for graduate work been rising, but the number completing the work for the doctorate has increased very rapidly. Between 1959–60 and 1969–70, the rate of increase in the number of doctor's degrees awarded exceeded the rate of increase in the number of master's degrees awarded, which in turn exceeded the rate of increase in earned bachelor's and first-professional degrees:

Earned degrees conferred, by level	*Bachelor's and first-professional*	*Master's*	*Doctor's*
1959–60	389,183	77,692	9,829
1969–70	827,234	208,291	29,866
Annual average rate of increase	7.8%	10.4%	11.8%

SOURCE: U.S. Office of Education.

The pronounced increase in graduate enrollment and in the number of advanced degrees awarded was stimulated by a number of developments—the increase in research and development expenditures which began, as we have seen, about 1952; the sharp increase in college enrollments, particularly in the 1960s, which created a buoyant demand for faculty members; the possibility of avoiding the draft, which was a particularly important influence on male graduate enrollment in the mid-1960s; and probably, also, the fact that a good many young persons found graduate work a pleasant way of life, and some showed an inclination to prolong it indefinitely.

The marked reduction in the rate of growth of R&D expenditures toward the late 1960s was an early adverse influence on the market for Ph.D.'s, and, although R&D expenditures are likely to increase in the 1970s, a reasonable expectation is that they will probably not increase more rapidly or, at most, not much more rapidly than the gross national product (GNP).

However, the major factor depressing the job market for Ph.D.'s in the 1970s and on into the 1980s will be the expected slowing down in the rate of increase and the subsequent decline in enrollment in higher education. On an FTE basis, the lowest of the Carnegie Commission's three projections indicates that the annual rate of increase in enrollment is likely to decline from about 5 to 6 percent in the very early 1970s to less than 1 percent by 1980 (Chart

CHART 23 *Annual percentage change in full-time-equivalent enrollment in higher education, actual, 1969–70, and projected, 1970–1990*

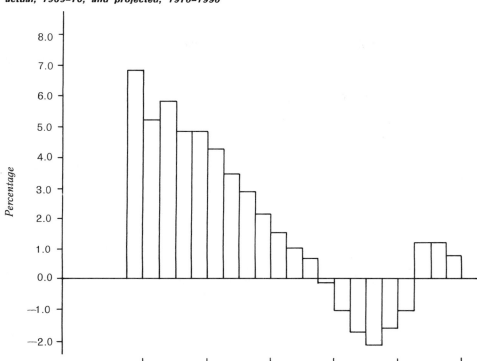

SOURCE: Projections developed for the Carnegie Commission by Gus W. Heggstrom of the Rand Corporation, formerly a member of the faculty of the University of California, Berkeley. The projections were revised (from 1986 on) in the spring of 1972 to reflect the behavior of the birthrate in the last few years.

23). After that, there is likely to be an absolute decline in enrollment until about 1987, when increases may resume at a modest rate.

These changes will reflect the fact that students entering college from about 1974 on will have been born in a period when the birthrate was declining, and that those entering from about 1978 on will have been born in a period when the absolute number of live births was declining.[2] The Commission's projections of undergraduate enrollment in the late 1980s have recently been revised to reflect the continued decline in the number of births in the last few years. The outlook for the 1990s is now very unclear because of uncertainties surrounding the future behavior of the birthrate.

[2] For birthrate data, see Carnegie Commission on Higher Education (29, p. 129).

CHART 24 *Ph.D.'s required to meet academic teaching needs*

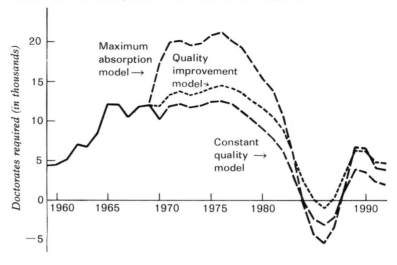

For our present purposes, the important point is that the demand for college faculty members is likely to decline somewhat in the 1970s and to begin a sharp descent toward the end of the decade. Three alternative projections developed by Cartter (129) incorporate varying assumptions with respect to future changes in the percentage of college faculty members holding the doctorate (Chart 24). Modified projections, incorporating additional alternative assumptions about the future behavior of student-faculty ratios in higher education, are presented in Chart 25.[3]

However, regardless of which projection of demand is the most realistic, the outlook for a growing imbalance between demand and supply appears inescapable. Traditionally, about one-half of new Ph.D.'s have entered college or university positions, and about 60 percent have ultimately been employed in academic institutions. The annual proportion of new Ph.D.'s entering college teaching has varied from about 40 to 52 percent, reflecting changes in the relative attractiveness of academic and other positions available (ibid.). But Chart 25, which presents a range of projections of the supply

[3] For a full discussion of these projections see Cartter (129). Balderston and Radner have also developed some estimates using Carnegie Commission enrollment projections and incorporating varied assumptions about student-faculty ratios (130), but their basic conclusions about a growing imbalance between demand and supply do not differ appreciably from Cartter's. They also showed that the academic demand for Ph.D.'s would be quite sensitive to alternative policies, particularly the funding policies of federal and state governments.

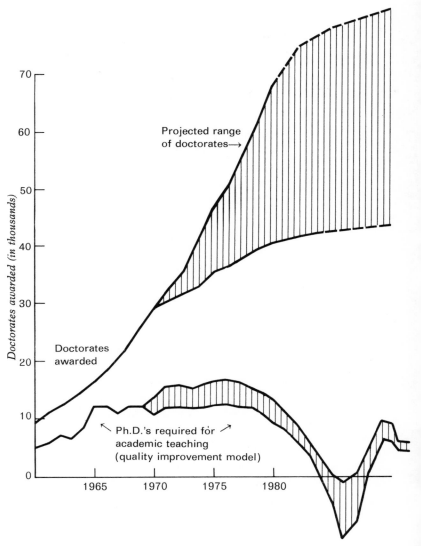

CHART 25 *Comparison of projected doctorates awarded academic teaching needs*

of new holders of doctor's degrees, along with projections of demand for college faculty, indicates clearly that college demand will rapidly fall farther and farther below 50 percent of the projected supply. And most observers consider it very unlikely that government and industry can absorb more than 50 percent of the future supply of Ph.D.'s, especially in view of the probability that R&D expenditures will rise considerably more slowly than they did prior to 1967–68. In any case, the demand from government and industry chiefly affects the natural sciences and a few other fields, such as economics.

We have suggested earlier that there is substantial divergence in projections of the supply of new holders of doctor's degrees. Among the series assembled by Wolfle and Kidd, the projected number of doctor's degrees to be awarded in 1980 (127, p. 6) ranged from 45,200 (National Science Foundation) to 77,700 (the highest of the Carnegie Commission's three projections).[4]

Just how many doctor's degrees will be awarded by 1980 depends, of course, on changes in graduate enrollment in the first half of the 1970s, when those who will receive their degrees toward the end of the decade will be entering the doctoral pipeline. Surveys conducted by the Council of Graduate Schools (CGS) in the fall of 1971 and in the fall of 1972 have indicated that the increase in graduate resident enrollment has been slowing down, as compared with projections based on past trends (131 and 132). In Chart 26, we have compared the lowest of three Carnegie Commission projections of graduate resident enrollment in 1971 and 1972 with actual enrollment as indicated by results of the CGS surveys.[5] The Commission's projection would have indicated an increase of 4.3 percent from 1970 to 1971 and of 4.5 percent from 1971 to 1972. It was based on the very conservative assumption that the past increase in first-time graduate enrollment rates would come to an end and that these rates would remain unchanged from 1969 on. But the Council of Graduate Schools surveys showed an increase of only 1.4 percent from 1970 to 1971 and of only 1.9 percent from 1971 to 1972.[6]

Enrollment for first-professional degrees has clearly been rising more rapidly than graduate resident enrollment. We had occasion in earlier sections to call attention to increases in enrollment in law and medical schools. The Carnegie Commission's fall 1971 enrollment survey (55) showed a 4.4 percent increase in total postbac-

---

[4] The Commission's projections have been developed under the direction of Dr. Gus W. Haggstrom of the Rand Corporation, formerly a member of the faculty of the University of California, Berkeley.

[5] For a discussion of the alternative assumptions used in the development of the three projections, see Carnegie Commission on Higher Education (29, p. 43).

[6] The two CGS surveys were not precisely comparable. The second covered more professional fields than the first.

CHART 26   *Graduate resident enrollment, actual, 1945 to 1970,* and actual and projected, 1971 and 1972 (logarithmic scale, in thousands)*

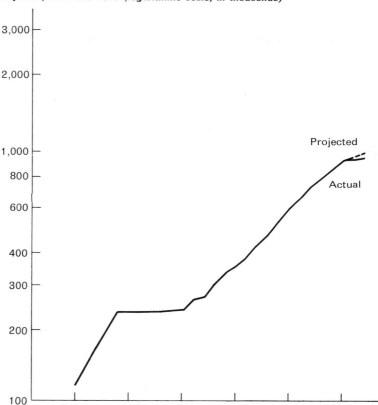

* Data are biennial to 1955 and annual thereafter; they are affected by a change in definition in 1953.

SOURCES: U.S. Office of Education data, adjusted by Carnegie Commission staff; and Council of Graduate Schools (131 and 132).

calaureate enrollment—3.7 percent for men and 6.0 percent for women.

Of particular interest were the indications from both the CGS surveys and the Carnegie Commission survey that very little of the gain in first-time enrollment was going to the universities. The CGS 1971 survey showed that public four-year colleges (those offering the master's as the highest degree) experienced an increase of 10.7 percent in first-time graduate enrollment, while private four-year colleges reported a gain of 6.1 percent. But public universities gained only 1.4 percent, and private universities lost 0.3 percent.

The CGS 1972 survey revealed a similar pattern of variation between four-year colleges and universities.

The Carnegie Commission survey also suggested that the slowing down of the rate of increase in graduate enrollment was attributable mainly to restrictive admissions policies rather than to changes in the desire to enter postbaccalaureate education. For all four groups of institutions mentioned above, the 1970–71 percentage increase in applications was considerably more pronounced than the percentage increase in enrollment, and the selection ratio (new enrollees or transfers as a percentage of applicants) declined somewhat.[7]

Probably the most significant results of the survey were those relating to changes in first-time enrollment by field—not in terms of precise percentages, but in terms of an indication of general trends. The sharpest increases were in architecture, nursing, urban studies/city planning, psychology, and biological sciences—in that order—while there was a decrease of about 12 percent in engineering and much more modest decreases in the humanities, sociology, physical sciences (including mathematics), and social sciences. (Sociology was reported separately and was not included in the social sciences). However, students did not necessarily succeed in entering their chosen fields. We have referred in earlier sections to the sharp increases in ratios of applications to admissions in law schools and medical schools. Other fields in which the percentage increase in applications substantially exceeded the percentage increase in enrollments were social work, psychology, social sciences, and sociology—the latter two, as we have seen, having experienced slight declines in enrollments.

The overall picture is one in which students are responding to changing labor market prospects in the various fields and also to rising concern about such problems as the urban crisis and the environment. The evidence on these points seems more clear and more significant than the evidence on the overall student demand for postgraduate education.

---

[7] However, the number of institutions providing information on applications was considerably smaller than the number reporting enrollments, and the data may therefore not be very reliable. Nevertheless, at least for leading research universities, they are consistent with reports of cutbacks in graduate programs at a number of these institutions.

SUPPORT OF GRADUATE EDUCATION Cutbacks in enrollments in leading graduate schools have been strongly influenced by a decline in federal government support of graduate fellowships and the discontinuation or phasing out of certain private foundation fellowship programs. The slowing of the rate of increase in federal R&D expenditures has also had an adverse impact on the number of graduate research assistantships available. According to Wolfle and Kidd, there was a 40 percent drop, from 57,600 to 36,000, in the total number of federally supported predoctoral fellows and trainees, as well as a drop in funding for these programs from $287 million in the peak year of 1968 to $182 million, in 1971 (127, p. 13).

In the immediate post-Sputnik years, the case for strong federal government support of graduate education seemed very clear to Congress and to the general public. Now that we appear to be producing an oversupply of holders of doctorates, there is an almost inevitable reconsideration. Another indication of this general attitude is the rather meager support of graduate education provided for by the Higher Education Amendments of 1972. These amendments, among other things, adopted a program of institutional aid for higher education, with 90 percent of the institutional aid funds to go to the support of undergraduate education and to be geared to student aid for needy students. The other 10 percent of the institutional aid funds would be based on the number of graduate students enrolled at each institution, allowing, if fully funded, a payment of $200 per student. There is no provision for grants awarded on the basis of financial need to students in their first two years of graduate work, nor for cost-of-education supplements related to these grants, as had earlier been recommended by the Carnegie Commission. Nor is there any provision for cost-of-education supplements related to holders of fellowships for advanced doctoral work. The flat across-the-board payments of $200 will represent only a modest contribution to the high cost of graduate education and do not differentiate between education at the master's level and at the far more costly advanced doctoral level. Thus, these payments will be relatively more beneficial to universities and colleges that award few or no doctor's degrees than to research universities that are heavily involved in doctoral education. The legislation does, however, provide for some degree of liberalization of loan programs for both undergraduate and graduate students and for consolidation of existing programs for the support of graduate education. But no decision has as yet (February 1973) been made on the funding of the new legislation.

To put it mildly, there is regrettable but perhaps understandable confusion at present about what the future course of national policy toward graduate education, and particularly education at the doctoral level, should be. We welcome the establishment of the new National Board on Graduate Education, recognizing that it could hardly have been appointed at a more appropriate time.

Although the Carnegie Commission does not, in general, believe that support of higher education should be geared to manpower requirements—we have made that clear in Section 2 in urging that there be no cutbacks in support of undergraduate education because of labor market trends—we do believe that there are certain exceptions to this general principle. These are concerned with ensuring the production of an adequate flow of able holders of doctorates who will contribute to the advancement of knowledge and of an adequate supply of physicians and dentists. There is a clear national interest in maintaining an adequate supply of highly educated manpower. Furthermore, the market for holders of doctor's degrees and of M.D. and D.D.S. degrees is more clearly a national market than for persons with less advanced levels of education—there is a high degree of interstate mobility on the part of holders of advanced degrees. Individual states cannot be assured of clearcut returns to their investment in these levels of education. There is evidence, also, from studies of age variations in creativity, that creativity tends to peak at relatively early ages in such fields as the physical sciences and mathematics. We cannot afford to obstruct the flow of young scholars into these fields.

We therefore believe that there is a case for consistent and sustained federal government support of graduate education, geared to continuous studies of the supply of, and demand for, highly educated scientists and other scholars. Stop and go policies are extremely undesirable, especially in view of the fact that they tend to have disruptive repercussions on the leading research universities that are best equipped to provide high-quality graduate education. Inevitably, federal government support through fellowships, traineeships, and research assistantships will have to differentiate among fields of study, providing the strongest support to those fields in which there is the least evidence that support will contribute to an excess supply.

In the midst of concern over the implications of predictions of an overall surplus of Ph.D.'s, we must not lose sight of the evidence, discussed in the previous section, that we may well witness a reappearance of shortages in engineering and in some of the physical sciences in the near future. Factors contributing to the probable reappearance of these shortages are the dramatic declines in enrollment that are occurring in a number of these fields, along with evidence that employers increasingly hire holders of advanced degrees, influenced at least in part by the minimal increases in starting salaries in the last few years.

In the market for Ph.D.'s, as in the job market for college graduates in general, there are, indeed, numerous possibilities of demand-supply adjustments. When the supply of doctorates is plentiful, employers—in industry, government, and in educational institutions—will tend to hire holders of doctorates for positions for which holders of master's or even of bachelor's degrees would previously have been considered satisfactory. (An important exception to this generalization is found in some community colleges, where it is felt that the research-oriented training given to Ph.D.'s produces graduates who are neither well trained nor well motivated to teach in community colleges. We shall return to this problem at a later point.) Ph.D.'s, as a result, will be underemployed in relation to previous standards and often in relation to their capabilities, but are not likely to experience prolonged unemployment. In addition, as our discussion of the field of physics indicated, foreign students receiving Ph.D.'s in this country will be less likely to remain here in the absence of desirable employment opportunities, and some United States citizens with doctorates will seek employment abroad.

There remains the problem of the unusually able student who wishes to pursue graduate work in a field in which a surplus of Ph.D.'s is likely to be a particularly intractable problem. The humanities and some of the social sciences are the chief examples. We believe that qualified students should not be denied the opportunity of participating in advanced education, to fulfill their own strong desires and aspirations.

In the debate over whether the social benefits of higher education exceed the individual benefits, we tend to agree with those who argue that individual benefits do not capture all the social benefits. Denison (133) and others have shown that the advancement of knowledge makes a contribution to economic growth over and above the contribution of the increase in individual earnings associated with increased education. We believe, also, that highly educated persons often make voluntary contributions to the quality of life in their communities, as studies conducted for the Commission by the Survey Research Center at the University of Michigan (6) and the National Bureau of Economic Research (134) have indicated. Such contributions are by no means confined to holders of degrees in fields with potential shortages of manpower.

Thus, on the basis of fulfilling the aspirations of some individuals and of the social benefits of advanced education, we believe the rights of qualified students to pursue graduate education should not be curtailed. But we strongly agree with Stone's argument relating to the field of history (135) on the desirability of vigorous efforts to ensure that these students will be able to pursue their graduate work, especially in the more distinguished institutions. We shall return to this issue later on.

THE DURATION OF DOCTORAL EDUCATION One of the hazards associated with the appearance of a less favorable job market for Ph.D.'s is the probability that the number of years spent in obtaining the degree will rise—a development which the Commission would consider most undesirable.[8]

As Folger, Bayer, and Astin (4, p. 191) have pointed out, there are a number of ways in which the length of Ph.D. training can be measured. They report the average time that elapses between graduate school entry and Ph.D. completion as 8.5 years for all fields combined. They also cite evidence indicating that the time required to obtain the Ph.D. has been "shortest in the physical sciences, next shortest in biological sciences, intermediate in the social sciences, longer in arts and humanities, and longest in education." Part of the explanation for the time elapsed is that students frequently leave to take a full-time job before completing the work for the degree, but the available data for 1957 to 1964 (ibid., p. 192) indicate that, depending on the field, two to four years were spent in full-time study and two to three years in part-time study (except in education, where the average number of years spent in part-time study was 5.5).

There is also considerable evidence that variations among fields in the average time elapsed reflect differences in the relative severity of requirements, particularly at the dissertation stage. Breneman

---

[8] See Appendix B for relevant recommendations.

(136) has analyzed the differences in average time elapsed between graduate school entry and receipt of the Ph.D. in selected departments at the University of California, Berkeley, and has found evidence suggesting that variations in departmental policies affecting the length of time required to complete the work for the degree were also related to differences in the relative ease or difficulty with which graduates could be placed.

Although it is not entirely clear from Breneman's evidence that variations in departmental policies were a result of deliberate decisions, and not a series of more or less unplanned adjustments to market situations, the pattern of variations among fields seems to be more or less uniform among institutions and does not seem to have varied greatly over time. The speed with which degrees have been obtained in the physical sciences in recent decades has been explained by the relative availability of full-time stipends, as well as by departmental policies encouraging rapid completion of the work for the degree.

The important point is that precisely those fields in which graduate work has tended to be most prolonged in the past are the disciplines that are likely to be most adversely affected by the changing job market for Ph.D.'s. We believe that any further prolongment would be a most unfortunate development and we urge doctoral-granting institutions to take vigorous steps to prevent it. Recently the Stanford University Faculty Senate has adopted a policy providing for graduate students, in most instances, to complete their doctorate work in four years rather than the nearly six years it has taken the average student in the past. The policy statements included the following provisions:

Every department shall present to the committee on graduate studies a clear timetable for the expected progress of its students, showing how the normal student will progress to the Ph.D.

Timetables requiring more than four years shall be subject to approval of the committee (137).

DOCTORAL-GRANTING INSTITUTIONS One of the most disturbing trends in graduate education is the proliferation of doctoral-granting institutions. Just in the two years from 1968 to 1970, the total number of institutions granting doctoral degrees increased by more than 20. In the latter year, there were slightly more than 280 institutions which awarded doctorates

(138). Of these, about 65 were specialized institutions, chiefly theological schools and medical schools.[9] Thus, more than 200 universities and colleges awarded doctorates in a variety of fields. But there were also many more that aspired to this status. A recent survey by Mayhew indicated that some 130 to 150 institutions that did not have doctoral programs had plans to develop such programs (139).

Despite the steady expansion in the number of doctoral-granting institutions, there has been a strong tendency historically for graduate education at the doctoral level to be concentrated in a limited number of leading research universities. This continues to be true. In 1968–69, 5 percent (or 16) of the doctoral-granting institutions each awarded 400 doctoral degrees or more and accounted for 34 percent of the doctorates, while another 24 institutions, awarding 200 to 399 doctorates, accounted for 24 percent of the degrees (127, p. 16).

There are significant economies of scale in the training of Ph.D.'s, and a "critical mass" of qualified faculty is necessary to develop a Ph.D. program of acceptable quality.[10] The tremendous expansion in the scope of knowledge required for expertise in most scholarly fields means that competence in the training of Ph.D.'s cannot readily be achieved in a small department, although this may be possible in some of the fine arts and in certain other fields. In addition, there is often interdisciplinary interdependence between such departments as chemistry and physics, or theoretical physics and mathematics.

There are also economies of scale associated with the need for large libraries for scholarly research and doctoral training in the social sciences and humanities, while extensive laboratories and other physical facilities are required for quality graduate work in the sciences. And today a graduate program of quality without access to at least one sizable computer is almost inconceivable; yet computers with reasonable capacities cannot be operated economically unless there are sufficient numbers of users.

Our studies of economies of scale have shown that, especially in universities and comprehensive colleges, factors contributing

---

[9] However, the majority of medical schools are not reported separately as degree-granting institutions but are included in reports of their parent universities.

[10] See the discussion in the Commission's report, *The More Effective Use of Resources,* Section 3.

to reduced educational costs per FTE student as institutions increase in size tend to be offset by factors making for rising costs that are associated with the growing complexity of the institution as it develops and adds new programs. However, studies at the University of Toronto and elsewhere have suggested that economies of scale are more clearcut in individual programs than in institutions as a whole.[11]

In any event, there is general agreement that advanced graduate education is considerably more costly than undergraduate education or graduate education at the master's level. Weights that are now in rather wide use have been developed on the basis of studies at the University of California, the University of Toronto, and elsewhere. The weights are intended to reflect the differing costs of education per FTE student at the various levels of instruction: for lower-division students, unity; for upper-division students, 1.5; for first-stage graduate students, 2.5; and for second-stage students, 3.5 (141, pp. 17–18). These analyses have been based on costs in universities with large numbers of doctoral students. There is some evidence that the overall ratio of graduate to undergraduate costs may be even higher in universities with relatively smaller doctoral programs (e.g., 132). Balderston has pointed out (141, p. 6):

Normally . . . a new doctoral program or a new professional school or a new experimental undergraduate college needs a nucleus investment for the initial phases in order to make it possible to open the doors. Then it will induce further costs for related departments, for the library and computer center, and for the administrative structure of the institution. And as the new program grows, it may take a long or a short time to reach a size of enrollment and faculty and a depth of resources that will enable it to be academically and fiscally viable for the long pull.

The inefficiencies associated with small doctoral programs impose a heavy burden on the taxpayers of states permitting the extension of doctoral-granting programs to public colleges that have not previously had them. Furthermore, attempts to develop com-

[11] A useful review of studies of economies of scale in particular fields, such as medical education and engineering, is included in one of the reports resulting from the study of costs in graduate education sponsored by the Council of Graduate Schools and the National Association of College and University Business Officers (140, pp. 110–111). Several of these studies have indicated that cost curves tend to be U-shaped, i.e., average costs decrease to a certain point as FTE enrollment rises, and then begin to increase.

prehensive doctoral programs in such institutions are not likely to result in high-quality advanced graduate education. Occasionally, however, such colleges have a few outstanding departments in which the development of doctoral programs might be justified.

The Commission believes that federal and state government policies should be designed to confine comprehensive doctoral programs to a relatively limited number of universities that have high-quality programs in many disciplines. The total number of universities in which comprehensive programs would be encouraged probably should not exceed 60 to 70, and, at the most, 100. The selection should be based on such criteria as the ACE studies of quality in graduate education (142 and 143), the Carnegie Commission classification of institutions of higher education,[12] and other sources of information on the quality of graduate programs. Other existing doctoral-granting institutions that have programs of generally inferior quality or high-quality programs in only a very limited number of disciplines should be encouraged to develop selective Ph.D. programs on the basis of regional or multicampus plans designed to limit each institution to specified disciplines but to ensure representation of all disciplines in the doctoral programs of the region or multicampus institution as a whole.

Regional approaches toward this type of objective have been developed by the New England Board of Higher Education and the Southern Regional Education Board and have been initiated in the mountain states under the auspices of the Western Interstate Commission on Higher Education (WICHE). The five private universities in Washington, D.C., are also a consortium under which graduate students at any one of the universities may register for courses any one of the others. It is not yet very effective and has not developed careful plans for limiting the number of fields in which each of the universities would offer doctoral education.

The primary instrument for implementing this policy at the federal government level should be a program along the lines of the policies previously recommended by the Commission for support of graduate education—a limited number of fellowships for advanced graduate students of exceptional ability. Such student aid would be accompanied by cost-of-education supplements going to the institutions in which grant holders or fellowship holders were enrolled. We believe that under this type of program students could

[12] See Carnegie Commission on Higher Education (29, Appendix A).

largely be relied upon to choose one of the universities with a high quality program in their chosen field of study. In order to help students make well-informed choices, there will need to be continuing research on the quality of graduate education in individual institutions.

However, student choice cannot be relied upon to solve the problem of preventing extension of doctoral programs to institutions that do not now have them or have them only to a very limited extent. This will require determined action by state and regional planning bodies because of the strength of the forces underlying the steady increase in the number of doctoral-granting institutions.

There should be particular emphasis on efforts by state coordinating councils and similar bodies to prevent the establishment of new doctoral programs and to require or recommend (depending on their powers) the discontinuation of degree programs that are very costly, or of low quality, or both.

The Commission has recommended that the doctor of arts (D.A.) degree become the standard degree for graduate students preparing to enter undergraduate or master's level college teaching, as well as for students planning on obtaining professional jobs that do not involve research responsibilities in government and industry. During the 1970s, the most rapid increases in enrollment and in demand for faculty will be in comprehensive colleges and community colleges.[13]

The D.A. degree represents, we believe, far more appropriate training for teaching in these institutions than the highly research-oriented Ph.D. Furthermore, the fact that the demand for faculty in universities will increase only slowly and at a rapidly diminishing rate strengthens the case for increased emphasis on the D.A. The D.A. is also designed to provide training that is less narrowly discipline-oriented than the Ph.D., and this will be an advantage as we move toward a period of stationary enrollment, with its difficult problem of adaptation of faculty resources to changing needs.

We believe that preparation for the D.A. can be successfully provided, not only in leading research universities, but also in other doctoral-granting universities and in some of the comprehensive universities and colleges that have developed faculties that are well equipped to offer graduate education. But we agree with the Council of Graduate Schools (144) that doctor of arts programs should

[13] See the projections in *New Students and New Places,* Section 4.

be developed only in those institutions and in those departments within institutions that have faculties of the requisite size and quality.

Recommendation 26: State coordinating councils and similar agencies should develop strong policies (where these do not now exist) for preventing the spread of Ph.D. programs to institutions that do not now have them. In addition, every effort should be made to prevent the establishment of new Ph.D. programs in particular fields of study in institutions that now have Ph.D. programs unless an exceptionally strong case can be made for them. We also strongly recommend the continuous review of existing degree programs with a view to eliminating those that are very costly or of low quality and the concentration of highly specialized degree programs on only one or two campuses of multicampus institutions.

Recommendation 27: Regional plans for the development of Ph.D. programs along the lines of those of the New England Board of Higher Education and the Southern Regional Education Board should be strengthened and extended to regions that do not now have them. We also recommend far more extensive use of consortium arrangements that involve planning for concentration of development of Ph.D. programs in particular fields in individual members of the consortium as well as the rights of students to cross-register for individual courses or fields of concentration. Such plans should call for developing the strength of an individual institution in a group of related fields, such as the physical sciences or the social sciences.

Recommendation 28: The continued development of doctor of arts programs should be encouraged. We consider the doctor of arts a more suitable degree than the Ph.D. for many types of employment.

Recommendation 29: Agencies and individuals that have been conducting studies of future supply and demand for Ph.D.'s should continue to review and update their work. We are impressed by the differences in outlook among fields and believe that the time has come for increased emphasis on projections relating to individual fields or groups of fields and less reliance on broad aggregative studies.

During the course of our work on this report, we have been impressed by the almost complete lack of analysis of the implications of the changing job market for holders of master's degrees and for master's programs in colleges and universities. Yet some of the fields that will be most affected by the changing job market, such as education, include a very large proportion of candidates for master's degrees.

Recommendation 30: Federal and state government agencies and other appropriate bodies should undertake studies of the implications of the changing job market for holders of master's degrees and for enrollment in master's programs.

9. Potential Adjustments in Demand and Supply

In earlier sections of this report we have referred to potential adjustments in supply-and-demand relationships, especially as they relate to the outlook in particular professional occupations. At this point, we shall consider in a more systematic way various types of supply-demand adjustments that are likely to affect the job market for college graduates more generally in the coming years.

As we suggested in Section 4, it is possible that an unfavorable job market for college graduates and other influences may depress future enrollment rates below those indicated by projections based on past trends. If this tendency were to persist through the 1970s, its effect in alleviating a potential imbalance in the job market for college graduates could be appreciable, but the evidence on this point is far from clear as yet.

In addition, a number of other types of probable demand-supply adjustments may well contribute to a more satisfactory job market for college graduates. These include (1) shifts in enrollment patterns by field, (2) educational upgrading, (3) alternative lifestyles and nontraditional careers, (4) the structuring of demand through public policy, and (5) a possible reversal, at least to some degree, of the brain drain.

SHIFTS IN ENROLLMENT PATTERNS BY FIELD

There has been considerable disagreement about the extent to which student choices of fields of study are responsive to changes in the job market. Folger, for example, has suggested that shifts in degree preferences in the 1960s did not seem to be closely related to changes in demand in the job market.

The largest increases have been in social sciences and humanities and arts. Those arts and sciences areas where a degree is not preparation for a specific job have been growing most rapidly in popularity, while those where job training is related to a specific profession (engineering, the health professions) have been growing more slowly (145, p. 211).

Adkins has also argued that shifts in student choices of fields have not been particularly responsive to changes in the job market (146).

On the other hand, in a series of recent studies, Freeman has presented findings that suggest a high degree of responsiveness of student choices of fields to changes in the relative outlook in various occupations (37, 38, and 122). Fogel and Mitchell have also developed data showing a positive relationship, with a lag between changes in employment in selected occupations employing college graduates and changes in the number of degrees awarded by field of study, but they are cautious in interpreting their results (147).

On net balance, the evidence seems to reveal a considerable degree of student responsiveness to changes in relative job opportunities, but within a framework of rather substantial stability in overall patterns of student tastes and abilities. The pronounced increases in numbers of degrees awarded in social sciences and arts and humanities in the 1960s occurred in large part in response to the marked rise in demand for teachers at all levels, as we have suggested earlier. But another factor was the rapid rise in enrollment rates of women, who have long displayed preferences for these fields, with the notable exception of economics. We must also keep in mind the evidence that the proportion of the college-age population with the requisite interests and abilities to complete the work for degrees in the physical sciences and engineering appears to be limited.

The Carnegie Commission's fall 1971 enrollment survey revealed pronounced shifts in enrollment patterns by field between 1970 and 1971 that were influenced not only by job market shifts but also by growing concern of students about ecology, urban problems, and other social issues (55). We have discussed the shifts in graduate enrollment in Section 8. Among undergraduates in four-year colleges, there were sharp increases in first-time enrollment in forestry (in which departments have tended to broaden their curricula to include increased emphasis on conservation), social work, nursing, biological sciences, and psychology, along with moderate increases in theology, religion, agriculture, architecture, fine arts, sociology, urban studies, and social sciences. On the other hand, there were pronounced declines in engineering (as mentioned earlier), education, and ethnic studies, as well as moderate declines in the humanities and physical sciences.

Shifts in first-time enrollment by field in public two-year colleges also revealed similar patterns. There were pronounced percentage increases in agriculture-related programs, health service programs, and trade and industrial programs, along with more modest rates of increase in science-related programs (a group that includes computer science), and public service programs (which include government, law enforcement, and social work). Only in engineering-related programs was there a decrease. In private two-year colleges, there were increases only in science-related programs, health service programs, and public service programs, but it must be kept in mind that total enrollment in private two-year colleges declined.

In addition to shifting among fields, students also shift among specialties within fields, often in response to job market changes. Some interesting data on enrollment in elementary education programs in Florida State University, Tallahassee, show only a slight drop in total enrollment—from 875 to 864—between 1968 and 1972, but there were sharp decreases in such subfields as elementary education (general), English education, science education, and social studies education, along with pronounced increases in art education, habilitative sciences, physical education, and "undecided in education."[1]

As we have pointed out earlier, the ACE data on career choices of entering college freshmen also reveal pronounced shifts in recent years that are clearly responsive to changes in the job market (Appendix A, Table A-14). But students frequently shift fields during their undergraduate careers. Astin and Panos, for example, have shown that well over one-half of a large sample of 1961-entering freshmen who were included in a follow-up survey in 1965 had shifted fields during their college careers, but substantial proportions of these shifts occurred between closely related fields (148).

Thus we may conceive of college entrants as falling into rather loosely defined "pools of potential majors" in various groups of fields. One pool would certainly consist of potential majors in a broad group embracing mathematics, statistics, the natural sciences, and engineering. Another group might consist of students destined to major in the social sciences, business administration, city and regional planning, or perhaps social welfare (especially among the women). Still another group might consist of students with strong interests in the humanities. Shifts would be more likely to take place within the pools than from one pool to another, and many of these shifts might be induced by changes in relative job op-

[1] Data supplied by Robert B. Mautz, State University System of Florida.

portunities or by improved information about such changes. However, some shifts would also occur between pools—for example, shifts out of the first broad group mentioned above by students who find that they do not have the requisite ability for college-level work in these fields.

Pronounced shifts in enrollment, such as those of the last few years, call, in general, for corresponding shifts in the distribution of course offerings, in the distribution of faculty members by field of specialization, and in the relative supply of various types of laboratory equipment and library materials—at least if they persist beyond a single year or so, in which adjustments can perhaps be made by using temporary personnel and makeshift facilities. When total enrollment is growing rapidly, it is not especially difficult to direct additions to the faculty and facilities largely toward the most rapidly growing fields. However, as the rate of growth of enrollment in higher education declines during the 1970s, and as enrollment levels off in the 1980s, shifts in the composition of faculty and facilities will be far more difficult to achieve.[2]

But the Astin and Panos findings on shifts in career choices suggest that colleges and universities must respond to changing student choices of careers and fields with all due deliberation, and with as much knowledge as possible of typical patterns of changes in occupational choice during the undergraduate period.

There is evidence that college graduates with liberal arts majors have had relatively severe difficulty in obtaining jobs in recent years (149). This should not be interpreted as an indication that, in general, students should be counseled away from liberal arts majors, but that they should be given as sound information as it is possible to gather about relative job prospects for persons trained in particular liberal arts disciplines. Those who continue to wish to major in liberal arts fields with poor job prospects should make the choice with full appreciation of the difficulties.

It also seems possible that there may be something of a swingback toward more frequent hiring of liberal arts majors before too long. The recent recession has been characterized by pronounced employer preferences for graduates with specific professional and occupational training, but, for a long time, there have been some business leaders who have expressed preferences for liberal arts majors, and there has been a strong tendency for the more success-

---

[2] See Appendix B for relevant earlier recommendations.

ful men in terms of income in the NBER-Thorndike sample (discussed in connection with Appendix A, Table A-11) to indicate that broad general education had been more valuable to them in their careers than specific occupational training (134).

Training in narrow specialties may also make it more difficult for college graduates to make desirable occupational shifts in the course of their adult lives. It has become widely recognized that the more rapid the pace of advancement of knowledge and technological change, the more rapidly specialized skills and knowledge become obsolescent. The current developments toward strengthening opportunities for adult education and retraining are thus of the utmost importance for future occupational flexibility.

Most of the available evidence indicates that vocational counseling has tended to be a relatively weak component of college and university student counseling programs, which have, in general, given greater emphasis to the students' personal and psychological problems. We believe that, in view of the pronounced changes that are occurring in the job market for college graduates, institutions of higher education should place considerably greater emphasis on vocational counseling.

Recommendation 31: Colleges and universities should take immediate steps to strengthen occupational counseling programs available to their students. We also recommend that college placement services be strengthened where they have not been well developed. Professional schools should maintain their own placement programs for those receiving master's, first-professional, and doctor's degrees, while arts and science departments should have their own placement programs for students at the doctoral level.

The recommendation at the end of Section 7 relating to the need for strengthening federal government analyses of supply and demand is also relevant in the present context.

EDUCATIONAL UPGRADING AND CREDEN-TIALISM In recent years, undoubtedly in part as a result of heightened interest in equal employment opportunities for racial minority groups and women, there has been an increased tendency to deplore "credentialism," or the imposition by employers of educational requirements that are not clearly indicated by the requirements of particular jobs. The U.S. Supreme Court, in the case of Griggs et al. *v.* Duke Power Company (March 8, 1971), decided that "employment practices," including education and test requirements, that "cannot be shown to be related to job performance" are contrary to the provisions of the Civil Rights Act of 1964.

One of the most vigorous recent attacks on credentialism is in the study, *Education and Jobs: The Great Training Robbery,* by Ivar Berg (9). Paul Taubman and Terence Wales have also developed data designed to show that educational requirements are widely used inappropriately (150), and we have earlier referred to Thurow's "job competition" model of the labor market, which is based on the assumption that educational requirements are "ubiquitous, if not universal" (11).

Although there is some justification in the charges, there is a tendency toward overgeneralization in the literature on this subject. Much of Berg's evidence on the lack of relationship, or of an actual inverse relationship, between educational attainment and productivity in employment, relates to blue-collar and relatively low-level white-collar jobs. We would expect that educational attainment would be more significant in relation to professional employment and top-level managerial jobs. In fact, Berg makes the point, with respect to data relating to selected industries, that "except at high levels (engineers and scientists) educational differences tend to wash out among employees at any organizational level" (9, p. 16). The very phrase, "the great training robbery," tends to ignore the fact we emphasized in Section 2—that preparation for the job market is only one of the functions of higher education. Yet we share Berg's criticism of overemphasis by employers on the college degree as the pathway to employment. We also share his criticism of other particular aspects of American education, including the overemphasis on length of training, as opposed to quality of training, for teachers for our public schools.

In Section 3, we showed that the growth in the number and diversity of professional occupations has been a major factor in explaining the growth in employment of college graduates over the decades, and that increased employment of college graduates has been primarily attributable to the growth of employment in occupations in which a college degree has been traditionally expected, rather than to educational upgrading of occupations. Furthermore, the tendency of employers to require a college degree is not as pervasive as is sometimes implied. A 1967–68 survey of a representative sample of about 300 of the larger employers in the San Francisco Bay Area indicated that the following percentages of employers required or preferred a college or more advanced degree in selecting workers for white-collar employment (151, p. 272):[3]

Major occupation group	Requiring College degree	Requiring Graduate degree	Preferring college degree
Professional	62.5	5.0	7.1
Technical	28.4		3.0
Managerial	34.1	2.4	6.9
Clerical			
Sales	17.2		

Rawlins and Ulman have explored the issue of credentialism quite fully (152). They find that, between 1950 and 1960, there was "a rather consistent increase in educational attainment . . . which 'bore' no statistically significant relationship to the changes in estimated requirements [for jobs]." On the other hand, they concede that "what may appear as an excess of college-trained manpower may simply be a further screening process which is perfectly consistent with profit maximization."

Even though educational requirements are not ubiquitous, there is no question that they have been rising. The less favorable job market anticipated for the 1970s will probably exacerbate this tendency, but so will the increasing complexity of managerial decision making, which will lead to increased preference for trained managers. On the other hand, civil rights pressure and court decisions, as in the Griggs case, will serve as a counterforce, but they will probably be more effective in discouraging formal educational requirements than in eliminating informal employer preferences.

It should also be kept in mind that the movement of college graduates into occupations in which they have not previously been employed to any considerable extent may have, in some cases, quite positive aspects. For example, during the recent recession, police departments in major cities found that they received increasing numbers of applications from college graduates or from persons with some college education (153), and some departments, like the one in Atlanta, adopted an apparently successful program of recruitment of college graduates. Increasingly it has come to be recognized that, in complex urban situations, the police officer is often

[3] A search for similar data from other studies has not proved fruitful.

in a situation in which he has to make a difficult decision on his own. Training in an analytical approach to decision making may be an advantage in such a situation. There has been some tendency for a slowly rising number of police departments to require one or two years of college, as well as a pronounced tendency to provide for released time plus educational costs to enable policemen to take appropriate courses in nearby colleges. In Section 3 we noted the recent rise in the percentage of associate's degrees and other awards in police technology and law enforcement (Appendix A, Table A-13).

However, college education requirements for policemen, as for other personnel, are a matter of controversy. It has recently been reported that New York City is contemplating requiring at least one year of college (133). On the other hand, in Berkeley, California, which has long required two years of college for patrolmen and which has been known as the city of "college cops," several members of the city council recently proposed reducing the educational requirement to high school graduation in order to get more blacks onto the police force. The proposal was rejected but is still a matter of controversy.

Recommendation 32: Employers should not raise educational requirements in response to changes in the job market for college graduates. We strongly recommend that educational requirements should not be imposed except where they are clearly indicated by job requirements.

ALTERNATIVE LIFESTYLES AND NON-TRADITIONAL CAREERS One of the great imponderables in looking ahead is the question of how far the choice of alternative lifestyles among young people will go and what its long-run effect on the job market will be. In a recent study of communes, for example, it was estimated that there were approximately 2,000 in the country as a whole (154). Members of communes sometimes pool their property and income, managing to live on very modest amounts by renting large old houses, sharing the preparation of meals and the care of children, adopting very inexpensive styles of dress, and the like. In rural areas they produce some of their own food. Some members are in the conventional labor market, but a number of communes have developed small business enterprises in which their members cooperate, often in arts or crafts fields. Overhead is minimal or nonexistent in some of these enterprises—sidewalk vending, for example, has been permitted in some cities and has been a matter of controversy in others. And the phenomenon of street musicians, living on the donations of passersby who enjoy their music, has become increasingly common in some large urban areas in the last few years.

Another phenomenon that has been of some significance in the last few years is the growing interest of recent or prospective college graduates in starting a small business, often of a somewhat unconventional kind, but on a more formal basis than sidewalk vending. Most of our information on this movement is impressionistic, but some college placement offices have taken pains to develop information on how students can go about starting a small business in a novel field. On the other hand, some placement officers also have been warning students about the risks involved in self-employment as a source of income.

The rejection of conventional careers as part of the emerging youth subculture has been interpreted as a manifestation of the onset of the postindustrialization stage of American economic development. The postindustrial society will be a society in which large-scale organizations and rapid technological change will be predominant. For some young people, the prevailing trends of this advanced technocracy are in conflict with their desires for a society that emphasizes basic human values and a concern about the preservation of the environment. Some observers regard the youth subculture as a counterrevolutionary force, others as a revolutionary force (155, pp. 376–381). It is also important to distinguish between young people who are primarily concerned with social and political change and those who may be broadly characterized as belonging to a "hippie" subculture—more interested in such developments as communal ways of living than in political action.

For our present purposes, the important point is that significant proportions of young people are rejecting conventional careers, and perhaps especially those careers that are most closely identified with corporate capitalism. Some are strongly motivated toward careers that involve efforts to improve the lot of the poor—through legal services, health services, and other similar activities. Some are oriented toward a philosophy that regards small-scale handicraft production as the most rewarding kind of activity for the intellectual. And still others embrace a Maoist-oriented philosophy of work for the intellectual, involving alternating participation in intellectual endeavors and manual work, including farming.

The Carnegie Commission Survey of Students and Faculty (1969) sheds some interesting light on the characteristics of undergraduates who do not see preparation for a career as an important goal for themselves or who appear to be alienated from aspiration toward a career.

One of the questions addressed to undergraduates was "how important it is for you to get each of the following at college: a detailed grasp of a special field, a well-rounded general education, training and skills for an occupation, learning to get along with people, preparation for marriage, and formulating the values and goals of my life." For each of these goals the student was asked to indicate whether it was (1) essential, (2) fairly important, or (3) not important. With respect to "training and skills for an occupation," 57 percent considered this an essential goal, 33 percent regarded it as fairly important, and 10 percent indicated that it was not important.

The students who regarded training and skills for an occupation as "not important" were by no means randomly distributed among institutions (Chart 27). More than one-fourth of the respondents in liberal arts colleges I (the more selective liberal arts colleges) did not regard this as an important goal. A relatively high percentage (16.9 percent) also responded in this manner in research universities I (the most heavily research-oriented universities). The lowest proportions of students who did not regard training and skills for an occupation as an important goal were found in comprehensive universities and colleges I and in two-year colleges. Students in public institutions were less likely to respond "not important" to this question than students in private institutions (data not shown), and in this connection it is appropriate to point out that liberal arts colleges I are the only group in the classification shown in Chart 27 that consist entirely of private institutions.

Probably consistent with this pattern of variation by type of institution is the finding that, when students were classified by family income, those from relatively well-to-do families, with incomes of $25,000 or more, were especially likely to respond that training and skills for an occupation were not an important goal. Such students would tend to be disproportionately represented in leading research universities and relatively selective liberal arts colleges. In general, however, variations with family income did not follow a consistent pattern.

The widest variations in responses to this question were associated with political leaning. Students who regarded themselves

CHART 27 *Percentage of undergraduates regarding training and skills for an occupation as not important among goals of a college education, by selected characteristics of students and their institutions.*

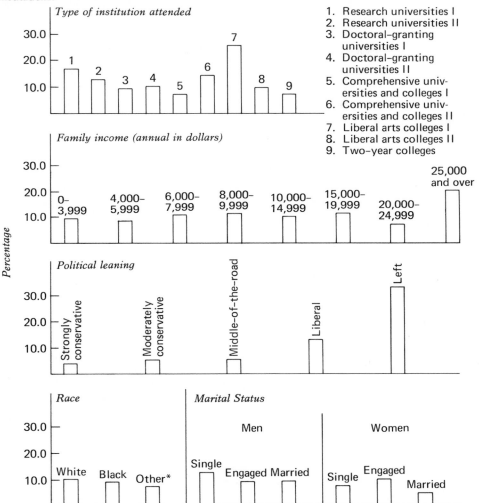

1. Research universities I
2. Research universities II
3. Doctoral–granting universities I
4. Doctoral–granting universities II
5. Comprehensive universities and colleges I
6. Comprehensive universities and colleges II
7. Liberal arts colleges I
8. Liberal arts colleges II
9. Two–year colleges

* Other includes Spanish-Americans, Mexican-Americans, American-Indians, and Asian-Americans.

SOURCE: Carnegie Commission Survey of Students and Faculty, 1969.

as conservative or middle of the road were relatively unlikely to respond "not important" to this question, whereas the proportion of liberals who responded in this manner was above average (13.6 percent), while as many as one-third of those who regarded themselves as leftists checked "not important" as their answer.

Variations by race, marital status, and sex were relatively minor and, for the most part, not statistically significant.

Perhaps the most interesting differences in response to this question were in relation to father's occupation (Chart 28). Especially high percentages who regarded training and skills for an occupation as unimportant were found among sons and daughters of lawyers, college professors, and physicians and dentists. But such responses may have been largely attributable to a feeling that specialized training for one's future occupation was to be found in graduate or

CHART 28 *Percentage of undergraduates regarding training and skills for an occupation as not important among goals of a college education, by father's occupation*

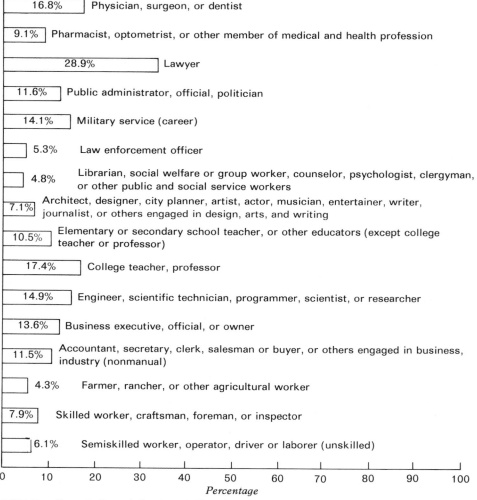

16.8%	Physician, surgeon, or dentist
9.1%	Pharmacist, optometrist, or other member of medical and health profession
28.9%	Lawyer
11.6%	Public administrator, official, politician
14.1%	Military service (career)
5.3%	Law enforcement officer
4.8%	Librarian, social welfare or group worker, counselor, psychologist, clergyman, or other public and social service workers
7.1%	Architect, designer, city planner, artist, actor, musician, entertainer, writer, journalist, or others engaged in design, arts, and writing
10.5%	Elementary or secondary school teacher, or other educators (except college teacher or professor)
17.4%	College teacher, professor
14.9%	Engineer, scientific technician, programmer, scientist, or researcher
13.6%	Business executive, official, or owner
11.5%	Accountant, secretary, clerk, salesman or buyer, or others engaged in business, industry (nonmanual)
4.3%	Farmer, rancher, or other agricultural worker
7.9%	Skilled worker, craftsman, foreman, or inspector
6.1%	Semiskilled worker, operator, driver or laborer (unskilled)

0   10   20   30   40   50   60   70   80   90   100

Percentage

SOURCE: Carnegie Commission Survey of Students and Faculty, 1969.

professional, rather than undergraduate, education. At the other end of the spectrum were children of farmers, librarians, social welfare workers, law enforcement officers, architects, city planners, and others. Most of these are occupations for which specific training is available at the undergraduate stage.

A somewhat different pattern of responses was found in the extent of agreement with the statement, "I cannot imagine being happy in any of the careers available to me" (Charts 29 and 30). Overall the distribution of responses on this item was as follows:

Strongly disagree	62.6%
Disagree with reservations	25.1
Agree with reservations	9.6
Strongly agree	2.7

In Charts 29 and 30 we have combined percentages who agreed with reservations and who strongly agreed.

Variations by type of institution were not as wide as in the responses to the previous question, but undergraduates in research universities I were especially likely to agree (15.7 percent), as were those in both groups of comprehensive universities and colleges (14.0 and 13.7 percent). Variations with family income were not very pronounced and followed no particular pattern. But again, political leaning was an important influence, and in this case undergraduates at the extremes of the political spectrum were especially likely to agree, although the tendency was considerably more pronounced among those considering themselves as left (26.3 percent) than among those regarding themselves as strongly conservative (16.9 percent). Differences related to major field of study were also significant, with students in the humanities agreeing to a somewhat greater than average extent (16 percent), whereas students in education and social welfare (combined) and those in health fields were especially unlikely to agree. Here the explanation seems fairly obvious. Students in education, social welfare, and health have generally chosen those fields with specific career objectives in mind, and it may well be that the fact that all three involve social service helps to explain the small percentage who felt they could not be happy in the careers open to them. Students in the humanities, on the other hand, are more likely to be somewhat uncertain about their career objectives. They were also somewhat more likely (52 percent) than average (44 percent) to regard themselves as liberal

CHART 29 *Percentage of undergraduates agreeing with the statement, "I cannot imagine being happy in any of the careers available to me," by selected characteristics of students and their institutions*

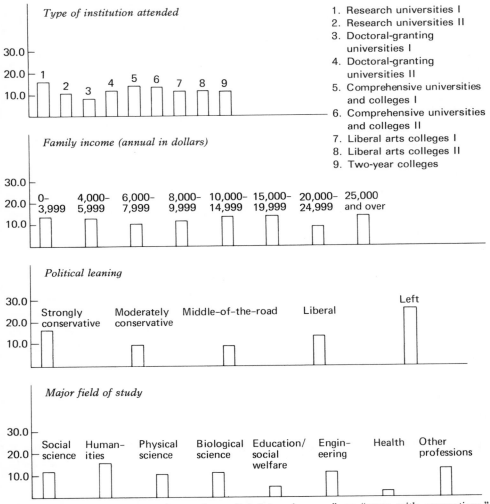

1. Research universities I
2. Research universities II
3. Doctoral-granting universities I
4. Doctoral-granting universities II
5. Comprehensive universities and colleges I
6. Comprehensive universities and colleges II
7. Liberal arts colleges I
8. Liberal arts colleges II
9. Two-year colleges

NOTE: Percentages include students who replied "strongly agree" or "agree with reservations." Other possible replies included "strongly disagree" and "disagree with reservations."

SOURCE: Carnegie Commission Survey of Students and Faculty, 1969.

or left, though not to the same extent as students in social science (62 percent).

Variations by father's occupation (Chart 30) fell into an interest-

CHART 30 *Percentage of undergraduates agreeing with the statement, "I cannot imagine being happy in any of the careers available to me," by father's occupation*

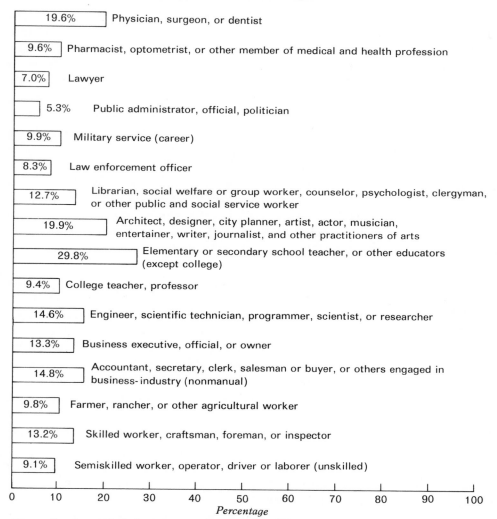

NOTE: Percentages include students who replied "strongly agree' or "agree with reservations." Other possible replies included "strongly disagree" and "disagree with reservations".
SOURCE: Carnegie Commission Survey of Students and Faculty, 1969.

ing pattern. Sons and daughters of teachers, architects, city planners, physicians and dentists, engineers, sales and clerical workers, and business executives tended to agree with this statement more frequently than the average student, whereas children of public administrators and politicians, lawyers, and law enforcement officers were relatively unlikely to agree.[4]

Beginning about the fall of 1971 there were numerous reports suggesting that students were becoming more serious about their academic work and disenchanted with participation in campus demonstrations. In particular, there were reports from a number of universities, including Berkeley and Yale, to the effect that students were spending more time in the library. Whether students have become more concerned about their studies in response to the difficulties that have developed in the job market for college graduates or because of disillusionment over the results of demonstrations is not yet clear. The change may mean that relatively fewer students would express lack of interest in careers today than at the time of our 1969 survey. Nevertheless, the results of the survey are probably still significant because of the light they shed on the characteristics of students who are relatively uninterested in conventional careers.

THE STRUC-TURING OF DEMAND Since World War II government policies have become a far more important determinant of the demand for college graduates and holders of advanced degrees than they were in earlier decades. They have also become an important determinant of demand for workers lacking a college degree. As Folger has put it, "governmental priorities are increasingly becoming the determinants of shifts in manpower demand" (145, p. 210). We have seen that the job market for school teachers may be somewhat more favorable than current projections suggest if increased federal and state aid makes it possible for school districts to reduce their student-faculty ratios and to improve compensatory education programs, and if the trend toward increased expenditures on day-care centers and early child development and education programs continues.[5]

Apart from the need to overcome the deficiencies in elementary and secondary education, to which the Commission attaches high priority, we should move forward, so far as possible, to meet the

[4] It would be interesting to determine whether responses to these questions would have indicated smaller proportions of students regarding preparation for a career as relatively unimportant 10 or 20 years ago, but unfortunately questions used in earlier surveys were not sufficiently comparable to permit an answer to this question.

[5] A modest reduction in student-faculty ratios is assumed in BLS projections of the demand for teachers, but teachers employed in settings other than kindergarten through the twelfth grade are not taken into account.

other critical unsolved problems of our society—to launch a more effective attack on urban problems, on environmental problems, on such glaring, but widely unrecognized, unmet needs as our inferior record in rehabilitating the seriously disabled, and on overcoming geographic maldistribution in the availability of health and other services. An effective attack on all these problems would not only create new demands for college-educated manpower but would also enable many young people to fulfill their aspirations for more useful roles in our society.

It is in the service industries generally, and especially in particular sectors of the service industries, that workers are most likely to have a college degree or at least some college education (Appendix A, Table A-7). And it is in the service industries that the most pronounced increases in employment are projected for the 1970s, with a particularly rapid increase projected for state and local government (2, p. 259). But many of the service industries are strongly affected by public policies, on which their future growth is heavily dependent.

Recommendation 33: As debates inevitably proceed in the coming years over the reordering of national goals, the goal of fulfilling the aspirations of many young people for more useful roles in our society should be given high priority, along with the more widely recognized goal of overcoming critical human, urban, and environmental problems.

LABOR MARKET RULES AND POLICIES In higher education circles, there has been increasing interest in the past few years in encouraging students to "stop out" for a year or more either immediately after high school or during the course of their college careers. There is also rising interest in encouraging various combinations of educational and work experience—part-time jobs that will lead to later careers (not just the kinds of manual and service jobs available to students around college campuses), cooperative education programs, open universities, "universities without walls," and related developments.[6]

Underlying this trend in thought in higher education circles is a recognition that too many students feel "locked in" to a prolonged educational process that often seems unrelated to the problems they will encounter as working adults and as active members of

[6]See Appendix B for relevant earlier recommendations.

their communities. Many faculty members also have vivid recollections of the hard-working and serious attitudes of the World War II veterans on college campuses in the late 1940s. They feel that the maturity of these veterans and the fact that many of them had wives and children tended to make them more serious and thoughtful students.

However, there is little evidence as yet of much interest in these concepts in employer circles. In fact, trends in employer, union, and public labor market regulations and policies in the United States have long been in a direction that runs counter to the easy entrance of young people into employment without a college degree or specific occupational training.

A REVERSAL OF THE BRAIN DRAIN? The immigration of scientists, engineers, physicians, and nurses was an important source of supply in these occupations during the 1950s and 1960s. The annual number of natural scientists and engineers immigrating to the United States rose from 1.3 percent of the number of domestic graduates in natural sciences and engineering[7] in 1949–50 to 7.3 percent in 1957–58. The percentage then dropped somewhat in the next several years, rose steadily after that to 9.6 percent in 1967–68, and dropped slightly to 9.2 percent in 1968–69 (156). Year-to-year fluctuations were not entirely attributable to changes in employment conditions but were also explained partly by changes in immigration legislation.

Considerably more important as a relative source of supply in the practice of medicine has been the flow of foreign medical graduates into the United States. The number of foreign medical graduates receiving their first licenses to practice in the United States rose from 5.1 percent of the total number of first licenses issued in 1950 to 22.9 percent in 1967 and then fell off slightly to 22.4 percent in 1968 (73, p. 19).[8] Foreign medical graduates represented 10 percent of all licensed M.D.'s and 37.4 percent of all unlicensed M.D.'s at the end of 1968 (ibid., p. 20). Unlicensed foreign medical graduates consisted in large part of interns and residents or persons engaged in research. We also noted in Section 6 that many Americans have been attending foreign medical schools in recent years. In addition, we presented data on the inflow of nurses from abroad.

---

[7] This includes recipients of bachelor's and advanced degrees.

[8] Canadian medical graduates are included with U.S. medical graduates, rather than with foreign medical graduates.

A 21 percent decline in the number of scientists and engineers and a 10 percent decline in the number of physicians immigrating in 1969, as compared with 1968, has been attributed primarily to changes in the immigration law: (1) a new preference system reducing the number of visas available for persons lacking familial preferences (relatives in the United States), and (2) initiation of a western hemisphere quota limiting the number of persons who would otherwise have been admitted (157, pp. 1–2).

It seems unlikely that the flow of foreign medical graduates to the United States will be greatly reduced as long as a shortage of physicians persists here. In fact, the number of foreign medical graduates rose appreciably between 1969 and 1970, both in numerical terms and as a percentage of graduates of U.S. medical schools. The situation in science and engineering, however, is quite different. Continuation of a sizable flow of scientists and engineers into the United States in the face of an unpromising employment situation seems improbable, especially in view of the fact that the U.S. Department of Labor revised its procedures for certifying the immigration of scientists and engineers in February 1971, requiring that, thereafter, such persons must have a job offer for which domestic workers are not readily available, and that their employment must not adversely affect the wages and working conditions of domestic workers (ibid., p. iv). There is also some potential for increased emigration of scientists and engineers who have received degrees in the United States. Information from a recent survey of doctorates, for example, indicates that between 5 and 10 percent of new doctors of science and engineering plan employment in a foreign country upon receipt of the degree. Most of these, however, are foreign students (ibid., pp. 11–12).[9]

Meanwhile, there have been some interesting recent reports of emigration of school teachers. In West Germany, the rising demand for technical experts in industry is reported to have led to a shortage of secondary school science and mathematics teachers. Notification of available teaching jobs by the state of Hamburg, requiring basic knowledge of German, with agencies in the United States in the summer of 1971 attracted 500 applicants within two weeks, of whom 100 received firm offers and 84 accepted positions—at salaries some 10 to 40 percent below the average U.S.

---

[9]For interesting data relating to Asian engineering students, see the recent study by Niland (159).

teacher's salary. All those who accepted the German jobs had previously been teachers at the college level; half held master's degrees and the remainder held doctoral degrees. There were indications that other West German states were moving to follow Hamburg's example.

In Australia, a rise in the mandatory school attendance age from 15 to 16 has created an acute shortage of high school teachers. Through a contact with a professor at California State College at Hayward, 1,500 applications for teaching flowed to California from Australia in the summer of 1971, and 110 American teachers, chiefly from California, sailed for Australia late in August.

It is virtually impossible to predict how important this type of movement might be in the 1970s without undertaking a detailed study of demand and supply of college-educated workers abroad. One point that is illustrated by the flow of teachers to West Germany and Australia, however, is significant. In both cases, the salaries offered were well below those of teachers in the United States, but, after allowance for lower living costs, the salaries would probably not be much lower in real terms. On the other hand, foreign work-permit requirements abroad are likely to limit the importation of U.S. college-trained manpower except where there are acute shortages.

There has, of course, been a substantial flow of American college graduates abroad to serve as executives of the rapidly increasing number of foreign branches of American corporations and as U.S. government officials or technical advisers in foreign countries, as well as in the Peace Corps. But opportunities in American corporations abroad are largely confined to executives with substantial managerial experience in this country, and unofficial American government policy discourages employment of United States citizens to exceed 5 percent of total employment in an American private organization abroad. Foreign companies recruit on U.S. college campuses, but only for their own nationals who have been studying here and expect to return to their own countries. We have been informed that attempts by college placement offices to place American college graduates abroad over the course of the last 10 years or so have been without much success, although there have been some opportunities in international banking. But where there is a problem of unemployment of the country's own university graduates, as has recently been the case in France and England, such opportunities as may have existed in the past are likely to dwindle.

All things considered, it does not seem likely that employment openings for United States college graduates abroad will be an appreciable factor in the overall demand for college graduates in the coming years, but in particular fields like science and engineering a reduced rate of immigration to this country seems probable.

Although there are some exceptions, many available projections of supply and demand for college graduates and holders of advanced degrees tend to be based on data relating to United States graduates and United States employment growth, without allowing for international movements. The intensive data-collection activities of the American Physical Society, noted in Section 7, have shed light on the flow of physicists abroad in the last few years. And in the changing job market picture, there is a very real danger that cutbacks in student places and in student aid, especially at the graduate level, will have an adverse effect on opportunities for foreign students to study in this country. Recently it was reported that expenditures on Fulbright scholarships and Agency for International Development grants—the two major sources of federal support for foreign students—have leveled off (159). Moreover, foreign students have been adversely affected by the increased flow of student aid to minority groups and by the recent sharp increases in tuition for out-of-state students at public institutions. We believe that this diminution in opportunities for foreign students is undesirable. We also believe that we should plan for a future in which we shall be exporting physicians, scientists, engineers, and other professionally trained workers to provide expert advice and assistance in developing countries, rather than importing such talent.

Recommendation 34: The international migration of students and professional personnel should be explicitly incorporated into analyses of changes in demand and supply, and opportunities for student places and student aid for foreign students in the United States should not be curtailed.

10. *Concluding Remarks*

In the introductory sections of this report, we expressed our explicit rejection of a "manpower planning" requirements model as the basic general criterion for the development of higher education. Our rejection of such a model was based in large part on philosophical considerations. We believe that individuals should enjoy maximum freedom in the choice of their career objectives. And we are keenly aware that freedom of choice is not meaningful for many young people in the absence of measures designed to ensure increased equality of educational opportunity, particularly for members of disadvantaged minority groups and generally for those from low-income families. In countries that use manpower requirements models for educational planning, young persons are sometimes altogether precluded from training for occupations that are given low priority in manpower planning, and those who choose the preferred occupations may receive higher student stipends and other types of preferred treatment. Such manpower-oriented educational models are more appropriate in countries with planned economies, where manpower objectives are designed to be consistent with other objectives of the plan, than in economies in which consumer choice is expected to be the major determinant of the composition of production of goods and services.

Our analysis in this report has also demonstrated that there are two other important reasons for rejecting a manpower model of higher education. In the first place, we have found that students' choices of fields of study are highly sensitive to shifts in the job market and can be relied upon to be a major factor in the process of adjustment to occupational shifts. Colleges and universities will be well advised to be guided by these changing student choices in the allocation of their resources among fields, except, as we have noted earlier, when there are indications that the shifts may be temporary. In the second place, we have called attention to many inadequacies in current long-term projections of the market for educated manpower.

Adequate long-range manpower forecasting—especially when it is concerned with the outlook in particular professions—is an exceedingly intricate affair. In varying degrees, the methods used in many of the projections that have been developed by federal government agencies in recent years have been deficient. They have relied too heavily on past trends and have failed to take into account probable adjustments on both the demand and the supply sides of the job market. And yet, it is not at all clear that enough is known about these adjustments to permit the development of adequately sophisticated models for long-range projections. The art of economic forecasting has made notable advances in the last few decades, but it is generally agreed that even the newer sophisticated forecasting equations are more reliable for predicting the situation one or two years ahead than for long-term projections. In predicting the future market for professional manpower, however, short-term forecasts are not particularly useful because of the lengthy duration of educational preparation for many of the professions. We want to know what the market will be like four years hence or even a dozen years hence when those who are choosing their undergraduate majors will have completed their training. Some progress has been made in recent years in developing a more adequate understanding of the types of adjustments that occur in the market for educated manpower, but there is a need for much more research before we are likely to develop adequate long-range predictions of the outlook in particular professions.

We have also called attention to other deficiencies in the data available for research in this field. For example, detailed occupational data from the 1970 census were not published until December 1972, and, when they did become available, it became apparent that there were quite pronounced differences between the numbers of persons revealed by the Census as employed in certain professions and the numbers in use in very recent years in connection with projections that have been developed by federal government agencies. Some of these projections now seem quite obsolete and in need of revision. Part of the problem is that the *Current Population Survey,* which provides much of our current intercensal labor market information, is not based on a large enough sample of households to permit the development of reliable occupational data in any detail. In addition, there are various conceptual and technical differences between occupational data derived from household surveys and data derived from other current sources, as we found in the case of lawyers, for example. And yet, in the case of one occupation—teachers, except college teachers, on which the *Current Population Survey* does provide reasonably reliable data[1] —we found indications that relatively recent increases in employment revealed by that survey were not taken into account in projections of supply and demand.

We believe that some of these deficiencies can be remedied: (1) through measures designed to make occupational data from decennial censuses available more promptly, (2) through more systematic collection of occupational data from employers, and (3) through more careful analyses of differences between occupational data derived from household surveys and from other sources, such as the data compiled by professional associations and collected from employers. The proposed survey of 1 million households in 1975 would be exceedingly useful.

In previous sections we have made recommendations relating to the need for improved counseling and for improved projections relating to the various professions. We also need to improve the flow of current occupational information more generally.

Recommendation 35: Federal government agencies should take steps to improve the flow of current occupational information and to make it available more promptly.

Despite the fact that this need has long been recognized by manpower experts, and has been the subject of recommendations by a number of advisory committees to the federal government, not much progress has been made.

If we are to rely in large part on the sensitivity of student choices of fields to occupational shifts, we need to provide students with the best possible information.

Finally, students are to some degree protected from the undesirable consequences of poor choices when their education has not been too narrowly specialized. We have noted that the men included in the NBER-Thorndike sample tended to feel that broad general

---

[1]Because of the large numbers of men and women employed as teachers, they are adequately represented in the sample.

education had been of greater value to them than specialized vocationally oriented education. We strongly favor an undergraduate program that combines well-designed and well-planned general education with more specialized work in the student's major field. And, in our discussion of selected professions, we have stressed the desirability of appropriate combinations of basic analytical training and clinical or operational training. As we look forward to the remainder of the present century, we can be certain that the pace of advancement of knowledge will be more rapid than ever before and that college graduates more than ever will have to be prepared to adapt to shifts of specialty within a given occupation and in some cases to shifts from one occupation to another during the course of their lifetime careers.

Appendix A: Statistical Tables

Major occupation group and sex	1900	1910
Total male workers		
Number (in thousands)	23,711	29,847
Percent	100.0	100.0
Professional, technical, and kindred workers	3.4	3.5
Managers, officials, and proprietors, except farm	6.8	7.7
Clerical and kindred workers	2.8	4.4
Sales workers	4.6	4.6
Craftsmen, foremen, and kindred workers	12.6	14.1
Operatives and kindred workers	10.3	12.5
Private household workers	0.2	0.2
Service workers, except private household	2.9	3.6
Nonfarm laborers	14.7	14.7
Farm workers	41.7	34.7
Total female workers		
Number (in thousands)	5,319	7,445
Percent	100.0	100.0
Professional, technical, and kindred workers	8.2	9.7
Managers, officials, and proprietors, except farm	1.4	2.9
Clerical and kindred workers	4.0	9.2
Sales workers	4.3	5.1
Craftsmen, foremen, and kindred workers	1.4	1.4
Operatives and kindred workers	23.7	22.0
Private household workers	28.7	24.0
Service workers, except private household	6.7	8.5
Nonfarm laborers	2.6	1.4
Farm workers	19.0	15.8

TABLE A-1 Percentage distribution of gainful workers, 1900 to 1930, of persons in the labor force, 1940, and of employed persons, 1950 to 1970, by major occupation group and sex

SOURCES: Gertrude Bancroft, *The American Labor Force,* John Wiley and Sons, Inc., New York, 1958, p. 209; *Statistical Abstract of the United States, 1970,* p. 225; and *Manpower Report of the President, 1971,* pp. 215–216. It should be noted that there are certain differences, for 1970 in particular, between the data in this table, which are based on the *Current Population Survey* of the U.S. Bureau of the Census, and the data in Table A-4, which are based on decennial census data.

1920	1930	1940	1950	1960	1970
33,569	37,933	39,168	42,156	44,485	48,960
100.0	100.0	100.0	100.0	100.0	100.0
3.8	4.8	5.8	6.4	10.7	14.0
7.8	8.8	8.6	12.9	13.4	14.2
5.3	5.5	5.8	7.2	7.1	7.1
4.5	6.1	6.4	5.6	6.1	5.6
16.0	16.2	15.5	17.7	18.7	20.1
14.4	15.3	18.1	21.0	19.4	19.6
0.1	0.2	0.3	0.3	0.1	0.1
3.6	4.6	5.7	6.1	6.5	6.6
14.0	13.7	12.1	8.1	8.1	7.3
30.5	24.8	21.7	14.7	9.9	5.3
8,637	10,752	12,574	17,493	22,196	29,667
100.0	100.0	100.0	100.0	100.0	100.0
11.7	13.8	12.8	10.3	12.2	14.5
2.6	2.8	3.3	5.7	5.0	4.5
18.7	20.9	21.4	26.2	29.8	34.5
6.3	6.8	7.4	8.2	7.6	7.0
1.2	1.0	1.1	1.1	1.0	1.1
19.9	17.3	19.5	19.1	15.0	14.5
15.7	17.8	18.1	10.0	9.8	5.1
8.1	9.7	11.3	12.0	14.7	16.5
2.3	1.5	1.1	0.5	0.4	0.5
13.5	8.4	4.0	6.9	4.5	1.8

TABLE A-2 Male college graduates in the experienced civilian labor force, by occupation, 1950 and 1960 (numbers in thousands)

Occupation	Total		Percentage change, 1950–1960	Percent of experienced labor force		Percent with four or more years of college		"Constant college" component, 1960*		Percent of total increase in labor force
	1950	1960		1950	1960	1950	1960	Number	Percent of change in college graduates	
Total experienced civilian labor force (male)	42,068.8	45,713.4	8.7	100.0	100.0	6.9	9.7	3,819.9	60.5	100.0
Professional, technical, and kindred workers	2,965.4	4,536.1	53.0	7.0	9.9	53.5	55.8	2,295.3	75.6	43.1
Accountants and auditors	326.5	396.1	21.3	0.8	0.9	35.6	43.6	141.0	45.4	1.9
Architects	22.8	29.7	29.9	0.0†	0.1	63.4	71.6	18.8	65.2	0.2
Artists and art teachers	51.7	67.7	31.1	0.1	0.1	27.1	31.7	18.4	59.2	0.4
Clergymen	158.2	196.4	24.1	0.4	0.4	63.2	70.9	124.1	63.3	1.0
College presidents, professors, and instructors, etc.	96.0	139.0	44.7	0.2	0.3	92.2	95.3	128.1	90.7	1.2
Dentists	66.5	85.3	28.2	0.2	0.2	91.2	91.8	77.8	97.8	0.5
Designers	29.4	55.1	87.7	0.1	0.1	18.2	21.3	10.0	45.6	0.7
Draftsmen	112.6	205.9	82.9	0.3	0.5	14.3	10.3	29.4	250.0	2.6
Editors and reporters	62.1	64.8	4.3	0.1	0.1	46.6	51.7	30.2	35.3	0.1
Engineers, technical	520.5	862.0	65.6	1.2	1.9	54.3	55.7	463.8	92.0	9.4
Foresters and conservationists	25.7	33.0	28.4	0.1	0.1	36.0	37.6	11.9	84.4	0.2
Lawyers and judges	165.3	202.3	22.4	0.4	0.4	89.0	89.7	180.1	96.2	1.0
Musicians and music teachers	79.7	85.6	7.3	0.2	0.2	27.8	43.7	23.8	13.4	0.2
Natural scientists	102.7	135.6	32.1	0.3	0.3	66.1	76.0	89.7	62.8	0.9
Optometrists	14.1	15.5	10.2	0.0†	0.0†	68.3	79.9	10.6	37.9	0.0†
Personnel and labor relations workers	37.9	69.3	83.1	0.1	0.2	39.9	49.2	27.7	66.8	0.9

Pharmacists	78.0	85.2	9.2	0.2	0.2	53.8	58.9	45.8	51.1	0.2
Physicians and surgeons	168.0	214.8	27.9	0.5	0.5	95.1	98.2	204.3	87.6	1.3
Public relations and publicity writers		24.0			0.1		52.0			
Religious workers	12.4	22.0	77.9	0.0†	0.0†	36.3	53.6	8.0	48.6	0.3
Social and welfare workers, except group	24.0	35.0	46.1	0.1	0.1	55.3	66.8	19.4	61.1	0.5
Social scientists	23.1	41.5	79.4	0.1	0.1	59.1	70.5	26.9	85.4	0.5
Sports instructors and officials	34.2	51.9	51.8	0.1	0.1	63.9	66.3	33.2	90.7	0.5
Teachers, except college	287.9	476.9	65.6	0.7	1.0	76.1	86.7	362.9	74.3	5.2
Technicians	117.2	360.2	207.3	0.3	0.8	12.8	10.7	46.1	132.2	6.7
Veterinarians	11.0	15.0	36.5	0.0†	0.0†	69.6	91.1	10.4	45.9	0.1
Professional, technical, and kindred workers, n.e.c.‡	337.9	566.3	67.6	0.8	1.2	27.0	35.0	152.9	58.4	6.3
Managers, officials, and proprietors, except farm	4,272.5	4,694.5	9.9	10.2	10.3	12.3	16.8	652.9	52.3	11.6
Buyers and department heads, store	108.5	184.7	70.3	0.3	0.4	15.7	17.2	29.0	82.0	2.1
Officials, administrators, and inspectors, n.e.c.‡, public administration	182.5	232.6	27.5	0.4	0.5	20.8	22.2	49.6	86.2	1.4
Purchasing agents and buyers, n.e.c.‡	59.3	94.8	59.8	0.1	0.2	15.8	21.7	15.0	50.4	1.0
Managers, officials, and proprietors, n.e.c.‡ —salaried	1,548.3	2,248.9	45.3	3.7	4.9	16.8	22.3	397.3	58.0	19.2
Managers, officials, and proprietors, n.e.c.‡ —self-employed	2,128.5	1,704.8	−19.9	6.0	3.7	8.4	9.5	144.8	328.2	−11.6

TABLE A-2 *(continued)*

Occupation	Total		Percentage change, 1950-1960	Percent of experienced labor force		Percent with four or more years of college		"Constant college" component, 1960*		Percent of total increase in labor force
	1950	1960		1950	1960	1950	1960	Number	Percent of change in college graduates	
Managers, officials, and proprietors, except farm cont.:										
Other managers, officials, and proprietors	245.5	228.7	−6.8	0.6	0.5	7.5	8.9	17.2	−29.2	−0.5
Clerical and kindred workers	2,670.8	3,133.6	17.3	6.3	6.9	7.1	7.8	207.5	37.3	12.7
Sales workers	2,639.5	3,060.6	16.0	6.3	6.7	9.6	12.2	300.7	41.0	11.6
All other occupation groups	29,520.6	30,288.5	2.6	70.2	66.3	1.2	1.7	363.5	2.3	21.1

* The "constant college" component is the number of college graduates there would have been in the occupation in 1960 if the percentage of college graduates were the same as in 1950. Subtotals and totals were computed by adding the numbers in individual occupation groups, including subgroups of clerical and sales workers that are not shown separately in the table.

† Less than 0.05 percent.

‡ Not elsewhere classified.

SOURCES: U.S. Bureau of the Census, *1950 Census of Population*, Special Report P-E, No. 1B, *Occupational Statistics*, Washington, D.C., 1956, pp. 107–109; and ibid., *1960 Census of Population*, Vol. PC(2)-7A, *Occupational Characteristics*, Washington, D.C., 1963, pp. 116–118 and 123–125.

TABLE A-3 *Female college graduates in the experienced civilian labor force, by occupation, 1950 and 1960 (numbers in thousands)*

Occupation	Total		Percentage change, 1950–1960	Percent of experienced labor force		Percent with four or more years of college		"Constant college" component, 1960*		Percent of total increase in labor force
	1950	1960		1950	1960	1950	1960	Number	Percent of change in college graduates	
Total experienced labor force (female)	16,481.9	22,293.2	35.3	100.0	100.0	7.7	7.9	1,799.4	106.1	100.0
Professional, technical, and kindred workers	1,972.4	2,788.8	41.4	12.0	12.5	44.9	47.5	1,254.8	84.7	14.0
Accountants and auditors	57.0	78.8	38.3	0.3	0.4	13.3	11.3	10.5	214.3	0.4
Artists and art teachers	30.0	36.8	22.6	0.2	0.2	38.8	43.8	14.3	61.7	0.1
College presidents, professors, and instructors, n.e.c.†	27.8	38.4	38.1	0.2	0.2	91.1	92.3	35.0	96.4	0.2
Dietitians and nutritionists	21.7	25.3	16.7	0.1	0.1	43.1	38.8	10.9	257.1	0.1
Editors and reporters	29.4	37.7	28.2	0.2	0.2	45.5	38.8	17.2	285.7	0.1
Farm and home management advisors	5.0	6.1	24.1	0.0‡	0.0‡	82.3	82.1	5.1	111.1	0.0‡
Lawyers and judges	7.0	7.3	5.1	0.0‡	0.0‡	74.9	64.1	5.5	§	0.0‡
Librarians	50.7	73.0	44.1	0.3	0.3	49.4	53.6	36.1	78.6	0.4
Musicians and music teachers	83.0	110.7	33.5	0.5	0.5	40.1	40.8	44.4	93.6	0.5

TABLE A-3 *(continued)*

Occupation	Total		Percentage change, 1950–1960	Percent of experienced labor force		Percent with four or more years of college		"Constant college" component, 1960*		Percent of total increase in labor force
	1950	1960		1950	1960	1950	1960	Number	Percent of change in college graduates	
Professional, technical, and kindred workers cont.:										
Natural scientists	12.6	14.6	15.7	0.1	0.1	69.5	69.9	10.2	96.0	0.0‡
Nurses, professional	399.2	576.2	44.3	2.4	2.6	19.7	13.4	113.5	2,145.4	3.0
Personnel and labor relations workers	15.0	30.0	−100.3	0.1	0.1	30.1	23.9	9.0	164.3	0.3
Physicians and surgeons	11.6	15.5	33.3	0.1	0.1	79.3	88.9	12.3	69.4	0.1
Recreation and group workers	7.7	16.9	−120.4	0.0‡	0.1	47.6	35.3	8.0	191.3	0.2
Religious workers	28.7	35.4	23.1	0.2	0.2	27.5	29.4	9.7	75.0	0.1
Social and welfare workers, except group	54.0	61.4	13.7	0.3	0.3	58.2	66.3	35.7	49.5	0.1
Social scientists	11.3	13.8	21.5	0.1	0.1	47.3	50.3	6.5	76.5	0.0‡
Sports instructors and officials	11.0	24.9	−127.5	0.1	0.1	82.9	73.1	20.7	126.9	0.2
Teachers, except college	842.2	1,205.5	43.1	5.1	5.4	63.1	71.2	760.7	70.9	6.3
Technicians	67.6	133.3	−97.1	0.4	0.6	27.0	17.7	36.0	321.4	1.1
Therapists and healers	11.7	20.0	−70.9	0.1	0.1	43.4	52.8	8.7	66.7	0.1
Professional, technical, and kindred workers, n.e.c.†	188.4	227.2	20.6	1.1	1.0	19.7	27.6	44.8	31.9	0.7
Managers, officials, and proprietors, except farm	680.8	794.4	16.7	4.1	3.6	7.6	7.9	64.6	1.2	2.0
Officials, administrators, and inspectors, public administration, n.e.c.†	28.6	41.9	46.5	0.2	0.2	14.6	12.6	6.1	168.8	0.2

Managers, officials, and proprietors, n.e.c.†—salaried	221.6	342.5	54.5	1.3	1.5	10.0	10.2	34.3	94.8	2.1
Managers, officials, and proprietors, n.e.c.†—self-employed	332.0	292.6	−11.9	2.0	1.3	5.3	5.2	15.5	41.9	−0.7
Other managers, officials, and proprietors	98.5	117.4	19.2	0.6	0.5	7.4	6.1	8.7	2,395.5	0.3
Clerical and kindred workers	4,376.2	6,484.2	48.2	26.6	29.1	4.9	3.4	317.0	1,654.7	36.3
Sales workers	1,374.7	1,747.0	27.1	8.3	7.8	2.5	2.0	47.7	1,400.0	6.4
All other occupation groups	8,077.7	10,478.7	29.7	49.0	47.0	1.1	1.2	115.3	67.5	41.3

* The "constant college" component is the number of college graduates there would have been in the occupation in 1960 if the percentage of college graduates were the same as in 1950. Subtotals and totals were computed by adding the numbers in individual occupation groups, including subgroups of clerical and sales workers that are not shown separately in the table.

† Not elsewhere classified.

‡ Less than 0.05 percent.

§ Computation of a percentage would not be meaningful in this case because there was an actual decline in the number of college graduates in the occupation between 1950 and 1960, but there would have been an increase if the percentage of college graduates in 1960 were the same as in 1950.

SOURCES: U.S. Bureau of the Census, *1950 Census of Population*, Special Report P-E, No. 1B, *Occupational Statistics*, Washington, D.C.., 1956, pp. 107–109; and ibid., *1960 Census of Population*, Vol. PC(2)-7A, *Occupational Characteristics*, Washington, D.C.., 1963, pp. 116–118 and 123–125.

TABLE A-4 *Employed persons, by occupation and sex, 1960 and 1970*

Occupation and sex	1960	1970	Percent of employed workers 1960	Percent of employed workers 1970	Percentage change 1960–1970
Male					
Total employed (number in thousands)	43,491.0	47,623.8	100.0§	100.0§	9.5
Professional, technical, and kindred workers	4,473.3	6,800.6	10.3	14.3	52.0
Accountants	392.3	520.6	0.9	1.1	32.7
Architects	29.4	54.2	0.1	0.1	84.4
Computer specialists	*	204.6	*	0.4	*
Engineers	852.0	1,187.9	2.0	2.5	39.4
Foresters and conservationists	31.3	38.2	0.1	0.1	22.0
Lawyers and judges	201.5	259.2	0.5	0.5	28.6
Mathematical specialists	20.2	23.0	0.1	0.1	13.9
Librarians	11.9	22.0	‡	0.1	84.9
Life and physical scientists	127.9	175.9	0.3	0.4	37.5
Agricultural	7.5	11.7	‡	‡	56.0
Biological	9.7	19.1	‡	‡	96.9
Chemists	74.6	95.6	0.2	0.2	28.2
Geologists	19.3	19.1	‡	‡	−1.0
Physicists and astronomers	*	21.1	*	‡	*
Other life and physical scientists	3.4†	9.3†	‡	‡	173.5†
Operations and systems researchers and analysts	*	71.8	*	0.2	*
Personnel and labor relations workers	68.7	201.4	0.2	0.4	193.2
Physicians, dentists, and related practitioners	*	493.1	*	1.0	*
Chiropractors	12.6	12.6	‡	‡	0.0
Dentists	85.1	87.7	0.2	0.2	3.1
Optometrists	15.5	16.5	‡	‡	6.5
Pharmacists	84.8	96.6	0.2	0.2	13.9
Physicians (including osteopaths)	217.9	255.1	0.5	0.5	17.1
Veterinarians	14.9	18.4	‡	‡	23.5
Other health practitioners	*	6.2	*	‡	*

| Occupation and sex | 1960 | 1970 | Percent of employed workers | | Percentage change |
			1960	1970	1960–1970
Registered nurses, dietitians, and therapists	32.7	53.1	0.1	0.1	62.7
Dietitians	1.8	3.2	‡	‡	77.8
Registered nurses	14.0	22.3	‡	‡	59.3
Therapists	16.9	27.6	‡	0.1	63.3
Health technologists and technicians	52.3	78.9	0.1	0.2	50.9
Religious workers	217.2	227.6	0.5	0.5	4.8
Clergymen	195.3	211.8	0.5	0.5	8.5
Other religious workers	21.9	15.8	0.1	‡	−27.9
Social scientists	26.8	87.7	0.1	0.2	227.2
Economists	16.0	58.6	‡	0.1	266.3
Psychologists	8.2	17.2	‡	‡	109.8
Other social scientists	2.6	11.9	‡	‡	357.7
Social and recreation workers	56.0	109.9	0.1	0.2	96.3
Social	34.5	80.8	0.1	0.2	134.2
Recreation	21.5	29.1	0.1	0.1	35.4
Teachers, college and university	138.3†	348.2†	0.3	0.7	151.8†
Teachers, except college and university	474.0†	815.7†	1.1	1.7	72.1†
Elementary and secondary school teachers	416.2†	741.0†	1.0	1.6	78.0†
Other teachers	57.8†	74.7†	0.1	0.2	29.2†
Engineering and science technicians	451.3	715.3	1.0	1.5	58.5
Technicians, except health, and engineering and science	*	137.9	*	0.3	*
Airline pilots	26.7	49.7	0.1	0.1	86.1
Radio operators	21.5	21.1	0.1	‡	−1.9
Other technicians	51.0	67.1	0.1	0.1	31.6
Vocational and educational counselors	*	60.1	*	0.1	*
Writers, artists, and entertainers	*	526.8	*	1.1	*

TABLE A-4 *(continued)*

Occupation and sex	1960	1970	Percent of employed workers		Percentage change 1960–1970
			1960	*1970*	
Professional, technical, and kindred workers cont.:					
Writers, artists, and entertainers cont.:					
Actors	6.0	5.8	‡	‡	−3.3
Athletes and kindred workers	*	35.0	*	0.1	*
Authors	19.8	18.0	0.1	‡	−9.1
Dancers	*	1.1	*	‡	*
Designers	53.8	83.1	0.1	0.2	54.5
Editors and reporters	63.7	87.6	0.2	0.2	37.5
Musicians and composers	*	56.3	*	0.1	*
Painters and sculptors	*	64.6	*	0.1	*
Photographers	44.9	55.8	0.1	0.1	24.3
Public relations men and publicity writers	23.3	54.4	0.1	0.1	133.5
Radio and television announcers	*	19.8	*	‡	*
Other writers, artists and entertainers	*	45.3	*	0.1	*
Research workers, not specified	*	86.0	*	0.2	*
Professional, technical and kindred workers, not elsewhere classified	548.0†	301.5†	1.3	0.6	†
Managers and administrators, except farm	4,627.8	5,315.8	10.6	11.2	14.9
Salaried	2,905.3†	4,399.3†	6.7	9.2	51.4†
Self-employed	1,722.5†	916.5†	4.0	1.9	−46.8†
Sales workers	2,983.7	3,303.8	6.9	6.9	10.7
Clerical and kindred workers	3,027.8	3,642.4	7.0	7.7	20.3
Craftsmen and kindred workers	8,500.5	10,088.5	19.5	21.2	18.7
Operatives	8,663.8	9,309.4	19.9	19.6	7.5
Laborers, except farm	2,982.9	3,147.0	6.9	6.6	5.5
Farm workers	3,587.3	2,143.0	8.3	4.5	−40.3
Service workers, including private household	2,660.1	3,873.3	6.1	8.1	45.6
Occupation not reported	1,983.8		4.6		

Occupation and sex	1960	1970	Percent of employed workers		Percentage change 1960–1970
			1960	1970	
Female					
Total employed (number in thousands)	21,155.6	28.929.9	100.0§	100.0§	36.8
Professional, technical, and kindred workers	2,749.9	4,550.6	13.0	15.7	65.5
Accountants	77.8	182.9	0.4	0.6	135.1
Architects	0.6	2.0	‡	‡	233.3
Computer specialists	*	49.9	*	0.2	*
Engineers	7.5	19.6	‡	0.1	161.3
Lawyers and judges	7.1	13.2	‡	0.1	85.9
Mathematical specialists	8.5	12.0	‡	‡	41.2
Life and physical scientists	12.2	26.6	0.1	0.1	118.0
Biological	3.7	10.3	‡	‡	178.4
Chemists	6.5	12.9	‡	0.1	98.5
Other life and physical scientists	2.0	3.4	‡	‡	70.0
Operations and systems researchers and analysts	*	7.6	*	‡	*
Personnel and labor relations workers	29.6	89.3	0.1	0.3	201.7
Physicians, dentists, and related practitioners	*	45.7	*	0.2	*
Dentists	1.8	3.1	‡	‡	72.2
Optometrists	0.7	0.7	‡	‡	0.0
Pharmacists	7.4	13.0	‡	0.1	75.7
Physicians, including osteopaths	15.9	25.8	0.1	0.1	62.3
Other health practitioners	*	3.1	*	‡	*
Registered nurses, dietitians, and therapists	583.5	891.9	2.8	3.1	52.8
Dietitians	24.6	36.9	0.1	0.1	50.0
Registered nurses	539.3	807.4	2.6	2.8	49.7
Therapists	19.6	47.6	0.1	0.2	142.9
Health technologists and technicians	86.6	180.9	0.4	0.6	108.9

TABLE A-4   *(continued)*

| Occupation and sex | 1960 | 1970 | Percent of employed workers | | Percentage change |
			1960	1970	1960–1970
Religious workers	39.6	26.0	0.2	0.1	−34.1
Clergymen	4.4	6.2	‡	‡	40.9
Other religious workers	35.2	19.8	0.2	0.1	−43.8
Social scientists	7.2	20.8	‡	0.1	188.9
Economists	2.6	7.4	‡	‡	184.6
Psychologists	3.6	10.6	‡	‡	194.4
Other social scientists	1.0	2.8	‡	‡	180.0
Social and recreation workers	76.5	156.0	0.4	0.5	104.1
Social	60.6	135.8	0.3	0.5	124.1
Recreation	15.9	20.2	0.1	0.1	27.0
Teachers, college and university	38.0†	138.1†	0.2	0.5	263.4†
Teachers, except college and university	1,196.7†	1,926.2†	5.7	6.7	61.0†
Elementary and secondary school teachers	1,104.5†	1,674.4†	5.2	5.8	51.6†
Other teachers	92.2†	251.8†	0.4	0.9	173.1†
Engineering and science technicians	27.7	87.8	0.1	0.3	217.0
Technicians, except health, and engineering and science	18.9	17.6	0.1	0.1	−6.9
Airline pilots	0.2	0.7	‡	‡	250.0
Radio operators	2.9	7.3	‡	‡	151.7
Other technicians	15.8	9.6	0.1	‡	−39.2
Vocational and educational counselors	*	46.6	*	0.2	*
Writers, artists, and entertainers	*	227.4	*	0.8	*
Actors	3.3	3.9	‡	‡	18.2
Athletes and kindred workers	*	13.5	*	0.1	*
Authors	7.7	7.4	‡	‡	−3.9
Dancers	*	4.9	*	‡	*
Designers	11.9	25.7	0.1	0.1	116.0
Editors and reporters	36.6	59.4	0.2	0.2	62.3
Musicians and composers	*	31.5	*	0.1	*

Occupation and sex	1960	1970	Percent of employed workers		Percentage change 1960–70
			1960	1970	
Writers, artists, and entertainers cont.:					
Painters and sculptors	*	36.3	*	0.1	*
Photographers	5.8	8.9	‡	‡	53.5
Public relations workers and publicity writers	7.3	19.4	‡	0.1	165.8
Radio and television announcers	*	1.5	*	‡	*
Other writers, artists, and entertainers	*	15.0	*	0.1	*
Research workers, not specified	*	29.9	*	0.1	*
Professional, technical, and kindred workers, not elsewhere classified	433.5†	352.7†	2.1	1.2	†
Managers and administrators, except farm	780.0	1,055.4	3.7	3.7	35.3
Salaried	482.6†	844.1†	2.3	2.9	74.9†
Self-employed	297.4†	211.3†	1.4	0.7	−29.0†
Sales workers	1,660.1	2,141.6	7.9	7.4	29.0
Clerical and kindred workers	6,275.5	10,105.8	29.7	34.9	61.0
Craftsmen and kindred workers	252.9	521.1	1.2	1.8	106.1
Operatives	3,256.7	4,147.1	15.4	14.3	27.3
Laborers, except farm	110.3	284.3	0.5	1.0	157.8
Farm workers	360.7	224.1	1.7	0.8	−37.9
Service workers, except private household	2,856.0	4,790.0	13.5	16.6	67.7
Private household workers	1,655.7	1,109.9	7.8	3.8	−33.0
Occupation not reported	1,197.8	*	5.7	*	*

* Not available or not comparable in 1960.

† Affected by reclassification. Art, dancing, and music teachers were classified under categories such as "artists and art teachers" in 1960 but were classified as teachers in 1970. This means that percentage increases in the number of college and university teachers as well as in other teacher categories between 1960 and 1970 are somewhat overstated. The increase in the number of salaried managers is also somewhat overstated because of a change in classification that occurred in 1967.

‡ Less than 0.05 percent.

§ In some cases, items do not add to subtotals because of rounding.

SOURCES: U.S. Bureau of the Census: *1960 Census of Population,* Subject Report PC(2)-7A, *Occupational Characteristics,* Washington, D.C. 1963, Table 3; and U.S. Bureau of the Census: *1970 Census of Population,* Subject Report PC(2)-7C, *Occupation by Industry,* Washington, D.C., 1972, Tables 1 and 8.

TABLE A-5 *Bachelor's and first-professional degrees awarded, by field, selected five-year periods, 1901 to 1950*

Field	1901–1905	1921–1925	1931–1935	1941–1945	1946–1950
Total number (in thousands)	149.5	360.2	684.8	779.9	1,412.2
Total percent	100.0	100.0	100.0	100.0	100.0
Natural science	13.3	12.7	10.4	10.9	10.7
Chemistry	3.7	4.1	2.9	3.3	2.8
Physical science	3.7	3.7	3.0	2.9	2.6
Earth science	1.1	1.4	1.0	1.0	0.8
Biological science	4.8	3.5	3.5	3.7	4.5
Social science	1.7	5.7	7.3	8.7	10.6
Economics	1.0	3.2	3.2	3.0	3.3
Psychology	0.3	0.9	1.3	1.7	2.2
Other	0.4	1.6	2.8	4.0	5.1
Humanities and arts	27.7	21.6	19.0	16.0	14.8
English	7.0	7.0	6.2	5.2	4.4
Fine arts	1.2	1.4	2.8	3.8	4.1
History	2.4	3.1	2.9	3.1	3.2
Language	12.2	8.0	5.3	2.6	1.5
Philosophy	4.9	2.1	1.8	1.3	1.6
Engineering	3.3	10.3	8.0	8.8	11.3
Applied biology	0.2	5.1	4.2	6.5	5.3
Agriculture	0.2	3.3	1.9	2.2	2.7
Home economics		1.8	2.3	4.3	2.6
Health fields	33.2	12.1	7.0	7.4	5.9
Medicine	18.6	4.5	3.6	3.4	2.1
Dentistry	8.0	3.3	1.4	1.5	0.8
Other	6.6	4.3	2.0	2.5	3.0
Business and commerce	0.2	5.8	6.9	8.6	14.6
Education	0.4	7.5	20.1	22.4	14.8
Other fields	20.0	19.2	17.1	10.7	12.0
Law	11.2	8.2	6.1	2.4	3.4
Other professions*	0.1	0.8	2.2	2.3	2.4
All other	8.7	10.2	8.8	6.0	6.2

* Includes architecture, journalism, library science, and social work.

SOURCE: D. Wolfle: *America's Resources of Specialized Talent: A Current Appraisal and a Look Ahead,* The Report of the Commission on Human Resources and Advanced Training, Harper and Brothers, New York, 1954, pp. 292–295.

TABLE A-6 *Doctor's degrees awarded, by field, selected five-year periods, 1911 to 1950*

Field	1911–1915	1921–1925	1931–1935	1941–1945	1946–1950
Total number	2,460	2,080	13,420	14,490	21,060
Total percent	100.0	100.0	100.0	100.0	100.0
Natural science	44.2	44.1	45.4	47.9	38.3
Chemistry	14.5	16.0	17.9	20.0	15.1
Physical science	10.7	9.4	8.4	7.0	8.5
Earth science	4.8	4.3	3.2	2.3	2.6
Biological science	14.2	14.4	15.9	18.6	11.7
Other					0.4
Social science	15.4	15.6	13.5	13.4	13.0
Economics	5.0	6.1	5.1	4.9	3.8
Psychology	4.8	4.6	4.0	3.6	4.1
Other	5.6	4.9	4.4	4.9	5.1
Humanities	33.1	26.0	22.7	22.2	19.5
English	7.7	6.1	5.8	5.3	4.1
Fine arts	0.2	0.3	0.5	2.0	3.5
History	6.2	5.9	5.6	4.4	4.2
Language	13.1	8.1	6.4	5.2	3.1
Philosophy	5.9	5.6	4.4	5.3	4.6
Engineering	0.4	1.3	2.5	1.6	5.6
Applied biology	1.6	1.6	2.4	2.7	4.8
Agriculture	1.6	1.6	2.4	2.5	4.5
Home economics				0.2	0.3
Health fields			0.4	0.4	1.0
Business and commerce					0.7
Education	4.9	10.9	12.4	11.3	14.2
Other fields	0.4	0.5	0.7	0.5	2.9
Law	0.4	0.5	0.6	0.3	0.5
Other professions*			0.1	0.2	0.3
All other					2.1

*Includes architecture, journalism, library science, and social work.

SOURCE: D. Wolfle: *America's Resources of Specialized Talent: A Current Appraisal and a Look Ahead,* The Report of the Commission on Human Resources and Advanced Training, Harper and Brothers, New York, 1954, pp. 298–301.

TABLE A-7
Industry of employed persons 18 years old and over by sex and years of school completed, 1968 and 1971

Sex, industry group, and selected industries	1968			
	Total employed (percent)	*No college*	*1–3 years college*	*4 years or more*
Male				
Agriculture	100	91	6	3
Nonagricultural industries	100	72	13	15
Mining	100	81	10	9
Construction	100	87	9	4
Manufacturing	100	79	11	10
Durable goods	100	79	11	10
Nondurable goods	100	79	11	10
Transportation and public utilities	100	82	12	6
Trade	100	76	16	8
Finance, insurance, and real estate	100	50	23	27
*Service**	100	51	12	37
Private households	100	90	9	1
*Other services**	100	51	12	37
Business and repair	100	76	13	11
Personal	100	83	12	5
Entertainment and recreation	100	70	18	12
Professional services	100	33	11	56
Medical	100	20	5	75
Hospital	100	67	10	23
Welfare	100	40	12	48
Education	100	27	11	62
Other	100	26	17	57
Public Administration	100	65	16	19
Postal	100	74	22	4
Other federal	100	56	14	30
State	100	55	14	31
Local	100	72	15	13

	1971		
Total employed (percent)	*No college*	*1–3 years college*	*4 years or more*
100	88	8	4
100	70	14	16
100	83	8	9
100	85	10	5
100	77	12	11
100	78	12	10
100	76	12	12
100	80	13	7
100	73	17	10
100	44	26	30
100	46	14	40
100	75	9	6
100	46	14	40
100	71	16	13
100	82	13	5
100	66	20	14
100	30	13	57
100	23	6	71
100	61	13	26
100	31	10	59
100	26	12	62
100	24	19	57
100	65	18	17
100	76	20	4
100	53	17	30
100	56	18	26
100	70	20	10

TABLE A-7 *(continued)*

Sex, industry group, and selected industries	1968			
	Total employed (percent)	No college	1–3 years college	4 years or more
Female				
Agriculture	100	91	6	3
Nonagricultural industries	100	76	13	11
Mining				
Construction	100	80	14	6
Manufacturing	100	90	8	2
Durable goods	100	89	9	2
Nondurable goods	100	92	6	2
Transportation and public utilities	100	80	16	4
Trade	100	88	10	2
Finance, insurance, and real estate	100	79	17	4
*Service**	100	64	15	21
Private households	100	95	4	1
*Other services**	100	58	17	25
Business and repair	100	75	19	6
Personal	100	91	7	2
Entertainment and recreation	100	77	14	9
Professional services	100	51	18	31
Medical	100	70	20	10
Hospital	100	70	21	9
Welfare	100	72	16	12
Education	100	31	17	52
Other	100	65	20	15
Public administration	100	73	17	10
Postal	100	78	19	3
Other federal	100	76	18	6
State	100	68	15	17
Local	100	69	16	15

* Includes forestry and fisheries.

SOURCES: U.S. Bureau of Labor Statistics, *Educational Attainment of Workers, March 1968,* Special Labor Force Report, No. 103, Washington, D.C., 1969, pp. A-17 and A-18; and U.S. Bureau of Labor Statistics, *Educational Attainment of Workers, March 1971,* Special Labor Force Report No. 140, Washington, D.C., 1972, pp. A-19 and A-20.

	1971		
Total employed (percent)	*No college*	*1–3 years college*	*4 years or more*
100	85	14	1
100	74	14	12
100	73	21	6
100	89	8	3
100	88	9	3
100	89	8	3
100	77	17	6
100	85	12	3
100	75	21	4
100	63	15	22
100	95	4	1
100	58	17	25
100	73	19	8
100	90	8	2
100	71	15	14
100	51	18	31
100	72	19	9
100	67	22	11
100	57	19	24
100	33	16	51
100	68	20	12
100	71	21	8
100	75	21	4
100	66	26	8
100	71	17	12
100	75	19	6

TABLE A-8
Employment by major nonagricultural industry group, 1950 to 1970

Major industry group	1950	1960	1970	Percentage change	
				1950–1960	1960–1970
Total employed workers (in thousands)	45,222	54,234	70,616	19.9	30.2
Mining	901	712	622	−21.0	−12.6
Construction	2,333	2,885	3,345	23.7	15.9
Manufacturing	15,241	16,796	19,369	10.2	15.3
Transportation and public utilities	4,034	4,004	4,504	− 0.7	12.5
Wholesale and retail trade	9,386	11,391	14,922	21.4	31.0
Finance, insurance, and real estate	1,919	2,669	3,690	39.1	38.3
Services	5,382	7,423	11,630	37.9	56.7
Government	6,026	8,353	12,535	38.6	50.1

SOURCE: U.S. Department of Labor: *Manpower Report of the President: Transmitted to the Congress, March 1972,* Washington, D.C., 1972, p. 215.

TABLE A-9 *Occupational distribution of men in the experienced civilian labor force, by years of college, 1960*

Occupation	All men	Men with some college		
		1 to 3 years	4 years	5 or more years
Total number (in thousands)	45,713	4,371	2,440	2,005
Total percent	100.0	100.0	100.0	100.0
Professional, technical, and kindred workers	9.9	19.3	43.3	73.6
Accountants and auditors	0.9	2.6	5.5	1.9
Architects	0.1	0.1	0.4	0.6
Clergymen	0.4	0.6	1.1	5.6
College presidents, professors, and instructors, n.e.c.	0.3	0.1	0.5	6.0
Dentists	0.2	0.1	0.6	3.2
Designers	0.1	0.4	0.4	0.3
Draftsmen	0.5	1.7	0.6	0.4
Editors and reporters	0.1	0.4	0.9	0.6

TABLE A-9 *(continued)*

Occupation	All men	Men with some college		
		1 to 3 years	*4 years*	*5 or more years*
Professional, technical, and kindred workers cont.:				
Engineers, technical	1.9	4.0	13.4	7.7
Lawyers and judges	0.4	0.3	1.0	7.8
Musicians and music teachers	0.2	0.3	0.6	1.2
Natural scientists	0.3	0.3	1.8	2.9
Personnel and labor relations workers	0.2	0.3	0.8	0.7
Pharmacists	0.2	0.6	1.5	0.7
Physicians and surgeons	0.5	0.0*	0.5	9.9
Social and welfare workers, except group	0.1	0.1	0.4	0.7
Social scientists	0.1	0.1	0.4	1.0
Sports instructors and officials	0.1	0.1	0.7	0.9
Teachers, elementary schools	0.3	0.4	2.2	3.5
Teachers, secondary schools	0.6	0.3	3.5	8.5
Teachers, n.e.c.	0.1	0.2	0.6	1.0
Technicians	0.8	2.4	0.9	0.8
Other professional, technical, and kindred workers	1.6	4.0	5.0	7.7
Managers, officials, and proprietors, except farm	10.3	19.0	22.9	11.4
Salaried managerial workers	6.5	13.5	17.9	9.3
Self-employed managerial workers	3.8	5.5	5.0	2.1
Clerical and kindred workers	6.9	12.4	7.1	3.6
Sales workers	6.7	12.5	12.1	3.9
Blue-collar workers (craftsmen, operatives, and nonfarm laborers)	47.3	24.2	8.0	3.3
Farm workers	8.1	3.4	1.9	0.6
Service workers	6.1	4.6	1.2	0.7
Occupations not reported	4.7	4.6	3.5	2.9

*Less than 0.05 percent.

SOURCE: U.S. Bureau of the Census: *1960 Census of Population,* Vol. PC(2)-7A, *Occupational Characteristics,* Washington, D.C., 1963, pp. 116–121.

TABLE A-10 *Occupational distribution of women in the experienced civilian labor force, by years of college, 1960*

		Women with some college		
Occupation	All women	1 to 3 years	4 years	5 or more years
Total number (in thousands)	22,293.2	2,473.4	1,156.3	611.7
Total percent	100.0	100.0	100.0	100.0
Professional, technical, and kindred workers	12.5	29.6	70.3	83.6
Accountants and auditors	0.4	0.9	0.6	0.3
Artists and art teachers	0.2	0.3	0.7	1.2
College presidents, professors, and instructors, n.e.c.	0.2	0.1	0.5	4.9
Designers	0.1	0.1	0.2	0.1
Dietitians and nutritionists	0.1	0.1	0.5	0.6
Draftsmen	0.1	0.1	0.1	0.1
Editors and reporters	0.2	0.4	1.0	0.6
Engineers, technical	0.0*	0.1	0.2	0.2
Lawyers and judges	0.0*	0.0*	0.1	0.6
Librarians	0.3	0.6	1.3	3.9
Musicians and music teachers	0.5	1.1	2.4	2.8
Natural scientists	0.1	0.1	0.5	0.7
Nurses, professional	2.6	9.3	4.6	4.0
Nurses, student professional	0.3	1.1	0.1	0.0*
Personnel and labor relations workers	0.1	0.3	0.4	0.3
Pharmacists	0.0*	0.1	0.3	0.2
Physicians and surgeons	0.1	0.0*	0.1	2.1
Recreation and group workers	0.1	0.2	0.3	0.3
Religious workers	0.2	0.3	0.5	0.7
Social and welfare workers, except group	0.3	0.4	1.7	3.5
Social scientists	0.1	0.1	0.2	0.7
Sports instructors and officials	0.1	0.1	1.0	1.1
Teachers, elementary schools	3.9	9.3	35.7	28.6
Teachers, secondary schools	1.1	0.7	10.0	17.0
Teachers, n.e.c.	0.4	0.9	2.7	3.3
Technicians, medical and dental	0.4	1.1	1.2	0.6

Occupation	All women	Women with some college		
		1 to 3 years	4 years	5 or more years
Professional, technicians and kindred workers cont.:				
Technicians, other	0.2	0.4	0.4	0.2
Therapists and healers	0.1	0.1	0.5	0.8
Other professional, technical, and kindred workers	0.3	1.3	2.5	4.3
Managers, officials, and proprietors, except farm	3.6	5.2	3.8	3.0
Salaried managerial workers	2.3	3.7	2.8	2.4
Self-employed managerial workers	1.3	1.5	1.0	0.6
Clerical and kindred workers	29.1	41.1	15.6	6.2
Sales workers	7.8	6.3	2.5	1.0
Blue-collar workers (craftsmen, operatives, and nonfarm laborers)	18.0	4.1	1.3	0.8
Farm workers	1.7	0.7	0.4	0.2
Service workers	21.5	8.3	2.1	1.1
Occupations not reported	5.8	4.7	4.0	4.3

*Less than 0.05 percent.

SOURCE: U.S. Bureau of the Census: *1960 Census of Population,* Vol. PC(2)-7A, *Occupational Characteristics,* Washington, D.C., 1963, pp. 124–128.

TABLE A-11 Men with some college education in NBER-Thorndike sample by educational attainment and major occupation group, 1955 and 1969	Major occupation group	Some college		Bachelor's degree		Master's degree		Ph.D., L.L.B. or M.D.	
		1955	1969	1955	1969	1955	1969	1955	1969
	Total number	978	1,060	1,199	1,152	299	401	233	385
	Total percent	100.0	100.0	100.0	100.0	100.0	100.0	100.0	100.0
	Professional	17.4	5.7	43.5	26.1	80.3	59.0	87.7	86.3
	Technical	5.0	9.5	1.7	3.1	0.7	1.3		0.3
	Managerial	36.4	59.4	31.5	63.3	13.3	39.1	6.4	12.5
	White collar	6.8	2.5	3.9	1.2	1.0	0.3	0.4	
	Sales	13.6	4.3	12.5	1.1	3.0		3.4	0.3
	Service	2.6	4.3	1.2	1.1	0.7		1.7	0.3
	Blue collar	15.9	10.9	3.8	2.0	0.3		0.4	
	Farm	2.3	3.4	1.9	2.1	0.7	0.3		0.3

NOTE: The data are based on a sample of male volunteers who had taken a battery of 17 tests administered by the Army Air Force during World War II and who were later included in a mailed questionnaire survey by Thorndike in 1955 and in a second mailed questionnaire survey conducted by the National Bureau of Economic Research in 1969. The data must be interpreted with caution because some of the respondents had experienced additional education between the two surveys and were classified in a higher education group in 1969 than in 1955. This was particularly true for those with master's or with Ph.D., LL.B., or M.D. degrees, as can be seen from the numbers in the top row of the table. The sample was also composed of men of above-average ability, for the volunteers had to pass the Aviation Cadet Qualifying Test with a score equivalent at least to that of the median of high school graduates to qualify for the other 17 tests. This may help to account for the fact that the proportions employed in managerial occupations were considerably higher than the data in Table A-4 would lead one to expect and may also suggest that the extent of shifting into the managerial group with advancing age was probably greater in the sample than for all men with some college education.

More detailed data on sources of movement into managerial positions between 1955 and 1969 (but not classified by educational level) indicate that the largest proportion of those who shifted into managerial positions (24 percent) had been in sales occupations in 1955. Other sources, in order of relative importance, were blue-collar and service occupations, engineering, other professions, clerical positions, technical positions, and contractors.

SOURCE: Adapted from data in P. Taubman and T. Wales: *Higher Education: An Investment and a Screening Device,* unpublished manuscript, National Bureau of Economic Research, New York.

High school graduates and men with some graduate education have been omitted.

		Men		Women	
		Major	*Minor*	*Major*	*Minor*
Reasons		*reason*	*reason**	*reason*	*reason**
Reasons related to career plans or interests and goals		48.5	37.8	43.1	29.8
Changed career plans		22.1	15.4	20.7	13.6
Wanted time to reconsider interests and goals		26.4	22.4	22.4	16.2
Academic and related reasons		53.5	59.4	34.1	44.8
Dissatisfied with college environment		26.7	22.3	22.3	19.7
Academic record unsatisfactory		15.5	20.8	5.8	11.1
Tired of being a student		11.3	16.3	6.0	14.0
Financial reasons		26.4	18.7	19.2	15.2
Scholarship terminated		2.8	3.1	1.4	2.5
Could not afford cost		23.6	15.6	17.8	12.7
Personal reasons		8.9	3.7	37.2	9.6
Marriage		7.8	3.1	29.0	6.1
Pregnancy		1.1	0.6	8.2	1.4
Draft		1.4	0.9	0.0	0.1

TABLE A-12 *Reasons for leaving college of matriculation, reported in 1965 by students who had entered four years earlier*

* A third alternative, "unrelated to my decision," is not shown.

SOURCE: A. W. Astin and R. J. Panos: *The Educational and Vocational Development of College Students,* American Council on Education, Washington, D.C., 1969, p. 31. Subgroups of reasons were developed by the Carnegie Commission staff.

TABLE A-13
Awards based on organized occupational curriculums at the technical or semi-professional level in institutions of higher education, by type of curriculum: aggregate United States, 1967–1968 to 1969–1970, by percent

Type of curriculum	Year		
	1967–68	*1968–69*	*1969–70*
All curriculums			
Total number	88,082	108,088	124,327
Total percent	100.0	100.0	100.0
Science- or engineering-related, total	48.4	49.2	49.3
Engineering-related, total	25.7	24.7	23.3
Science-related, total	3.0	3.0	3.1
Health service curriculums, total	19.2	20.2	21.5
Dental assistant, dental hygiene	3.0	3.0	3.1
Nursing, practical	5.0	5.2	5.0
Nursing, associate degree or diploma	7.9	8.3	9.4
All other health	3.4	3.8	4.1
Scientific data processing curriculums	.6	1.2	1.3
Non-science- and non-engineering-related, total	51.6	50.8	50.7
Business- and commerce-related, total	39.6	38.4	37.3
General business, business related	11.5	11.7	11.8
Secretarial studies	15.6	13.8	12.4
All other business and commerce related	12.5	13.0	13.2
Other nonscience and nonengineering, total	11.9	12.4	13.4
Education	2.3	2.5	2.6
Fine, applied, or graphic arts	3.9	3.3	3.4
Police technology, law enforcement	2.1	2.7	3.3
All other nonscience and non-engineering	3.7	4.0	4.1

SOURCE: U.S. Office of Education, *Associate Degrees and Other Formal Awards Below the Baccalaureate 1969–70,* Washington, D.C., 1971, p. 55.

TABLE A-14 *Probable career choices of college freshmen, by sex (weighted national norms), 1966 to 1971*

Career choice	1966	1967	1968	1969	1970	1971
Men						
Total*	100.3%	100.1%	100.1%	99.8%	100.1%	100.0%
Businessman	18.6	17.5	17.5	16.9	17.4	16.1
Lawyer	6.7	5.8	5.5	5.6	6.2	6.8
Engineer	16.3	15.0	14.6	14.5	13.3	9.7
College teacher	2.1	1.4	1.3	1.3	1.2	0.8
Teacher, elementary and secondary	11.3	11.2	12.7	10.9	9.6	7.5
Physician or dentist	7.4	6.4	5.6	4.9	5.9	6.4
Other health professions	3.2	2.7	2.9	2.8	3.0	4.1
Research scientist	4.9	3.9	3.8	3.3	3.5	3.3
Farmer or forester	3.2	3.3	2.9	3.0	3.1	4.8
Clergyman	1.2	1.9	1.1	1.4	1.3	1.0
Artist (including performer)	4.6	4.1	4.2	4.3	5.1	4.9
Other choice	15.8	16.7	16.7	19.3	19.0	21.7
Undecided	5.0	10.2	11.3	11.6	11.5	12.9
Women						
Total*	99.8	99.8	99.9	100.1	100.2	100.0
Businesswoman	3.3	3.3	3.3	3.6	4.2	4.4
Lawyer	0.7	0.6	0.6	0.8	1.0	1.4
Engineer	0.2	0.2	0.2	0.3	0.4	0.2
College teacher	1.5	0.9	0.9	0.8	0.9	0.6
Teacher, elementary and secondary	34.1	36.4	37.5	36.5	31.0	24.8
Physician or dentist	1.7	1.5	1.3	1.3	1.5	2.0
Nurse	5.3	5.4	6.1	6.0	8.7	8.6
Other health professions	6.6	6.3	5.7	6.0	6.4	8.8
Research scientist	1.9	1.6	1.7	1.4	1.6	1.5
Farmer or forester	0.2	0.1	0.1	0.2	0.4	0.7
Clergywoman	0.8	0.3	0.2	0.3	0.2	0.2
Artist (including performer)	8.9	8.1	7.8	7.6	7.6	7.2
Other choice	31.0	25.2	23.7	24.3	24.5	26.1
Undecided	3.6	9.9	10.8	11.0	11.8	13.5

*Totals may differ from 100.0 because of rounding.

SOURCE: American Council on Education: *National Norms for Entering College Freshmen,* Washington, D.C., annual, 1966 to 1971 (title varies slightly).

TABLE A-15 *Degrees awarded to men, by level and field, 1948 and 1970*

Field	Bachelor's and first-professional 1948	Bachelor's and first-professional 1970	Master's 1948	Master's 1970	Doctor's 1948	Doctor's 1970	Total 1948	Total 1970
Total number (in thousands)	176.0	486.9	28.9	126.1	3.7	25.9	208.6	639.0
Total percent	100.0	100.0	100.0	100.0	100.0	100.0	100.0	100.0
Mathematical sciences	1.5	3.5	1.9	3.2	3.2	4.4	1.6	3.5
Mathematics	n.a.	3.4	n.a.	2.9	n.a.	3.8	n.a.	3.4
Statistics	n.a.	0.1	n.a.	0.3	n.a.	0.6	n.a.	0.1
Computer sciences		0.3		1.1		0.4		0.4
Physical sciences	5.0	3.8	7.7	4.0	21.0	15.7	5.6	4.3
Chemistry	3.0	2.0	4.0	1.3	14.6	7.7	3.3	2.0
Earth sciences	n.a.	0.1	n.a.	0.3	n.a.	1.5	n.a.	0.2
Physics	1.1	1.0	2.3	1.6	5.2	5.4	1.4	1.3
Other physical sciences	0.9	0.7	1.4	0.8	2.1	1.1	0.9	0.8
Life sciences	8.4	7.8	7.4	4.5	14.5	14.0	8.4	7.4
Biological sciences	4.6	5.6	3.5	3.1	9.4	10.9	4.6	5.3
Agriculture	3.3	1.8	3.2	1.1	4.8	2.7	3.3	1.7
Forestry	0.5	0.4	0.7	0.3	0.3	0.4	0.5	0.4
Engineering	17.6	9.1	14.5	12.2	7.0	14.1	16.9	9.9
Health professions	6.4	3.8	2.6	1.8	2.5	1.2	5.8	3.3
Dentistry	0.9	0.8	0.3				0.8	0.6
Medicine	3.6	1.6	0.8			0.3	3.1	1.2
Other health professions	1.9	1.4	1.5	1.8	2.2	1.2	1.9	1.5
Social sciences	10.2	18.7	11.0	11.8	11.1	14.8	10.3	17.2
Anthropology	*	0.3	0.1	0.3	0.4	0.6	0.1	0.4
Economics (including agricultural economics)	4.4	3.4	2.8	1.7	2.9	3.6	4.0	3.1
Political science	2.1	4.3	2.3	1.3	2.4	1.8	2.2	3.5
Psychology	1.6	3.9	2.3	2.0	3.3	5.0	1.7	3.6
Sociology	1.0	2.6	1.0	0.9	1.5	1.7	1.0	2.2
Other social sciences	1.1	4.2	2.5	5.6	0.6	2.1	1.3	4.4
Arts and humanities	9.2	15.0	13.5	10.6	12.2	12.4	9.9	14.0
English	2.5	3.8	3.6	2.6	3.4	3.2	2.7	3.6
Fine and applied arts	2.0	3.2	4.0	3.3	1.9	2.3	2.3	3.2
Foreign languages	0.7	1.2	1.5	1.5	2.0	2.2	0.8	1.3
History	3.2	5.8	3.7	2.7	3.7	3.5	3.3	5.0
Philosophy	0.8	1.0	0.7	0.5	1.2	1.2	0.8	0.9

Field	Bachelor's and first-profes- sional		Master's		Doctor's		Total	
	1948	1970	1948	1970	1948	1970	1948	1970
Professional fields (other than health and education)	28.8	27.9	13.0	21.4	12.8	4.4	26.4	25.7
Architecture	0.5	0.8	0.5	0.5	0.1	*	0.5	0.7
Business and commerce	18.2	19.8	6.7	16.3	1.0	2.3	16.3	18.4
Journalism	1.2	0.7	0.7	0.5		0.1	1.1	0.6
Law	6.0	3.1†	1.3	0.7	6.5	0.1†	5.4	2.5
Religion and theology	1.7	1.9	2.8	1.8	5.0	1.5	1.9	1.9
Other professions	1.2	1.6	1.0	1.6	0.2	0.4	1.2	1.6
Education	6.6	8.5	25.5	28.3	11.7	18.1	9.3	12.8
Broad and general cur- ricula and miscellaneous	6.3	1.6	2.9	1.1	3.1	0.5	5.8	1.5

*Less than 0.05 percent.
†Data for 1948 and 1970 are not comparable, because a J.D. was classified as a doctor's degree in 1948 and as a first-professional degree in 1970.
SOURCE: U.S. Office of Education, *Earned Degrees Conferred,* Washington, D.C., annual.

TABLE A-16 *Degrees awarded to women, by level and field, 1948 and 1970*

Field	Bachelor's and first-profes- sional		Master's		Doctor's		Total	
	1948	1970	1948	1970	1948	1970	1948	1970
Total number (in thousands)	96.2	246.4	13.5	83.2	0.5	4.0	110.2	433.6
Total percent	100.0	100.0	100.0	100.0	100.0	100.0	100.0	100.0
Mathematical sciences	1.7	3.0	1.1	2.0	2.0	2.4	1.6	2.8
Mathematics	n.a.	3.0	n.a.	1.9	n.a.	1.9	n.a.	2.8
Statistics	n.a.	*	n.a.	0.1	n.a.	0.5	n.a.	*
Computer sciences		0.1		0.2		0.1		0.1
Physical sciences	2.5	0.9	2.1	1.0	8.2	5.9	2.5	0.9
Chemistry	2.1	0.6	1.6	0.5	6.0	4.2	2.1	0.6
Earth sciences		0.1		0.2		0.4		0.1
Physics	0.2	0.1	0.3	0.2	1.2	0.9	0.2	0.1
Other physical sciences	0.2	0.1	0.2	0.1	1.0	0.4	0.2	0.1
Life sciences	4.9	3.2	3.2	2.4	16.0	12.5	4.7	3.1
Biological sciences	4.7	3.1	3.1	2.3	15.4	11.8	4.5	3.0
Agriculture	0.2	0.1	0.1	0.1	0.6	0.7	0.2	0.1

Field	Bachelor's and first-professional 1948	1970	Master's 1948	1970	Doctor's 1948	1970	Total 1948	1970
Life Sciences cont.:								
Forestry	*	*	0.0	*	0.0		*	*
Engineering	0.2	0.1	0.1	0.2	0.0	0.6	0.2	0.1
Health professions	5.2	5.2	2.8	2.9	4.6	1.5	4.9	4.7
Dentistry	0.1	*	0.0	0.0	0.0	0.0	*	*
Medicine	0.8	0.2	0.2	0.0	0.8	0.0	0.7	0.2
Nursing	3,4	3.2	1.5	1.8	0.0	0.3	3.2	2.9
Other health professions	0.9	1.8	1.1	1.1	3.8	1.2	1.0	1.6
Social sciences	13.3	16.9	16.5	10.1	13.6	18.4	13.7	15.6
Anthropology	0.1	0.6	0.1	0.4	0.4	1.5	0.1	0.6
Economics (including agricultural economics)	1.4	0.6	0.9	0.3	2.0	1.3	1.3	0.5
Political science	1.2	1.5	1.0	0.5	1.8	1.4	1.2	1.3
Psychology	3.7	4.3	3.9	1.9	6.4	9.4	3.8	3.9
Sociology	4.7	5.2	1.1	0.8	2.4	2.6	4.2	4.4
Other social sciences	2.2	4.7	9.5	6.2	0.6	2.2	3.1	4.9
Arts and humanities	24.0	26.1	20.8	16.7	27.1	24.8	23.6	24.3
English	8.6	11.0	7.3	6.2	10.3	9.3	8.4	10.0
Fine and applied arts	8.2	5.9	6.7	4.4	4.2	3.6	8.0	5.6
Foreign languages	3.2	4.6	3.0	3.9	6.0	7.4	3.2	4.5
History	3.7	4.3	3.6	2.0	5.4	3.4	3.7	3.9
Philosophy	0.3	0.3	0.2	0.2	1.2	1.1	0.3	0.3
Professional fields (other than health and education)	18.1	7.5	10.5	10.5	6.0	3.2	17.2	8.1
Business and commerce	6.4	2.8	2.6	0.9	0.6	0.3	5.9	2.4
Journalism	1.4	0.7	0.4	0.4	0.0		1.3	0.6
Home economics	7.5	2.8	4.0	1.5	2.4	2.0	7.0	2.7
Law	0.4	0.3†	0.2	0.1	1.6	0.1†	0.4	0.2
Library science	1.2	0.3	0.7	6.5	0.2	0.4	1.2	1.5
Religion and theology	1.0	0.5	2.5	0.9	1.2	0.3	1.2	0.6
Other professions	0.2	0.1	0.1	0.2	0.0	0.1	0.2	0.1
Education	24.3	35.9	40.7	53.0	17.5	30.1	26.2	39.2
Broad and general curricula and miscellaneous	5.8	1.1	2.2	1.0	5.0	0.5	5.4	1.1

*Less than 0.05 percent.

† Data for 1948 and 1970 are not comparable, because a J.D. was classified as a doctor's degree in 1948 and as a first professional degree in 1970.

SOURCES: U.S. Office of Education, *Earned Degrees Conferred,* Washington, D.C., annual.

TABLE A-17 *Scientists in the National Roster of Scientific and Technical Personnel, by field and type of employer, 1970*

Field	Total	Educational institutions	Industry and business	Federal government	Nonprofit organizations	Other*
Total (percent)	100	42	31	10	3	14
Physical sciences	100	30	47	9	2	12
Chemistry	100	23	58	6	2	11
Earth and marine sciences	100	28	42	13	1	16
Atmospheric and space sciences	100	15	12	31	1	41
Physics	100	50	27	11	2	10
Mathematics and related fields	100	43	38	7	3	9
Mathematics	100	57	26	5	2	10
Computer sciences	100	14	66	8	4	8
Statistics	100	36	26	20	4	14
Biological sciences	100	60	10	10	6	14
Agricultural sciences	100	23	16	36	1	24
Social sciences	100	63	7	7	6	17
Psychology	100	56	7	6	8	23
Economics	100	59	14	11	4	12
Sociology	100	74	2	3	4	19
Political science	100	77	2	5	3	13
Anthropology	100	81	1	2	3	13
Linguistics	100	74	3	3	7	13

*Includes "other government," military," "self-employed," "other," and "no report."

SOURCE: National Science Foundation, *American Science Manpower,* 1970, NSF 71–45, Washington, D.C., 1971, pp. 19, 22, 24, 26, 45–46.

Type of employer	Total	Ph.D.	Master's	Bachelor's	Other*
Total (percent)	100	40	30	27	3
Educational institutions	100	58	29	10	3
Federal government	100	29	28	40	3
Other government	100	25	34	37	4
Military	100	14	36	38	12
Nonprofit orgs.	100	47	27	16	10
Industry and business	100	26	28	43	3
Self-employed	100	34	23	31	12
Other	100	35	31	30	4
No report	100	22	41	32	5

TABLE A-18 Scientists in the National Roster of Scientific and Technical Personnel, by type of employer and level of degree, 1970

* Includes "medical professional," "less than bachelor's," and "no report."

SOURCE: National Science Foundation, *American Science Manpower 1970,* NSF 71-45, Washington, D.C., 1971, pp. 13, 15, 17, 45–46.

Appendix B: Previous Commission Recommendations Relating to Issues Discussed in This Report

All the recommendations that have previously been made by the Commission are relevant, directly or indirectly, to the issues discussed in the present report, but we have attempted to select for inclusion in this Appendix those that are most directly concerned with the relationship of higher education to the job market for young people emerging from colleges and universities. A digest of Commission recommendations through June 1972 is available,[1] and a complete digest of all Commission recommendations will be published in connection with our final report, to be issued later in 1973.

1 *Quality and Equality: Revised Recommendations, New Levels of Federal Responsibility for Higher Education* (1970)

This report repeated some of the recommendations included in the Commission's first report, issued in 1968,[2] but also included some revised recommendations. All the recommendations relating to student aid and to cost-of-education supplements to institutions are relevant to the issues considered in the present report. Some of them were revised in minor ways in the Commission's report *Institutional Aid: Federal Support to Colleges and Universities* (1972).

Other especially pertinent recommendations in the revised *Quality and Equality* report are the following:

---

[1] Carnegie Commission on Higher Education: *A Digest and Index of Reports and Recommendations: December 1968–June 1972*, Berkeley, Calif., 1972.

[2] *Quality and Equality: New Levels of Federal Responsibility for Higher Education*, McGraw-Hill Book Company, New York, 1968.

- That the present federal aid program of guidance, counseling, and testing for identification and encouragement of able students be expanded to include development of better ways to identify potentially able students; that training courses for high school teachers and counselors should keep them up to date on financial aid, college programs, and career possibilities; and that establishment of centers should provide information about career possibilities and opportunities for postsecondary education to parents and students (p. 17).

- That the Veterans' Educational Benefit programs be continued and that benefits under such programs be revised automatically to keep pace with rising living and educational costs.

  To encourage students to seek noncollege alternatives early in their postsecondary years, . . . that a national service educational benefit program be established making educational grants available for service in various programs such as the Peace Corps or VISTA, with the amount of the benefits set at some percentage of veterans' educational benefits (p. 19).

- That federal grants for university-based research (not including federal contract research centers), regardless of changing priorities for defense and space research, be increased annually (using grants in 1967–68 as a base) at a rate equal to the five-year moving average annual rate of growth in the gross national product (p. 26).

- That there be established within the federal government a National Foundation for the Development of Higher Education whose functions would be to encourage, advise, review, and provide financial support for institutional programs designed to give new directions in curricula, to strengthen essential areas that have fallen behind or have never been adequately developed because of inadequate funding, and to develop programs for improvement of educational processes and techniques (p. 27).

2 *A Chance to Learn: An Action Agenda for Equal Opportunity in Higher Education* (1970)

- That state and federal funds be allocated to colleges and universities for specific programs to meet the present needs of inner-city schools and of desegregated schools with heterogeneous classroom enrollments (p. 6).

- That institutions of higher education, either alone or in conjunction with local school districts, establish educational opportunity centers to serve areas with major concentrations of low-income populations (pp. 7–8).

- That graduate and professional departments coordinate recruiting of disadvantaged students (p. 8).

- That programs be initiated for an individualized "foundation year" on an optional basis to all interested students (p. 14).

- That every student accepted into a program requiring compensatory education receive the necessary commitment of resources to allow his engagement in an appropriate level of course work by the end of no more than two years (p. 14).

3 *The Open-Door Colleges: Policies for Community Colleges* (1970)

- That all state plans for the development of two-year institutions of higher education should provide for comprehensive community colleges, which will offer meaningful options for college-age students and adults among a variety of educational programs, including transfer education, general education, remedial courses, occupational programs, continuing education for adults, and cultural programs designed to enrich the community environment. Within this general framework there should be opportunities for varying patterns of development and for the provision of particularly strong specialties in selected colleges (p. 17).

- That there should be coordinated efforts at the federal, state, and local levels to stimulate the expansion of occupational education in community colleges and to make it responsive to changing manpower requirements (p. 21).

- That all community colleges should provide adequate resources for effective guidance, including not only provision for an adequate professional counseling staff but also provision for involvement of the entire faculty in guidance of students enrolled in their courses (p. 22).

- That all community college districts provide for effective coordination of their guidance services with those of local high schools and for coordination of both counseling and placement services with those of the public employment offices and other appropriate agencies (p. 22).

- That, through the coordinated efforts of federal, state, and local governments, the goal of providing a community college within commuting distance of every potential student should be attained by 1980 (p. 38).

4 *Higher Education and the Nation's Health: Policies for Medical and Dental Education* (1970)

- That the number of medical school entrants should be increased to 15,300 by 1976 and to 16,400 by 1978. Toward the end of the 1970s, the question of whether the number of entrant places should continue to be increased will need to be reappraised. The expansion in the number of medical school entrants should be accomplished through an average expansion of about 39 to 44 percent in existing and developing schools by 1978, with nine new schools accounting for about 900 to 1,350 entrant places, adding another 8 to 13 percent. The number of dental school entrants should be increased at least to 5,000 by 1976 and to 5,400 by 1980 (pp. 44–45).

- That all university health science centers consider the development of programs for the training of physician's and dentist's associates and assistants, where they do not exist, and that, wherever feasible, such programs be initiated forthwith (p. 45).

- That university health science centers should adopt programs designed to recruit more women and members of minority groups as medical and dental students (p. 45).

- That university health science centers should be responsible, in their respective geographic areas, for coordinating the education of health care personnel and for cooperation with other community agencies in improving the organization of health care delivery (p. 47).

- That all universities with health science centers develop plans for accelerating premedical and medical education. That plans be developed for shortening the total duration of predental and dental education where it is unnecessarily prolonged (p. 49).

- That all universities with health science centers, and especially those developing new centers, consider plans for (1) greater integration of preprofessional and professional curricula, (2) increasing the student's options so that basic training in health-related sciences can lead on to training for a variety of health-related professions as well as medicine and dentistry, (3) awarding a master's degree at the end of this basic training period, and (4) integrating instruction in the basic sciences on main university campuses if this can be accomplished without major costs associated with the shift, without interfering with integration of basic science and clinical science instruction, and without delaying the opportunities for students to have early contact with patients (p. 52).

- That area health education centers be developed in areas at some distance from university health science centers which do not have sufficiently large populations to support university health science centers of their own, and in a few metropolitan areas needing additional training facilities but not full health science centers. These area centers would be affiliated with the nearest appropriate university health science center and would perform somewhat the same functions recommended for university health science centers, except that the education of M.D. and D.D.S. candidates would be restricted to a limited amount of clinical education on a rotational basis, and research programs would be largely restricted to the evaluation of local experiments in health care delivery systems (p. 58).

- That the federal government play a major role in the financing of health manpower education (p. 61). (Detailed recommendations were made relating to federal aid, and these recommendations played a central role in influencing the provisions of the Comprehensive Health Manpower Training Act of 1971.)

- That the federal government support the expansion and strengthening of the health manpower research programs in the Department of Health, Education and Welfare, in cooperation with the Department of Labor, to encompass broad continuous studies of health manpower supply and demand. Research funds should be made available for specialized studies of these problems in university health science centers and appropriate university research institutes (p. 77).

- That a National Health Manpower Commission be appointed to make a thorough study of changing patterns of education and utilization of health manpower, with particular reference to new types of allied health workers, to changing patterns of health care delivery, and to national licensing requirements for all health manpower (p. 78).

5 *Less Time, More Options: Education Beyond the High School* (1971)

- That service and other employment opportunities be created for students between high school and college and at stop-out points in college through national, state, and municipal youth programs, through short-term jobs with private and public employers, and through apprenticeship programs in the student's field of interest; and that students be actively encouraged to participate (p. 13).

- That postsecondary educational opportunities outside the formal college in apprenticeship programs, proprietary schools, in-service training in industry, and in military programs be expanded. Appropriate educational credit should be given for the training received, and participants should be eligible, where appropriate, for federal and state assistance available to students in formal colleges (p. 13).

- That employers, both private and public, hire and promote on the basis of talent as well as on prior certification (p. 14).

- That professions, wherever possible, create alternate routes of entry other than full-time college attendance, and reduce the number of narrow, one-level professions that do not afford opportunities for advancement (p. 14).

- That a degree (or other form of credit) should be made available to students at least every two years in their careers (and in some cases every year) (p. 15).

- That opportunities be created for persons to reenter higher education throughout their active careers in regular daytime classes, nighttime classes, summer courses, and special short-term programs, with degrees and certificates available as appropriate (p. 19).

- That opportunities be expanded for students to alternate employment and study, such as the "sandwich" programs in Great Britain and the programs at some American colleges (p. 19).

· That alternative avenues by which students can earn degrees or complete a major portion of their work for a degree be expanded to increase accessibility of higher education for those to whom it is now unavailable because of work schedules, geographic location, or responsibilities in the home (p. 20).

6 *From Isolation to Mainstream: Problems of the Colleges Founded for Negroes* (1971)

· That colleges founded for Negroes utilize the present period of transition for curriculum innovation and enrichment and that most of them concentrate on developing, in addition to general liberal arts courses, strong comprehensive undergraduate programs in preprofessional subjects and in subjects that prepare students for advanced education and high-demand occupations (p. 29).

· That more colleges founded for Negroes provide education for adult members of the black community and that the federal government and foundations give favorable consideration to requests for the support of such activities (p. 34).

7 *The Capitol and the Campus: State Responsibility for Postsecondary Education* (1971)

· That states showing a low proportion of their students within commuting distance of free-access colleges immediately undertake an evaluation of their higher education system to determine if, in fact, it lacks open access as a system and, if so, what steps need be taken to achieve reasonably open access (p. 56).

· That states enter into agreements, or make grants, for the purpose of continuing certain educational programs at private institutions (for example, Florida and Wisconsin grants to private medical schools). These should be selected after consideration of special manpower needs, evaluation of existing student places for these programs in public institutions, and the relative costs of expanding public capacity or supporting and expanding private programs (p. 97).

8 *New Students and New Places: Policies for the Future Growth and Development of American Higher Education* (1971)

· That colleges and universities continue to seek ways of sharing facilities, courses, and specialized programs through cooperative arrangements; that existing consortia make continuous efforts toward increasing the effectiveness of their cooperative programs; and that institutions — especially small colleges — that are not now members of consortia carefully consider possibilities for forming consortia with neighboring institutions (p. 94).

- That state and federal government agencies, as well as private foundations, expand programs of support for the development of external degree systems and open universities along the lines of programs initiated within the last year or so. It will also be important for governmental bodies and foundations to provide funds for evaluation of these innovative programs as they develop (p. 117).

9 *The Fourth Revolution: Instructional Technology in Higher Education* (1972)

- That the early advancement of instructional technology should be encouraged by the adequate commitment of colleges and universities to its utilization and development and by adequate support from governmental and other agencies concerned with the advancement of higher learning (p. 46).

- That a major thrust of financial support and effort on behalf of instructional technology for the next decade should be toward the development and utilization of outstanding instructional programs and materials. The academic disciplines should follow the examples of physics and mathematics in playing a significant role in such efforts (p. 48).

- That the federal government should continue to provide a major share of expenditures required for research and development in instructional technology and for introduction of new technologies more extensively into higher education at least until the end of the century (p. 118).

- That colleges and universities supplement their instructional staffs with qualified technologists and specialists to assist instructors in the design, planning, and evaluation of the new teaching-learning technology, and that institutions develop their potentials for training specialists and professionals needed to perform the functions that are associated with the increasing utilization of instructional technology (p. 74).

10 *The More Effective Use of Resources: An Imperative for Higher Education* (1972)

- That institutions of higher education seek to increase their retention rates through improved counseling programs, where these are deficient, and through establishing the practice of conducting an "exit interview" with every student who plans to withdraw (p. 61).

- That high school counseling programs be strengthened and improved, not only for the purpose of guiding students to appropriate colleges or to appropriate jobs or occupational programs, but also to dissuade poorly motivated students from entering college (p. 62).

- That leading research universities refrain from cutbacks in graduate programs except on a carefully considered, selective basis. We also recommend that institutions with less emphasis on research consider curtailment or elimination, on a selective basis, of Ph.D. programs that are not of high quality or that are too small to be operated economically. We urge great caution in the development of new Ph.D. programs in particular fields at existing doctoral-granting institutions and do not believe that there is a need for any new Ph.D.-granting institutions, although some or even many institutions will be introducing the D.A. degree (p. 97).

- That colleges and universities use great caution in adopting new degree programs and conduct periodic reviews of existing degree programs, with a view to eliminating those in which very few degrees are awarded, whether or not they are required to do so by state coordinating bodies (p. 130).

- That campuses consider the following special policies for increasing their flexibility to adjust to a period of declining rate of growth:

  Recapturing certain vacated positions for central reassignment.

  Hiring temporary and part-time faculty members.

  Providing that tenure does not necessarily apply only to the specific original assignment of a specialized field and location.

  Employing persons with subject-matter flexibility, as made easier in the training for the Doctor of Arts degree, and by encouraging persons to shift fields where this is desirable and possible.

  Providing opportunities for early retirements on a full-time or part-time basis (pp. 116–117).

- That colleges and universities review their student services, with particular reference to reducing the extent of subsidization of these services where it seems justified. However, in view of the critical need for counseling services for disadvantaged students, the changes that are occurring in patterns of participation in higher education, and the complex shifts that are taking place in the labor market for college graduates, we believe that counseling services will need to be expanded rather than contracted in many colleges and universities (p. 142).

11 *Reform on Campus: Changing Students, Changing Academic Programs* (1972)

- That diversity among institutions and within them should be a major goal of higher education, and one test of institutions and of their major segments should be how successful they have been in defining their special characters and how successful they are in achieving them (p. 40).

- That cluster and theme colleges within large institutions provide particularly good opportunities for diversity (p. 40).

- That consideration should be given to establishing campus by campus a series of coherent options for a broad learning experience among which students may choose (p. 45).

- That students should be added more generally as voting members to curriculum committees in the departments and the group majors and the professional schools where they are majors, and on committees concerned with broad learning experiences, or be given some other forum for the expression of their opinions (p. 47).

- That the process of change in each institution should be examined to assure (a) that innovation can be initiated without unnecessary impediments, (b) that all innovations of significance are subject to subsequent evaluation and review, and (c) that all experimental programs include a specific time plan for their termination or for their incorporation into the mainstream of the academic program (pp. 64–65).

- That 1 to 3 percent of all funds should be taken each year from existing programs, set aside as a self-renewal fund, and directed to new or expanded programs (p. 65).

12 *The Campus and the City: Maximizing Assets and Reducing Liabilities* (1972)

- That urban campuses, in appropriate instances, offer certain portions of their programs in off-campus facilities—at industrial plants, in business and government offices, and at public libraries and schoolrooms in residential areas (p. 50).

- That consideration should be given to the establishment of *learning pavilions* at community colleges and comprehensive colleges located in central cities (p. 50).

- That the Urban Corps provide an excellent mechanism for giving opportunities to students to have experience in city government and that cities that do not now have such programs should seriously consider developing them (p. 72).

- That in each metropolitan area with population in excess of one million, there should be established:
  (1) A metropolitan higher education council
  (2) A metropolitan educational opportunity counseling center (p. 113).

References

1   Folger, J. K., and C. B. Nam: *Education of the American Population,* U.S. Bureau of the Census, Washington, D.C., 1967.

2   U.S. Department of Labor: *Manpower Report of the President: Transmitted to the Congress, March 1972,* Washington, D.C., 1972.

3   Flanders, R. B.: "Employment Patterns for the 1970s," *Occupational Outlook Quarterly,* vol. 14, pp. 2–17, Summer 1970.

4   Folger, J. K., H. S. Astin, and A. E. Bayer: *Human Resources and Higher Education: Staff Report of the Commission on Human Resources and Advanced Education,* Russell Sage Foundation, New York, 1970.

5   U.S. Office of Manpower, Automation, and Training: *Formal Occupational Training of Adult Workers,* Washington, D.C., 1964.

6   Withey, S., et al.: *A Degree and What Else? Correlates and Consequences of a College Education,* McGraw-Hill Book Company, New York, 1972.

7   Bowen, H. R.: *Manpower and Higher Education,* unpublished paper presented at meeting of Association of Graduate Schools, Oct. 19, 1972.

8   Carnegie Commission on Higher Education: *Reform on Campus: Changing Students, Changing Academic Programs,* McGraw-Hill Book Company, New York, 1972.

9   Berg, I.: *Education and Jobs: The Great Training Robbery,* Praeger Publishers, Inc., New York, 1970.

10 Bowen, W. G., and T. A. Finegan: *The Economics of Labor Force Participation,* Princeton University Press, Princeton, N.J., 1969.

11 Thurow, L. B.: "Measuring the Economic Benefits of Education," in M. S. Gordon (ed.), *Higher Education and the Labor Market,* McGraw-Hill Book Company, New York, forthcoming.

12 Psacharopoulos, G.: "The Economic Returns to Higher Education in Twenty-Five Countries," *Higher Education: An International Journal of Higher Education and Educational Planning,* vol. 1, pp. 141–158, May 1972.

13 Spaeth, J. L., and A. M. Greeley: *Recent Alumni and Higher Education: A Survey of College Graduates,* McGraw-Hill Book Company, New York, 1970.

14 Keniston, K., and M. Gerzon: "Human and Social Benefits," in American Council on Education, *Universal Higher Education: Costs and Benefits,* Washington, D.C., 1971.

15 Smith, A.: *The Wealth of Nations,* The Modern Library, Inc., Random House, Inc., New York, 1937.

16 Rudolph, F.: *The American College and University,* Alfred A. Knopf, Inc., New York, 1962.

17 U.S. Bureau of the Census: *1950 Census of Population,* special report PE, no. 1B, *Occupational Statistics,* Washington, D.C., 1956.

18 U.S. Bureau of Labor Statistics: *Special Labor Force Report,* selected issues, Washington, D.C., 1959 to 1972.

19 Edwards, A. M.: *Comparative Occupation Statistics for the United States, 1940,* Washington, D.C., 1943.

20 Folk, H.: *The Shortage of Scientists and Engineers,* D. C. Heath & Company, Lexington, Mass., 1970.

21 National Science Foundation: *National Patterns of R&D Resources: Funds and Manpower in the United States, 1953–1972,* NSF 72-300, Washington, D.C., 1971.

22 *Economic Report of the President: Transmitted to the Congress, March 1972,* Washington, D.C., 1972.

23 U.S. Bureau of the Census: *1960 Census of Population,* subject report PC(2)-7A, *Occupational Characteristics,* Washington, D.C., 1963.

24 U.S. Bureau of the Census: *1970 Census of Population,* subject report PC(2)-7C, *Occupation by Industry,* Washington, D.C., 1972.

25 U.S. Bureau of Labor Statistics: *College Educated Workers, 1968–80: A Study of Supply and Demand,* Bulletin 1673, Washington, D.C., 1970.

26 U.S. Bureau of Labor Statistics: *The U.S. Economy in 1980: A Summary of BLS Projections,* Bulletin 1673, Washington, D.C., 1970.

27 U.S. Office of Education: *Projections of Educational Statistics to 1980–81: 1971 Edition,* Washington, D.C., 1972

28 Kreps, J. M.: *Sex in the Market Place: American Women at Work,* Johns Hopkins Press, Baltimore, 1971.

29 Carnegie Commission on Higher Education: *New Students and New Places: Policies for the Future Growth and Development of American Higher Education,* McGraw-Hill Book Company, New York, 1971.

30 Carnegie Commission on Higher Education: *The Open-Door Colleges: Policies for Community Colleges,* McGraw-Hill Book Company, New York, 1970.

31 Astin, A. W.: *College Dropouts: A National Profile,* American Council on Education, research reports, vol. 7, no. 1, Washington, D.C., 1972.

32 Haber, S.: "The Professions and Higher Education in America: A Historical View," in M. S. Gordon (ed.), *Higher Education and the Labor Market,* McGraw-Hill Book Company, New York, forthcoming.

33 U.S. Bureau of the Census: *1950 Census of Population,* special report PE, no. 5B, *Education,* Washington, D.C. 1953.

34 U.S. Bureau of the Census: *1960 Census of Population,* vol. 1, part 1, *Characteristics of the Population: U.S. Summary,* Washington, D.C., 1964.

35 U.S. Bureau of the Census: "Income in 1969 of Families and Persons in the United States," *Current Population Reports: Consumer Income,* ser. P-60, no. 75, Washington, D.C., 1970.

36 Becker, G.: *Human Capital: A Theoretical and Empirical Analysis,* Columbia University Press, New York, 1964.

37 Freeman, R. B.: "The Implications of the Changing Labor Market for Members of Minority Groups," in M. S. Gordon (ed.), *Higher Education and the Labor Market,* McGraw-Hill Book Company, New York, forthcoming.

38 Freeman, R. B.: *Black Elite,* unpublished manuscript, Department of Economics, University of Chicago, Chicago, Ill.

39 U.S. Bureau of Labor Statistics: *Special Labor Force Report,* no. 140, Washington, D.C., 1972.

40 Endicott, F. S.: *Trends in Employment of College and University Graduates in Business and Industry,* Northwestern University, Evanston, Ill., 1971.

41 National Education Association: *Economic Status of the Teaching Profession, 1970–71,* Washington, D.C., 1971.

42 Kuznets, S.: "Economic Growth and Income Inequality," *American Economic Review,* vol. 45, pp. 1–28, March 1955.

43 Clark, C.: *Conditions of Economic Progress,* Macmillan and Company, London and New York, 3d ed., 1957.

44 Keat, P. G.: "Long-Run Changes in Occupational Wage Structure, 1900–1956," *Journal of Political Economy,* vol 68, pp. 584–600, December 1960.

45 Chiswick, B. R., and J. Mincer: "Time-Series Changes in Personal Income Inequality in the United States from 1939, with Projections to 1985," *Journal of Political Economy,* vol 80, pp. S34–S36, May–June 1972.

46 Gordon, M. S.: "The Changing Labor Market for College Graduates,"

in M. S. Gordon (ed.), *Higher Education and the Labor Market,* McGraw-Hill Book Company, New York, forthcoming.

47 *Chronicle of Higher Education,* Feb. 16, 1970.

48 *Economic Report of the President: Transmitted to the Congress, February 1971,* Washington, D.C., 1971.

49 *Chronicle of Higher Education,* June 7, 1971.

50 *Monthly Labor Review,* vol. 95, October 1972.

51 *New York Times,* Jan. 8, 1973.

52 **U.S. Bureau of Labor Statistics:** *The College Graduate and the World of Work,* New York, September 1972.

53 "Graduate Unemployment in the United Kingdom," *Bulletin, International Association of Universities,* vol. 20, pp. 8–11, February 1972.

54 "France: Mass Higher Education Produces Diplomas but not Jobs," *Science,* vol. 176, pp. 264–267, Apr. 21, 1972.

55 **Peterson, R. E.:** *American College and University Enrollment Trends in 1971,* Carnegie Commission on Higher Education, Berkeley, Calif., 1972.

56 *New York Times,* July 16, 1972.

57 *New York Times,* Apr. 20, 1972.

58 *San Francisco Chronicle,* Dec. 25, 1972.

59 **Coleman, J. S., et al.:** *Equality of Educational Opportunity.* Government Printing Office, Washington, D.C., 1966, 2 vols.

60 **Jencks, C., et al.:** *Inequality: A Reassessment of the Effect of Family and Schooling in America,* Basic Books, Inc., Publishers, New York, 1972.

61 **Bowles, S. E.:** "Toward Equality of Educational Opportunity?" *Harvard Educational Review,* vol. 38, pp. 89–99, Winter 1968.

62 **Perl, L. J.:** *The Role of Educational Investment and Family Background in the Production and Distribution of Educational Services,* unpublished manuscript, School of Industrial Relations, Cornell University, Ithaca, N.Y.

63 **Armor, D. J.:** "The Evidence of Busing," *The Public Interest,* no. 28, pp. 90–120, Summer 1972.

64 **Pettigrew, T. F.:** *A Brief Critique of the Armor Anti-Busing Article,* Memorandum to the Commissioners, U.S. Commission on Civil Rights, Washington, D.C., Sept. 29, 1972. (The memorandum is a brief summary of a longer article to be published in *The Public Interest,* Winter 1973).

65 **Conant, J. B.:** *Slums and Suburbs: A Commentary on Schools in Metropolitan Areas,* McGraw-Hill Book Company, New York, 1961.

66 **Carnegie Commission on Higher Education:** *A Chance to Learn: An Action*

Agenda for Equal Opportunity in Higher Education, McGraw-Hill Book Company, New York, 1970.

67   *New York Times,* Feb. 7, 1972.

68   **Dunham, A. E.:** *Colleges of the Forgotten Americans: A Profile of State Colleges and Regional Universities,* McGraw-Hill Book Company, New York, 1969.

69   **Hodgkinson, H. L.:** *Institutions in Transition: A Profile of Change in Higher Education,* McGraw-Hill Book Company, New York, 1971.

70   **New York State Education Department:** *Master's Degrees in the State of New York, 1969–70,* Albany, N.Y., 1972.

71   **Stone, J.:** *Breakthrough in Teacher Education,* Jossey-Bass, Inc., San Francisco, 1968.

72   *Chronicle of Higher Education,* Jan. 24, 1972.

73   **Blumberg, M. S.:** *Trends and Projections of Physicians in the United States, 1967–2002,* Carnegie Commission on Higher Education, Berkeley, Calif., 1971.

74   **National Commission for the Study of Nursing and Nursing Education:** *An Abstract for Action,* McGraw-Hill Book Company, New York, 1970.

75   *Nursing Outlook,* vol 18, December 1970.

76   **National Education Association:** *Salary Schedules for Teachers, 1970–71,* research report, Washington, D.C., 1970.

77   **Altman, S. H.:** *Present and Future Supply of Registered Nurses,* U.S. Public Health Service, Bethesda, Md., 1971.

78   *Nursing Outlook,* vol. 19, December 1971.

79   **Brown, E. L.:** *Nursing Reconsidered: A Study of Change,* J. B. Lippincott Co., Philadelphia and Toronto, 1971, part 2.

80   **Leininger, M.:** "This I Believe . . . about Interdisciplinary Health Education for the Future," *Nursing Outlook,* vol. 19, pp. 787–791, December 1971.

81   **Koch, M. S., and P. M. Woolley:** "Allied Health Training at Johns Hopkins Hospital," *Journal of Medical Education,* vol. 47, pp. 333–338, May 1972.

82   **U.S. Public Health Service:** *The Allied Health Professions Personnel Training Act of 1966, as Amended: Report to the President and the Congress,* Washington, D.C., 1969.

83   **Grupenhoff, J. T., and S. P. Strickland:** *Federal Laws: Health/Environment Manpower,* Science and Health Communications Group, Washington, D.C., 1972.

84   **Greenfield, H. I.:** *Allied Health Manpower: Trends and Prospects,* Columbia University Press, New York, 1969.

85   **Carnegie Commission on Higher Education:** *Higher Education and the Na-*

tion's Health: Policies for Medical and Dental Education, McGraw-Hill Book Company, New York, 1970.

86   **American Bar Association:** *Annual Review of Legal Education,* Chicago, selected issues.

87   **Hughes, E. C., et al.:** *Education for the Professions of Medicine, Law, Theology, and Social Welfare,* McGraw-Hill Book Company, New York, forthcoming.

88   *San Francisco Chronicle,* Dec. 13, 1972.

89   **American Bar Foundation:** *Lawyer Statistical Report: 1971,* Chicago, 1972.

90   **U.S. Bureau of the Census:** *Statistical Abstract of the United States, 1971,* Washington, D.C., 1971.

91   **Packer, H. L., and T. Ehrlich:** *New Directions in Legal Education,* McGraw-Hill Book Company, New York, 1972.

92   *Chronicle of Higher Education,* Aug. 28, 1972.

93   **Schein, E. H.:** *Professional Education: Some New Directions,* McGraw-Hill Book Company, New York, 1972.

94   **Gordon, R. A., and J. E. Howell:** *Higher Education for Business,* Columbia University Press, New York, 1959.

95   **Pierson, F. C.:** *The Education of American Businessmen,* McGraw-Hill Book Company, New York, 1959.

96   **Cox, R. G.:** "Challenge to Graduate Education for Business," *Wharton Quarterly,* vol. 6, pp. 4–8, Summer 1972.

97   **American Association of Collegiate Schools of Business:** *Business Enrollments and Faculty Projections: 1970–1971,* St. Louis, n.d.

98   **American Association of Collegiate Schools of Business:** *Teaching Loads— Class Sizes and Admission and Degree Requirements, 1969–70,* St. Louis, n.d.

99   **Brimmer, A. F.:** "Long-Term Economic Outlook and Demand for Managerial Personnel," *Wharton Quarterly,* vol. 6, pp. 9–13 and 46–54, Summer 1972.

100   "Jobs: The Market Outlook for 1972-73," *MBA: The Master in Business Administration,* vol. 6, pp. 54–55, April 1972.

101   **Zsoldos, K. A.:** "The Job Market: More of the Same," *MBA: The Master in Business Administration,* vol. 6, pp. 57–60, October 1971.

102   "B - School Grads Are Back in Demand," *Business Week,* Dec. 16, 1972, pp. 70–73.

103   **Froomkin, J., J. R. Endriss, and R. W. Stump:** *Population, Enrollment, and Costs of Public Elementary and Secondary Education, 1975–76 and*

1980–81: A Report to the President's Commission of School Finance, Simat, Heilleisen, and Eichner, Inc., Washington, D.C., 1971.

104 **Graduate School of Business, Stanford University:** *A Proposal for a Program in Urban Management,* May 24, 1971.

105 **Borelli, A. J.:** "Blacks and Graduate Business Schools: Statistics and Comment," *AACSB Bulletin,* vol. 8, pp. 27–34, October 1971.

106 **Freeman, R. B.:** *The Market for College-Trained Manpower: A Study in the Economics of Career Choice,* Harvard University Press, Cambridge, Mass., 1971.

107 **Naughton, K.:** "Characteristics of Jobless Engineers," *Monthly Labor Review,* vol. 95, pp. 16–21, October 1972.

108 *New York Times,* Aug. 7, 1971.

109 **Office of Information, U.S. Department of Labor:** *News,* Sept. 12, 1972.

110 *New York Times,* Jan. 19, 1972.

111 **U.S. Bureau of the Census:** *Historical Statistics of the United States: Colonial Times to 1957,* Washington, D.C., 1960.

112 **Brode, W. R.:** "Manpower in Science and Engineering on a Saturation Model," *Science,* vol. 173, pp. 206–213, July 16, 1971.

113 **National Science Foundation:** *1969 and 1980 Science and Engineering Doctorate Supply and Utilization,* NSF 71-20, Washington, D.C., 1971.

114 **National Science Foundation:** *Science Resources Studies: Highlights,* NSF 71-14, Washington, D.C., May 26, 1971.

115 *Chronicle of Higher Education,* March 6, 1972.

116 *Business Week,* Nov. 4, 1972.

117 *Engineering Education,* February 1971.

118 *Engineering Education,* April 1972.

119 **Thompson, M., E. Smithberg, and L. B. Andersen:** "Engineering Opportunity Program: A Special Program for Disadvantaged Students," *Engineering Education,* pp. 794–798, April 1972.

120 **Jencks, C., and D. Riesman:** *The Academic Revolution,* Doubleday and Company, Inc., Garden City, N.Y., 1968.

121 **National Science Foundation:** *Science Resources Studies: Highlights,* NSF 71-26, Washington, D.C., July 2, 1971.

122 **Freeman, R. B.:** *The Scientific Manpower Market in the 1970s,* unpublished paper, Department of Economics, University of Chicago, Chicago, Ill.

123 **Moses, L. E.:** "The Response of Graduate Enrollment to Placement Opportunities," *Science,* vol. 177, pp. 494–497, Aug. 11, 1971.

124 Grodzins, L.: "The Manpower Crisis in Physics," *Bulletin of the American Physical Society,* pp. 737–749, June 1971.

125 National Academy of Sciences and Social Science Research Council: *The Behavioral and Social Sciences: Outlook and Needs,* A Report of the Behavioral and Social Sciences Survey Committee, Prentice-Hall, Inc., Englewood Cliffs, N.J., 1969.

126 Subcommittee on Scientific, Professional, and Technical Manpower, Manpower Advisory Committee, U.S. Department of Labor: *Recommendations to the Secretary of Labor,* draft of report as submitted to Manpower Advisory Committee, Nov. 27, 1972.

127 Wolfle, D., and C. V. Kidd: "The Future Market for Ph.D.'s," *AAUP Bulletin,* vol. 58, pp. 5–16, March 1972.

128 Wolfle, D., and C. V. Kidd: "The Future Market for Ph.D.'s," *Science,* vol. 173, pp. 784–793, Aug. 27, 1971.

129 Cartter, A. M.: "The Academic Labor Market," in M. S. Gordon, (ed.), *Higher Education and the Labor Market,* McGraw-Hill Book Company, New York, forthcoming.

130 Balderston, F., and R. Radner: *Academic Demand for New Ph.D.s, 1970-1990: Its Sensitivity to Alternative Policies,* University of California Ford Foundation Program for Research in University Administration, no. P-26, Berkeley, Calif., 1971.

131 Educational Testing Service: *Report on Council of Graduate Schools— Graduate Record Examination 1971–72 Survey of Graduate Enrollment,* Princeton, N.J., 1971.

132 Educational Testing Service: *Report on Council of Graduate Schools— Graduate Record Examinations Board 1972–73 Survey of Graduate Enrollment,* Princeton, N.J., 1972.

133 Denison, E. F.: *The Sources of Economic Growth in the United States and the Alternatives Before Us,* Committee for Economic Development, New York, 1962.

134 Juster, T., (ed.): *Education, Income, and Human Behavior,* McGraw-Hill Book Company, New York, forthcoming.

135 Stone, L.: "The AHA and the Job Market for Graduate Students," *AHA Newsletter,* pp. 22–27, March 1972.

136 Breneman, D.: *The Ph.D. Production Function: The Case at Berkeley,* University of California Ford Foundation Program for Research in University Administration, no. P-16, Berkeley, Calif., 1970.

137 *San Francisco Chronicle,* Nov. 11, 1972.

138 U.S. Office of Education: *Earned Degrees Conferred: 1969–70,* Washington, D.C., 1972.

139   Mayhew, L.B.: *Graduate and Professional Education, 1980: A Survey of Institutional Plans,* McGraw-Hill Book Company, New York, 1970.

140   Powell, J. H., Jr., and R. D. Lamson: *Elements Related to the Determination of Costs and Benefits in Graduate Education,* Council of Graduate Schools, Washington, D.C., 1972.

141   Balderston, F. E.: *Cost Analysis in Higher Education,* University of California Ford Foundation Program for Research in University Administration, no. P-33, Berkeley, Calif., 1972.

142   Cartter, A. M.: *An Assessment of Quality in Graduate Instruction,* American Council on Education, Washington, D.C., 1966.

143   Roose, K. D., and C. J. Andersen: *A Rating of Graduate Programs.* American Council on Education, Washington, D.C., 1970.

144   Council of Graduate Schools: *Supplemental Statement on the Doctor of Arts Degree, 1972,* Washington, D.C., 1972.

145   Folger, J. K.: "The Job Market for College Graduates," *The Journal of Higher Education,* vol. 43, pp. 203–222, March 1972.

146   Adkins, D. L.: "The American Educated Labor Force," in M. S. Gordon (ed.), *Higher Education and the Labor Market,* McGraw-Hill Book Company, New York, forthcoming.

147   Fogel, W., and D. J. B. Mitchell: "Higher Education Decision Making and the Labor Market," in M. S. Gordon (ed.), *Higher Education and the Labor Market,* McGraw-Hill Book Company, New York, forthcoming.

148   Astin, A. W., and R. J. Panos: *The Educational and Vocational Development of College Students,* American Council on Education, Washington, D.C., 1969.

149   Thal-Larsen, M.: *Placement and Counseling in a Changing Labor Market: Report of the San Francisco Bay Area Placement and Counseling Survey,* Institute of Industrial Relations, University of California, Berkeley, 1970.

150   Taubman, P., and T. Wales: "Education as an Investment and Screening Device," in T. Juster (ed.), *Education, Income, and Human Behavior,* McGraw-Hill Book Company, New York, forthcoming.

151   Gordon, M. S., and M. Thal-Larsen: *Employer Policies in a Changing Labor Market: Report of the San Francisco Bay Area Employer Policy Survey,* Institute of Industrial Relations, University of California, Berkeley, 1969.

152   Rawlins, V. L., and L. Ulman: "The Utilization of College Trained Manpower in the United States," in M. S. Gordon (ed.), *Higher Education and the Labor Market,* McGraw-Hill Book Company, New York, forthcoming.

153   *New York Times,* Nov. 6, 1971.

154   Fairfield, R.: *Communes USA: A Personal Tour,* Penguin Books Inc., Baltimore, 1972.

155 Keniston, K.: *Youth and Dissent: The Rise of a New Opposition,* Harcourt Brace Jovanovich, Inc., New York, 1971.

156 **U.S. Office of Education and National Science Foundation:** various publications.

157 **National Academy of Sciences, National Research Council:** *Doctorate Recipients from United States Universities, 1958–66, and Summary Report for 1967, 1968, 1969, 1970,* Washington, D.C., 1971.

158 Niland, J. R.: *The Asian Engineering Brain Drain,* D. C. Heath & Company, Lexington, Mass., 1970.

159 *New York Times,* June 25, 1972.

Carnegie Commission on Higher Education
Sponsored Research Studies

THE NEW DEPRESSION IN HIGHER
EDUCATION:
A STUDY OF FINANCIAL CONDITIONS AT 41
COLLEGES AND UNIVERSITIES
Earl F. Cheit

FINANCING MEDICAL EDUCATION:
AN ANALYSIS OF ALTERNATIVE POLICIES
AND MECHANISMS
Rashi Fein and Gerald I. Weber

HIGHER EDUCATION IN NINE COUNTRIES:
A COMPARATIVE STUDY OF COLLEGES AND
UNIVERSITIES ABROAD
*Barbara B. Burn, Philip G. Altbach, Clark Kerr,
and James A. Perkins*

BRIDGES TO UNDERSTANDING:
INTERNATIONAL PROGRAMS OF AMERICAN
COLLEGES AND UNIVERSITIES
Irwin T. Sanders and Jennifer C. Ward

GRADUATE AND PROFESSIONAL EDUCATION,
1980:
A SURVEY OF INSTITUTIONAL PLANS
Lewis B. Mayhew

THE AMERICAN COLLEGE AND AMERICAN
CULTURE:
SOCIALIZATION AS A FUNCTION OF HIGHER
EDUCATION
Oscar Handlin and Mary F. Handlin

RECENT ALUMNI AND HIGHER EDUCATION:
A SURVEY OF COLLEGE GRADUATES
Joe L. Spaeth and Andrew M. Greeley

CHANGE IN EDUCATIONAL POLICY:
SELF-STUDIES IN SELECTED COLLEGES AND
UNIVERSITIES
Dwight R. Ladd

STATE OFFICIALS AND HIGHER EDUCATION:
A SURVEY OF THE OPINIONS AND
EXPECTATIONS OF POLICY MAKERS IN NINE
STATES
Heinz Eulau and Harold Quinley

ACADEMIC DEGREE STRUCTURES:
INNOVATIVE APPROACHES
PRINCIPLES OF REFORM IN DEGREE
STRUCTURES IN THE UNITED STATES
Stephen H. Spurr

COLLEGES OF THE FORGOTTEN AMERICANS:
A PROFILE OF STATE COLLEGES AND
REGIONAL UNIVERSITIES
E. Alden Dunham

FROM BACKWATER TO MAINSTREAM:
A PROFILE OF CATHOLIC HIGHER
EDUCATION
Andrew M. Greeley

THE ECONOMICS OF THE MAJOR PRIVATE
UNIVERSITIES
William G. Bowen
(Out of print, but available from University Microfilms.)

THE FINANCE OF HIGHER EDUCATION
Howard R. Bowen
(Out of print, but available from University Microfilms.)

ALTERNATIVE METHODS OF FEDERAL
FUNDING FOR HIGHER EDUCATION
Ron Wolk
(Out of print, but available from University Microfilms.)

INVENTORY OF CURRENT RESEARCH ON
HIGHER EDUCATION 1968
Dale M. Heckman and Warren Bryan Martin
(Out of print, but available from University Microfilms.)

*The following technical reports are available from the Carnegie Commission on Higher Education, 1947
Center Street, Berkeley, California 94704.*

RESOURCE USE IN HIGHER EDUCATION:
TRENDS IN OUTPUT AND INPUTS, 1930–1967
June O'Neill

TRENDS AND PROJECTIONS OF PHYSICIANS
IN THE UNITED STATES 1967–2002
Mark S. Blumberg

MAY 1970:
THE CAMPUS AFTERMATH OF CAMBODIA
AND KENT STATE
Richard E. Peterson and John A. Bilorusky

MENTAL ABILITY AND HIGHER EDUCATIONAL
ATTAINMENT IN THE 20TH CENTURY
Paul Taubman and Terence Wales

AMERICAN COLLEGE AND UNIVERSITY
ENROLLMENT TRENDS IN 1971
Richard E. Peterson

PAPERS ON EFFICIENCY IN THE
MANAGEMENT OF HIGHER EDUCATION
*Alexander M. Mood, Colin Bell,
Lawrence Bogard, Helen Brownlee,
and Joseph McCloskey*

The following reprints are available from the Carnegie Commission on Higher Education, 1947 Center Street, Berkeley, California 94704.

ACCELERATED PROGRAMS OF MEDICAL EDUCATION, by Mark S. Blumberg, reprinted from JOURNAL OF MEDICAL EDUCATION, vol. 46, no. 8, August 1971.*

SCIENTIFIC MANPOWER FOR 1970–1985, by Allan M. Cartter, reprinted from SCIENCE, vol. 172, no. 3979, pp. 132–140, April 9, 1971.

A NEW METHOD OF MEASURING STATES' HIGHER EDUCATION BURDEN, by Neil Timm, reprinted from THE JOURNAL OF HIGHER EDUCATION, vol. 42, no. 1, pp. 27–33, January 1971.*

REGENT WATCHING, by Earl F. Cheit, reprinted from AGB REPORTS, vol. 13, no. 6, pp. 4–13, March 1971.

COLLEGE GENERATIONS—FROM THE 1930s TO THE 1960s by Seymour M. Lipset and Everett C. Ladd, Jr., reprinted from THE PUBLIC INTEREST, no. 25, Summer 1971.

AMERICAN SOCIAL SCIENTISTS AND THE GROWTH OF CAMPUS POLITICAL ACTIVISM IN THE 1960s, by Everett C. Ladd, Jr., and Seymour M. Lipset, reprinted from SOCIAL SCIENCES INFORMATION, vol. 10, no. 2, April 1971.

THE POLITICS OF AMERICAN POLITICAL SCIENTISTS, by Everett C. Ladd, Jr., and Seymour M. Lipset, reprinted from PS, vol. 4, no. 2, Spring 1971.*

THE DIVIDED PROFESSORIATE, by Seymour M. Lipset and Everett C. Ladd, Jr., reprinted from CHANGE, vol. 3, no. 3, pp. 54–60, May 1971.*

JEWISH ACADEMICS IN THE UNITED STATES: THEIR ACHIEVEMENTS, CULTURE AND POLITICS, by Seymour M. Lipset and Everett C. Ladd, Jr., reprinted from AMERICAN JEWISH YEAR BOOK, 1971.

THE UNHOLY ALLIANCE AGAINST THE CAMPUS, by Kenneth Keniston and Michael Lerner, reprinted from NEW YORK TIMES MAGAZINE, November 8, 1970 .

PRECARIOUS PROFESSORS: NEW PATTERNS OF REPRESENTATION, by Joseph W. Garbarino, reprinted from INDUSTRIAL RELATIONS, vol. 10, no. 1, February 1971.*

. . . AND WHAT PROFESSORS THINK: ABOUT STUDENT PROTEST AND MANNERS, MORALS, POLITICS, AND CHAOS ON THE CAMPUS, by Seymour Martin Lipset and Everett C. Ladd, Jr., reprinted from PSYCHOLOGY TODAY, November 1970.*

DEMAND AND SUPPLY IN U.S. HIGHER EDUCATION: A PROGRESS REPORT, by Roy Radner and Leonard S. Miller, reprinted from AMERICAN ECONOMIC REVIEW, May 1970.*

RESOURCES FOR HIGHER EDUCATION: AN ECONOMIST'S VIEW, by Theodore W. Schultz, reprinted from JOURNAL OF POLITICAL ECONOMY, vol. 76, no. 3, University of Chicago, May/June 1968.*

INDUSTRIAL RELATIONS AND UNIVERSITY RELATIONS, by Clark Kerr, reprinted from PROCEEDINGS OF THE 21ST ANNUAL WINTER MEETING OF THE INDUSTRIAL RELATIONS RESEARCH ASSOCIATION, pp. 15–25.*

NEW CHALLENGES TO THE COLLEGE AND UNIVERSITY, by Clark Kerr, reprinted from Kermit Gordon (ed.), AGENDA FOR THE NATION, The Brookings Institution, Washington, D.C., 1968.*

PRESIDENTIAL DISCONTENT, by Clark Kerr, reprinted from David C. Nichols (ed.), PERSPECTIVES ON CAMPUS TENSIONS: PAPERS PREPARED FOR THE SPECIAL COMMITTEE ON CAMPUS TENSIONS, American Council on Education, Washington, D.C., September 1970.*

STUDENT PROTEST—AN INSTITUTIONAL AND NATIONAL PROFILE, by Harold Hodgkinson, reprinted from THE RECORD, vol. 71, no. 4, May 1970.*

WHAT'S BUGGING THE STUDENTS?, by Kenneth Keniston, reprinted from EDUCATIONAL RECORD, American Council on Education, Washington, D.C., Spring 1970.*

THE POLITICS OF ACADEMIA, by Seymour Martin Lipset, reprinted from David C. Nichols (ed.), PERSPECTIVES ON CAMPUS TENSIONS: PAPERS PREPARED FOR THE SPECIAL COMMITTEE ON CAMPUS TENSIONS, American Council on Education, Washington, D.C., September 1970.*

INTERNATIONAL PROGRAMS OF U.S. COLLEGES AND UNIVERSITIES: PRIORITIES FOR THE SEVENTIES, by James A. Perkins, reprinted by permission of the International Council for Educational Development, Occasional Paper no. 1, July 1971.

FACULTY UNIONISM: FROM THEORY TO PRACTICE, by Joseph W. Garbarino, reprinted from INDUSTRIAL RELATIONS, vol. 11, no. 1, pp. 1–17, February 1972.

MORE FOR LESS: HIGHER EDUCATION'S NEW PRIORITY, by Virginia B. Smith, reprinted from UNIVERSAL HIGHER EDUCATION: COSTS AND BENEFITS, American Council on Education, Washington, D.C., 1971.

ACADEMIA AND POLITICS IN AMERICA, by Seymour M. Lipset, reprinted from Thomas J. Nossiter (ed.), IMAGINATION AND PRECISION IN THE SOCIAL SCIENCES, pp. 211–289, Faber and Faber, London, 1972.

POLITICS OF ACADEMIC NATURAL SCIENTISTS AND ENGINEERS, by Everett C. Ladd, Jr., and Seymour M. Lipset, reprinted from SCIENCE, vol. 176, no. 4039, pp. 1091–1100, June 9, 1972.

THE INTELLECTUAL AS CRITIC AND REBEL: WITH SPECIAL REFERENCE TO THE UNITED STATES AND THE SOVIET UNION, by Seymour M. Lipset and Richard B. Dobson, reprinted from DAEDALUS, vol. 101, no. 3, pp. 137–198, Summer 1972.

THE POLITICS OF AMERICAN SOCIOLOGISTS, by Seymour M. Lipset and Everett C. Ladd, Jr., reprinted from THE AMERICAN JOURNAL OF SOCIOLOGY, vol. 78, no. 1, July 1972.

THE DISTRIBUTION OF ACADEMIC TENURE IN AMERICAN HIGHER EDUCATION, by Martin Trow, reprinted from THE TENURE DEBATE, Bardwell Smith (ed.), Jossey-Bass, San Francisco, 1972.

THE NATURE AND ORIGINS OF THE CARNEGIE COMMISSION ON HIGHER EDUCATION, by Alan Pifer, reprinted by permission of The Carnegie Foundation for the Advancement of Teaching.

*The Commission's stock of this reprint has been exhausted.